No Kids Allowed

No Kids Allowed

Children's Literature for Adults

MICHELLE ANN ABATE

Johns Hopkins University Press
Baltimore

© 2020 Michelle Ann Abate
All rights reserved. Published 2020
Printed in the United States of America on acid-free paper
9 8 7 6 5 4 3 2 1

Johns Hopkins University Press
2715 North Charles Street
Baltimore, Maryland 21218-4363
www.press.jhu.edu

Library of Congress Cataloging-in-Publication Data

Names: Abate, Michelle Ann, 1975– author.
Title: No kids allowed : children's literature for adults / Michelle Ann Abate.
Description: Baltimore : Johns Hopkins University Press, 2020. | Includes
  bibliographical references and index.
Identifiers: LCCN 2019057784 | ISBN 9781421438856 (hardcover) | ISBN
  9781421438863 (paperback) | ISBN 9781421438870 (ebook)
Subjects: LCSH: Juvenile-style literature for adults—United States. |
  American literature—20th century—History and criticism. | American
  literature—21st century—History and criticism.
Classification: LCC PS492 .A23 2020 | DDC 810.9/9282—dc23
LC record available at https://lccn.loc.gov/2019057784

A catalog record for this book is available from the British Library.

Figures 1–5: Graphic novel excerpt from *In the Shadow of No Towers* by Art
Spiegelman, copyright © 2004 by Art Spiegelman. Used by permission of
Pantheon Books, an imprint of the Knopf Doubleday Publishing Group, a
division of Penguin Random House LLC. All rights reserved.

Figures 6–11: Illustrations by Viviana Garofoli copyright © 2008 by Viviana
Garofoli; from *MA! There's Nothing to Do Here! A Word from Your Baby-in-
Waiting* by Barbara Park. Used by permission of Random House Children's
Books, a division of Penguin Random House LLC. All rights reserved.

*Special discounts are available for bulk purchases of this book. For more
information, please contact Special Sales at specialsales@press.jhu.edu.*

Johns Hopkins University Press uses environmentally friendly book
materials, including recycled text paper that is composed of at least
30 percent post-consumer waste, whenever possible.

CONTENTS

Rick Schroder, the American actor who is most well-known for his role in the popular 1980s sitcom *Silver Spoons*, once reflected: "I spent my whole childhood wishing I were older—and now I'm spending my adulthood wishing I were younger."

This book charts a literary phenomenon that emerges from a similar sentiment. It examines the growing number of narratives released since the closing decades of the twentieth century that have been issued in a physical format—like a picture book or a board book—or belong to a narrative style—such as a bedtime story or an ABC text—that is commonly and even primarily associated with young people. However, these titles were written intentionally and exclusively for adults. Taken collectively, these narratives constitute a paradoxical new genre: what I call "children's literature for adults."

My discussion of children's literature for adults may be titled *No Kids Allowed*, but plenty of individuals of all ages supported and assisted me as I worked on these pages. First and foremost, I want to express my deep gratitude to Catherine Goldstead, my editor at Johns Hopkins University Press, for her help and encouragement. This project has benefited greatly from her interest, her insight, and her editorial investment. I am equally thankful to the various sets of anonymous outside readers of my manuscript. Their thoughtful and detailed suggestions made my project stronger and sharper.

I am indebted to many colleagues and friends for their assistance and their encouragement. I wish to thank Joe Sutliff Sanders, whose comments on the book's introduction augmented my analysis. I am grateful to Karly Marie Grice, who read several chapters in their early stages and provided helpful suggestions. I also want to relay my tremendous appreciation to Annette Wannamaker, Gwen Athene Tarbox, and Caroline Clark. Thank you for being not simply such wonderful professional colleagues but equally fabulous friends.

Portions of some chapters have appeared previously in various journals. A version of chapter two was published in *Literature and Theology*, volume 30, issue 2 (2016), pages 164–81. A modified edition of chapter three was released in *Jeunesse: Young People, Texts, Cultures*, volume 7, issue 2 (2015), pages 40–64. An earlier take on chapter four appeared in *Children's Literature in Education*, volume 44, issue 4 (2013), pages 326–43. Furthermore, an analysis of chapter five that predated the inauguration of Donald J. Trump was published in *The Lion and the Unicorn*, volume 38, issue 1 (2014), pages 1–29. I am grateful to both the editors and the publishers of these journals for permission to re-use this material.

Finally, I'd like to dedicate this book to the countless other fellow travelers who, though they are technically in adulthood, continue to thoroughly enjoy their childhood. The emergence of children's literature for adults affirms that these two states need not be mutually exclusive. On the contrary, we not only can, but even should, enjoy both simultaneously. As the pages that follow explain, childhood is not just for children anymore.

No Kids Allowed

A Is for Adult

Coloring Books, Bedtime Stories, and Picture Books for Grown-Ups

> Kids are getting older faster, but adults are getting younger later.
>
> —Brian Goldner, President/CEO of Hasbro toys, 2006

In early December 2015, journalist Ann Cannon aptly observed: "Walk into any local bookstore these days and you're likely to find extensive displays of coloring books . . . for adults" (par. 1). The ellipsis in her sentence was deliberate. It was a sign that for Cannon, coloring books as items for children are common, but ones intended for adults are odd and unexpected. During the second decade of the twenty-first century, however, this exact situation began to occur: companies began making and marketing coloring books for a demographic of grown-ups rather than kids. As journalist Susannah Cahalan explained, "The trend began in 2011 when Scottish freelance illustrator Johanna Basford was approached by a small UK publishing house, Laurence King Publishing. An editor there had stumbled across her work online and thought that her intricate drawings would make the perfect coloring book" (par. 7). The result was *Secret Garden: An Inky Treasure Hunt and Colouring Book*. While the coloring book was advertised as a more sophisticated item intended for older children, "something funny happened. Adults started buying them" (Cahalan, par. 8). Debra Masumoto, the publicity and marketing manager at Lawrence King Publishing, explained how the trend began. "We started noticing the Amazon reviews," she observed, "They all sort of said the same thing: 'Oh, it was so pretty and I bought it for my niece's birthday but then I just had to get one for myself'" (qtd in Cahalan, par. 9).

William Brennan, in an article that appeared in the *Atlantic* in April 2015, was among the first to document the trend as it spread across Europe. He commented that *Jardin Secret*, as Basford's book was titled in France, had sold hundreds of thousands of copies, primarily to adults (par. 3). Meanwhile, another series of coloring books with similarly intricate designs but released by a different publisher boasted "nearly 2 million copies" in print (Brennan, par. 4).

As customer feedback indicated, the bulk of the titles, akin to *Jardin Secret*, had been purchased by grown-ups for use themselves (Brennan, par. 4).

From there, coloring books for adults quickly spread to countries around the world. As Cahalan reported, "China followed suit. Four months after publication, 'Secret Garden' sold 3 million copies" (par. 11). Events in Brazil were even more astounding. When coloring books for adults arrived in the country, they "sold so many copies that news agencies reported the nation had a shortage of colored pencils" (Cahalan, par. 11).

In early summer 2015, the adult coloring book craze reached the United States. In an article that appeared in *Publishers Weekly*, Jim Milliot relayed some eye-popping statistics: "*Lost Ocean*, Johanna Basford's newest book (and her first published by Penguin), sold more than 55,000 copies in the first week" (par. 1). Meanwhile, Basford's first two coloring books, *Secret Garden* and *Enchanted Forest*, tallied sales figures of "more than 453,000 copies and 350,000 copies, respectively, so far this year" (Milliot, par. 1). A variety of other titles were experiencing similar levels of success. As Evan Porter remarked in a story that appeared in *Upworthy*, coloring books for adults "are selling at breakneck pace. Publishers are even having trouble keeping them in stock" (par. 10).

These events did not go unnoticed by cultural commentators. Over the fall and winter of 2015, articles about the meteoric rise of coloring books for adults appeared in venues ranging from the *New Yorker*, *Vogue*, and the *Atlantic* to *Slate*, the *New York Times*, and *CNN*. With these items equally popular among young urban hipsters and small-town retirees, they were rightly called a "smash hit" (Pierleoni, par. 4). The factors fueling their success were simple. In addition to possessing the nostalgic appeal of an activity that many loved in childhood, coloring books provided practitioners with a combination of relaxation, stress relief, and creative outlet (Martinez, par. 9). Moreover, with titles such as *Mandala Coloring Book*, *Creative Cats Coloring Book*, and *Fantastic Cities: A Coloring Book of Amazing Places Real and Imagined*, there was a text for seemingly every taste, interest, and personality type.

By the time the Christmas shopping season arrived, coloring books for adults were one of the hottest gifts. Featured in display cases in bookstores around the United States, the texts were "*wildly* popular, selling millions of copies" (Campbell-Dollaghan, par. 2; emphasis in original). By mid-December 2015, in fact, nine of the twenty titles listed on Amazon's list of current bestsellers were coloring books for adults, a genre that many journalists pointed out "didn't exist two years ago" (Cahalan, par. 1).

The end of the holiday shopping season did not signal the end of the adult coloring book craze. As Jim Milliot commented, "It is hard to find a publisher that hasn't entered the adult coloring book market" (par. 3). Even so, the field was far from reaching a saturation point: "Though the market seems flooded . . . it shows no signs of slowing," Cahalan observed (par. 3). Lesley O'Mara, an industry insider, echoed this observation, asserting that "We've never seen a phenomenon like it in our thirty years of publishing" (qtd in Raphel, par. 2). As these comments suggested, coloring books for adults—at least for the foreseeable future—were here to stay.

In the present study, I demonstrate that the cultural appearance and the commercial success of coloring books for adults were anything but anomalous occurrences. Rather, these events represent the latest development in a larger and heretofore overlooked phenomenon: the growing genre of what I call "children's literature for adults." Beginning in the closing decades of the twentieth century and accelerating rapidly in the new millennium, an array of narratives appeared that were aligned with a literary school or issued in a physical format that was commonly and even primarily associated with young people—picture books, bedtime stories, board books, and so on—despite being written for adults. Examples range from Mabel Maney's campy mystery novels about "Nancy Clue" and "The Hardly Boys" (1993–1995) and Erich Origen and Gan Golan's popular political parody *Goodnight Bush* (2008) to Barbara Park's baby-shower staple *MA! There's Nothing to Do Here!: A Word from Your Baby-in-Waiting* (2008) and Adam Mansbach's irreverent bedtime story *Go the F**k to Sleep* (2011). In aiming for an adult audience, these texts differentiate themselves from narratives for young readers that have become popular among adults, such as the Harry Potter series or the Hunger Games trilogy. As the moniker "children's literature for adults" suggests, these books represent the next literary step or cultural progression of this phenomenon: they are juvenile-styled texts intended for an adult readership. Prominent articles in *Slate*, the *New York Times*, and the *Guardian* revealed that the impressive sales figures of books such as *Twilight* and *The Fault in Our Stars* can be attributed, in large part, to their popularity with adult readers.[1] These discussions, however, neglect to mention their close corollary: children's literature not simply enjoyed *by* adults, but written *for* them.

Although it might be tempting to see such texts as a passing fad or isolated novelty, both the sales figures and the staying power of these narratives suggests otherwise. Children's literature for adults encompasses some of the most commercially successful narratives released over the past few decades in the United States. Both *Goodnight Bush* and *Go the F**k to Sleep*, for example, were *New York Times* bestsellers. Meanwhile, Mabel Maney's *The Case of the Not-So-Nice Nurse* is a cult classic within the LGBTQ+ (Lesbian, Gay, Bisexual, Transgender, Queer, and Questioning) community. These exemplary titles demonstrate that children's literature for adults embodies a vibrant new genre that engages with an array of complex social, political, and aesthetic issues. Through their form and their content, these texts question the generic boundaries of children's literature while also challenging the longstanding Western assumption that adulthood and childhood are separate and even mutually exclusive entities. Children's literature for adults raises questions such as: In what ways do the designations "childhood" and "adulthood" change from an intellectual and an ontological standpoint if they begin to blend, blur, and overlap? What does it mean if the human life span is no longer conceived as unidirectional but instead conceptualized as recursive, looping and twisting back around on itself? Furthermore, does the classification "children's literature" retain its literary integrity if it can be expanded to include the seemingly oxymoronic category of texts intended for adults? Phrased in a different way, children's literature has long been defined by its intended audience. What happens to this genre when its readership expands to include titles that are not merely being enjoyed by adults, but are designed exclusively for them? Finally, does calling juvenile-styled narratives intended for a readership of grown-ups "children's literature for adults" ultimately reinforce the boundaries of age and audience that these works destabilize? Do we need an entirely different name, category, or term for these texts?

In spite of the growing cultural presence, strong commercial success, and compelling literary implications of children's literature for adults in the United States, little work has been done on the subject. Although this phenomenon has been a facet of American print culture for several decades, the phrase "children's literature for adults" is not a recognized subject category by the Library of Congress or an existing genre tag for the American Library Association. Even more astoundingly, no scholarly books, academic essays, or research articles about this wholesale phenomenon have been published.[2] To date, the bulk of references to "children's literature for adults" have appeared sporadically, sparingly, and primarily online. In October 31, 2017, for example, Alex Conway wrote a blog post about the growing number of adult-audience parodies of classic children's texts, along with the proliferation of coloring books for adults and their connection to nostalgia.[3] Additionally, over the past few years, books that comprise this growing new genre have been collected in listicles (a term coined to describe articles that are presented wholly or partly in the form of a list). In 2013, for example, Stephanie Bonjack posted "Twisted and Wrong: 6 Children's Books Intended for Adults" on the website *LitReactor*. In this article, she enumerated "titles that look like children's books—they tend to be cute and small and richly illustrated—but were clearly never meant for children" (par. 1). Three years later, Amanda Long created a similar list for the parenting website *Mum's Grapevine*. In a telling barometer of the massive growth of books of this nature, her discussion featured "23 of the Naughtiest Kids Parody Books for Adults."

Together with lists on various websites, there have been a few book chapters and journal articles over the years that have explored the parodic treatment of well-known narratives for young readers. As Eric L. Tribunella commented in an essay that appeared in 2008, "As of late, children's literature, or works with some claim to being children's literature, has been frequently targeted for retelling, in many cases for adult readers" (135). Many of these new versions have been humorous in nature, while others, as Tribunella's essay documents, can be most accurately classified as erotica.[4] Indeed, in examples ranging from Angela Carter's reimagining of classic fairy tales in *The Bloody Chamber* (1979) to the massive growth of fanfiction—and especially slash fiction—in recent decades, characters, plots, and even an author's entire literary *oeuvre* that was originally intended for children have been creatively coopted by adults.

While my work is certainly in dialogue with the observations made by Tribunella and other scholars who have written on these events, it also differs from them in a significant way. Previous discussions have spotlighted a specific sampling: a selection of picture book parodies, a literary lineage of slash fiction, or a retelling of various fairy tales.[5] Such analyses have not identified these narratives as belonging to a larger literary movement, which is my interest here. Eric Tribunella gestures towards this phenomenon, affirming that "adult-audience retellings of children's books clearly constitute a vital literary and cultural phenomenon" (136). However, other than providing a survey of some titles that can be classified in this category in the opening pages of his essay, he does not explore the origins, evolution, and significance of children's narratives for adult audiences, as I do in the pages that follow. In sum, my interest is in examining these books as part of a new, growing, and vibrant genre, rather than just seeing them as a cluster of compelling but otherwise unrelated examples.

This project is the first book-length study of the growing genre of children's literature for adults in the United States.[6] While much has been written about the development of the concept of childhood, surprisingly little work has been done about the cultural notion of adulthood by scholars of children's literature. Accordingly, in this book, I probe the etymological root and societal evolution of the terms *adult* and *adulthood* in the United States.[7] While these concepts are commonly regarded as clear and concrete, I argue they are actually far more malleable, even mercurial. As my discussion reveals, adulthood is not a social certainty but a cultural construction, one changing with historical circumstances. Next, I discuss how, in spite of the vicissitudes of being an adult, conformity to this stage is compulsory and deviance is commonly met with opprobrium. For centuries, a variety of individuals have been associated—by choice or by force—with childishness, immaturity, and infantilization. Placing children's literature for adults in dialogue with past instances in which people have defied traditional notions about age and maturity, I discuss the social, cultural, economic, and political circumstances that gave rise to this phenomenon and distinguish it from previous incarnations. This introduction thus provides the necessary background information for framing, contextualizing, and understanding children's literature for adults.

In the chapters that follow, I offer case studies of narratives written in a literary style or using a material format long associated with books for children, although each of these texts was intended for adults. Encompassing picture books, bedtime stories, series novels, and board books, these narratives embody a cross-section of the categories that constitute contemporary children's literature. At the same time, these texts engage with a wide range of the topics facing American adults in the present era. Encompassing subjects such as the trials of parenthood, the terrorist attacks of 9/11, and the highly partisan nature of national politics, they demonstrate how literary styles commonly associated with children can be effective platforms for adults.

Much has been written in recent years about the steadily shrinking duration of childhood. As Neil Postman, Peggy Orenstein, and Susan Linn have all discussed, young people grow up faster today than in previous generations. Commenting about this phenomenon in an article that appeared in the *New York Times Magazine* in May 2009, Orenstein wondered, "How did 5 become the new 7, anyway?" (MM13). In the field of advertising, this issue has become such an essential consideration that it has its own acronym: "what marketers refer to as KGOY—Kids Getting Older Younger—their explanation for why 3-year-olds now play with toys that were initially intended for middle-schoolers" (Orenstein, par. 3). With thong underwear marketed to pre-adolescent girls and children as young as eleven experiencing their first sexual encounters, the late twentieth century and opening decade of the new millennium marked what Postman termed the "disappearance of childhood."

I also chart the presence of an opposite but equally important trend. As Brian Goldner, the president and CEO of the Hasbro toy company, remarked in 2006, "Kids are getting older faster, but adults are getting younger later" (qtd in Noxon 101). Children's literature for adults serves as a telling barometer about millennium-era modifications to literary categories and, perhaps more importantly, to the social construction of the human life cycle. The board books, alphabet texts, and bedtime stories that comprise this genre are equal parts topical and timeless. Titles such as *Goodnight Bush* and *Go the F**k to Sleep* have been popular and successful during the past few years, but their emergence and appeal have implications that are much longer-lasting as well as farther-reaching. Accordingly, this book examines these narratives as artistically rich and intellectually complex in their own right, while also revealing how they engage with larger literary and cultural phenomena. Ultimately, I spotlight one of the most revolutionary developments to happen to books for young readers since their inception: the name notwithstanding, "children's literature" is not just for children anymore.

"Because I Said So": The Both Obvious and Elusive Meaning of Adulthood

While the historical origins, cultural characteristics, and social purpose of childhood has been the subject of both scholarly and popular inquiry for generations, adulthood has not received the same level of sustained interest. Unlike the earlier, more malleable, and seemingly more influential phases of the human life cycle, adulthood is regarded as requiring little discussion: its point, purpose, and practices are as clear as they are concrete. Indeed, as James Côté has written, adulthood has a "taken-for-granted quality" (48). Becoming an adult is something that no individual can seemingly avoid; it is an inescapable part of the process of growing older. In the words of Daniel Donahoo, "You see, the job of a child is to become an adult. To grow, to learn, to develop. It's not a simple process, but it *is* an inevitable one" (11; emphasis in original).

In spite of such longstanding beliefs in the inevitability and the universality of adulthood, the social conception of adults and the cultural construction of adulthood have surprisingly rich and varied histories. While the word "adult" would seem to have a long etymological past extending back to the origins of the English language, it is actually a far more recent construct. As the *Oxford English Dictionary* reveals, *adult* "remained rare in English until at least the second quarter of the 17th cent." Indeed, the term *adult* only came into widespread use when the concept of children and the notion of childhood took shape. In this way, adults were defined by what they were not: children. Prior to this occurrence, the concept of an "adult" was so broad that it was unspoken. After all, if this term could be used to describe virtually everyone, it hardly needed to be uttered.

When the term "adult" did finally come into widespread use, it had a seemingly simple definition. According to the *OED*, an adult is a person "having reached the age of maturity; a grown-up." However, as disciplines ranging from biology and sociology to psychology and anthropology have all pointed out, this explanation is anything but clear. After all, the "age of maturity" can vary greatly by individual but also by family, region, socioeconomic class, race, religion, ethnicity, nationality, and historical time period. From a biological standpoint, the "age of maturity" has often been regarded as the time when children enter puberty and are thus able to procreate. However, the onset of menses in girls as well as sexual potency in boys is far from universal—or even stable. As the Office of Women's Health at the US Department of Health and Human Services reports, "A girl can start her period anytime between the ages of 8 and 15." A similarly sizable expanse of time applies to boys. Jonathan Mar and Grace Norwich highlight this fact on one of the opening pages of their nonfiction text, *The Body Book for Boys*: "For some boys, this process starts as early as the age of nine. For others, it doesn't begin until they're fourteen or fifteen" (61).

Nevertheless, few Americans would likely regard the mere attainment of a certain chronological age or development of a specific physiological trait as a sufficient qualification for adulthood. Consequently, "the age of maturity" also has powerful sociocultural components. As Jordan Stanger-Ross, Christina Collins, and Mark J. Stern have noted, Americans have commonly conceived of the process of becoming an adult in the context of five key life events: "marrying, leaving parents' homes, establishing new households, leaving school and entering the workforce" (626). The rationale fueling these benchmarks is simple: "Together these choices transform young people from their positions as dependents living in houses headed by other people to economic independence and procreative households of their own" (Stanger-Ross, Collins, and Stern 626). Less clear, however, are the requisite number of these traits that need to be achieved, the comparative importance assigned to each of them, and the expected age at which these conditions need to be satisfied. For example, must an individual have completed all five of these "core transitions" in order to be considered an adult? If not, what is the minimum number for entry? For instance, would only one be sufficient, or are at least two required? Moreover, are some of these milestones more important than others—and, if so, do they have the power to nullify other benchmarks? For example, what if an individual has completed school, left home, and even entered the workforce but is not financially independent—is he or she an adult? Likewise, what if they are married or even if they have children, but still live with their own natal family—can they be regarded as having reached "the age of maturity"?

The answers to these questions have changed significantly even during the relatively brief period since the end of the Second World War. As Roger A. Stetterson, Jr. and Barbara Ray discuss, during the "the 1950s and 1960s, most Americans viewed family roles and adult responsibilities as being nearly synonymous" (21). By contrast, during the opening decade of the twenty-first century, this link between family and adulthood was no longer paramount. Stetterson and Ray report: "Unlike their parents' and grandparents' generations, for whom marriage and parenthood were prerequisites for adulthood, young people today more often view these markers as life choices rather than requirements" (22). For them, other milestones take precedence. To ascertain the order of these elements, the MacArthur Research Network on Transitions to Adulthood[8] began administering a biennial opinion poll "to a national representative sample of Americans" in 2002 (Stetterson and Ray 22). Their findings revealed that "Today, more than 95 percent of Americans consider the most important markers of adulthood to be completing school, establishing an independent household, and being employed full-time—concrete steps associated with the ability to support a family" (Stetterson and Ray 22).

In the same way that attitudes regarding the relative importance of certain life milestones have changed over time, so too have perceptions about the age by which young people are expected to have reached these benchmarks. Once again, beliefs have shifted greatly just during the second half of the twentieth century. In the period directly following World War II, plentiful numbers of well-paying as well as "stable jobs made it possible for couples to marry and form families at a young age"—often directly after graduation from high school (Stetterson and Ray 21). As a result, leaving "home quickly in the 1950s was 'normal' because opportunities were plentiful and societal expectations of the time reinforced the need to do so" (Stetterson and Ray 24). By comparison, the situation sixty years later is much different. Changing economic conditions—beginning with the decline of American manufacturing during the 1970s and accelerating rapidly amidst the worldwide economic recession that occurred in 2008—have radically altered the economic prospects of recent generations. In the words of Stetterson and Ray, "Globalization increased competition, markets became internationalized, and new technologies spread networks and knowledge. All these forces gave rise to new economic and employment uncertainties that now complicate young people's decisions about living arrangements, educational investments, and family formation" (29). In contrast to the baby boomers, both members of Generation X and millennials are living at home longer, delaying getting married, and deciding to further their education though college and graduate school. As journalist Stephanie K. Taylor observed, whereas higher education was once reserved for a small minority of the cultural elite, by 2006 "more than 40 percent of high school graduates now go on to college" (A2). Not only are larger numbers of young people seeking postsecondary education, but they are taking longer to obtain their degree. Factors such as the increased cost of college tuition, necessitating that students work more hours while they go to school, as well as the difficulty of being able to complete all the required courses, especially if a student changes their major, have extended the amount of time to graduation. As the National Center for Education Statistics reported, by 2009, the time to completion for a four-year degree had reached six years for 59 percent of the nation's undergraduates ("Fast Facts"). Taken collectively, these decisions are increasing the age at which young people are reaching various milestones compared to even a generation or two before them. According to Taylor, "In 1960 the average 25-year-old U.S. woman, according to Census Bureau statistics, was a married mother of two nearing her fifth wedding anniversary. Today, most 25-year-old women are single and childless" (A2).

Changing conceptions about at what age and in what order young people ought to reach milestones such as moving out and getting married prompted a wholesale reconsideration of what it means to be an "adult." Dorothy Rogers, in her influential book *The Adult Years: An Introduction to Aging* (1986), noted how fragmented adulthood had become. Pointing to changes ranging from an increase in human life expectancy to the declining number of young people who married and became parents when they were in their twenties, she argued that the formerly homogenous perception of "adulthood" had begun to erode. To more accurately reflect these alterations, Rogers divided her discussion into sections: "The Young Adult," the "Middle-Aged Adult," and

"Older Adults." As she explained, while each of these categories can be regarded simply as a subset of the larger concept of "the age of maturity," they possess such unique characteristics that they can be viewed as their own distinct period of life (1–3).

Of course, all historical generalizations are just that—generalizations. Their veracity within any given era can vary greatly by race, ethnicity, geographic region, religious background, socioeconomic class, and even gender. As Stetterson and Ray report, during almost any time period, "Americans who are less educated and less affluent give earlier deadlines for leaving home, completing school, obtaining full-time employment, marrying, and parenting" (22). Not surprisingly, beliefs about when and how one becomes an "adult" also vary greatly by race and ethnicity. Consider the issue of establishing an independent household: "Since the 1970s, black men have lived more often with parents than their white peers" (Stetterson and Ray 23). Similarly, foreign-born individuals routinely hold differing attitudes about what it means to be an "adult" than native-born Americans. According to Stetterson and Ray once again, "residential independence has been and continues to be one of the markers of attaining independence in the United States, particularly among native-born youth" (25). However, this trait is far less important for individuals whose families originated from outside of the United States. As data collected during the opening decade of the twenty-first century revealed, "Immigrants of the second generation are more likely to live at home than native-born blacks and especially whites" (Stetterson and Ray 24). Finally, but far from inconsequentially, any of these attitudes can vary greatly within demographic groups based on factors such as family dynamics, religious background, and, of course, gender identity. The postwar period forms a powerful illustration of this condition. During the 1950s, middle-class white men and women held varying beliefs on how and when they would reach adulthood: "For men, the defining characteristic of adulthood was having the means to marry and support a family. For women, it was getting married and becoming a mother" (Stetterson and Ray 21). Given that the conventional gender roles for this demographic dictated that men worked outside the home and women did not, obtaining a full-time job and becoming financially independent were not important benchmarks of adulthood for middle-class women.

If reaching the "age of maturity" and becoming an "adult" are unclear milestones, then the period of "adulthood" is even more elusive. "Adulthood is the one stage of life that lacks a history," historian Steven Mintz has written (x). He continues: "We know a great deal about childhood, adolescence, and old age in the past, but adulthood remains a historical black hole" (x). The *Oxford English Dictionary* defines this term tautologically, as simply "The condition or state of being an adult." Moreover, this period has a surprisingly short history. Contrary to conceptions of adulthood as a timeless or, at least, longstanding construct, the *OED* lists the first textual reference to it at the astoundingly late date of 1850—and this remark is made in a discussion concerning animals, not humans: "At five years old, the horse arrives at adult-hood." It was not until twenty-five years later, in 1875, that the *OED* recorded the inaugural usage of the term "adulthood" in reference to human beings. The example provided, from John Brookes's treatise *Manliness*, muses: "We know of no lovelier trait in childhood or adulthood than *openness* of character."

Prior to this period, another now-archaic term was more common: "adultness." Defined as (according to the *Oxford English Dictionary*) "The state, condition, or fact of being adult, or an adult; (possession of) adult qualities, attributes, or characteristics," this word has its origins in the mid-seventeenth century and seems to have come into use around the same time that the word "adult" experienced increased cultural currency and intellectual traction. While "adultness" and "adulthood" are both nouns that signify maturation, they possess significant sociolinguistic differences. As the *OED* indicates, the former, "adultness," suggests mere possession of traits that are associated with the "age of maturity." Meanwhile, the latter word, "adulthood," signifies an individual's residence in this period of the human life cycle. While the term "adultness" is no longer used today, its core concept remains relevant. Many teens and even tweens today, given their technological prowess, social savvy, and sexual precocity, possess "adultness." However, few would likely argue that these traits mean that they have now entered "adulthood."

As even this brief discussion demonstrates, being an "adult" and occupying the period of "adulthood" in the United States is a complex, variable, and highly individuated phenomenon—and it always has been. Indeed, as Côté has asserted, "there is no definition [of adulthood] and . . . the term has no definite meaning either among the public or among social scientists" (48). Both in the past and in the present, the harder we try to pin it down, the more it eludes us. In this way, while adults are commonly seen to have "settled down," adulthood itself has historically resisted, avoided, and even evaded this condition.

In spite of the historical, cultural, and even personal vicissitudes of adulthood, one feature has remained constant—it has been conceptualized as the antithesis of childhood. While sociologists, psychologists, and historians might disagree about the definition of adulthood, most agree about what it is not. Adulthood is the stage that does not simply succeed childhood; it supplants it. From the time of its initial inception through understandings in the present day, one of the benchmarks of being an adult is how thoroughly and successfully the individual has shed the traits, habits, and behaviors associated with children.

"I Don't Wanna Grow Up": Defying the Norms of Adulthood—by Choice and by Force—in US History

In spite of the mercurial nature of adulthood, conformity to it is culturally expected. After all, becoming an "adult" is as much of a societal imperative as it is a biological inevitability. Every culture depends upon the presence of physically, intellectually, and emotionally "mature" individuals not simply for its ongoing development, but for its basic survival. As Jordan Stanger-Ross, Christina Collins, and Mark J. Stern have written, these figures provide "the bedrock of social organization" (626).

Given the indispensability of reaching "the age of maturity," individuals who defy its expectations are viewed in a negative light—or, at least, with reproach. In a telling indication of lingering beliefs that adulthood is a rigid requirement that simply must be embraced with age, a common way to deride individuals who do not adhere to its conventions is by likening them to children. Beverly Lyon Clark has discussed this powerful paradox in American culture. In spite of pervasive rhetoric regarding the value and importance of young people during the twenty-first century, an effective method for insulting a grown man or woman, she observes, is to call them "juvenile," "childish," or "immature" (4).

This phenomenon has a long history in the United States. Throughout the nineteenth century, individuals who existed outside of the hegemonic order were commonly denigrated by being likened to children. Fueled by prevailing beliefs in Darwinian theory, a variety of perceived similarities to children were used to affirm the inferiority of groups like women, blacks, and indigenous tribal peoples and thus justify denying them full social, economic, and political rights. Thomas Jefferson, writing in 1814, for example, expressed his belief that blacks were "as incapable as children" (qtd in Dierksheide, par. 5). Such views were shared by many other white men and women during this era and were used as the basis for arguments about slavery being a "paternalistic" and even "beneficial" institution. These social attitudes were supported by scientific arguments. For example, "[t]he celebrated German anatomist Carl Vogt wrote in 1864: 'By its rounded apex and less developed posterior lobe the Negro brain resembles that of our children. . . . The grown-up Negro partakes, as regards intellectual faculties, of the nature of the child'" (qtd in Gould, 135). Analogous remarks were made about women in the nineteenth century. As Corinne T. Field has written, "In the antebellum United States, law and public opinion defined adult independence as a stage of life specific to white men, while classifying women as perpetual dependents" (113). Such beliefs allowed for an easy linguistic slippage: since women were perpetual dependents, they were also like perpetual children. Figures ranging from politicians to physicians argued that women were unfit to engage in activities such as voting, managing their own finances, or enrolling in higher education because they were evolutionarily closer to children than adults. Edward Drinker Cope, a well-respected comparative anatomist during the nineteenth century, for instance, asserted that women's "metaphysical characteristics" were "very similar in essential nature of those which men exhibit at an early stage of development" (158–59).

Of course, this same historical period witnessed the heyday of white Western imperialism and extensive colonialist efforts. Indigenous peoples, especially on the continent of Africa, were routinely likened to children in social and scientific efforts to justify their subjugation. Under the auspices of various pseudosciences like phrenology, craniometry, and anthropometry, authorities proclaimed that the intellectual, physical, and psychological development of tribal peoples halted in late childhood or early adolescence. G. Stanley Hall, a leading American psychologist, argued in 1904 that "Most savages in most respects are children, or, because of sexual maturity, more properly, adolescents of adult size" (649). As before, such sentiments were shared by many other prominent physicians, psychologists, and anthropologists. In 1895, for example, "Herbert Spencer, the apostle of social Darwinism, asserted: 'The intellectual traits of the uncivilized . . . are traits recurring in the children of the civilized'" (Gould 146).

While the scientific basis for deriding certain demographic groups by likening them to children lost credibility during the Progressive era, the social tendency to engage in this practice did not. Throughout the twentieth century, individuals who did not conform to conventional notions of maturity faced criticism. As countless self-help books, informational websites, and daytime talk shows assert, adults who act like children—in the workplace, on the athletic field, during a romantic relationship, or in a friendship—need to be chastised and changed; failing that, they must be avoided and even shunned.

Stephanie Marston, for example, matter-of-factly informs the readers of her 1994 advice book that "Some people are simply too angry, unreliable, immature or unstable" to have an adult relationship (163).

Such pronouncements are commonly directed at individual people. However, during times of widespread rebellion against established norms of adult behavior, they become applied to large groups. Perhaps the best example of this phenomenon occurred during the 1960s and 1970s. Fueled by factors such as the growing discontent with the Vietnam War and advent of the sexual revolution, the nation's college-aged young people engaged in a wholesale rejection of many signature traits of adulthood. In gestures that were often regarded as being selfish and childish, they refused to wear "respectable" clothing, get "proper" hairstyles, or settle down into marriage. As Gary Cross has discussed, in the minds of many parents, psychologists, and politicians, the nation's twenty-somethings were seeking to create "a life in which one remained a youth" (135). This assessment was only partially accurate. To many individuals from this generation, being an adult did not indicate a time of responsibility and respectability. Instead, amidst the injustices of the Vietnam War and the inequities made visible by the black, feminist, disability, and LGBTQ civil rights movements, this stage of life was more strongly associated with hypocrisy, corruption, and stifling conformity. In the words of Cross once again, these young people did not wish "to face the expected limitations and boredoms of ordinary adult life" (136).

That said, popular opinion largely believed otherwise. For much of the nation, the hippies were not viewed as brave iconoclasts calling adult norms into question. Instead, as Leonard Steinhorn has relayed, they were regarded as "self-absorbed hedonists and Peter Pans who never will grow up and accept their duty" (xii). In 1976, Tom Wolfe famously gave this era's cohort of iconoclastic young people the puerile label of the "Me Generation." As Cross recalled, for their refusal to fight in war, get married, or take a nine-to-five corporate job, "the pundits and politicians called us babies" (132).

During the 1980s, such sentiments surfaced again with the publication of Dan Kiley's book *The Peter Pan Syndrome: Men Who Have Never Grown Up* (1983). As journalist Robert McGill Thomas Jr. explained, "Dr. Kiley got the idea for 'The Peter Pan Syndrome' after noticing that, like the famous character in the James M. Barrie play, many of the troubled teen-age boys he treated had problems growing up and accepting adult responsibilities" (7). Kiley believed that this phenomenon was not an isolated issue, but a national problem.

The Peter Pan Syndrome struck a chord. The book was an immediate success and went on to become a bestseller (Thomas 7).

Over the past decade or so, Kiley's concept has surfaced again. In films such as *Failure to Launch* (2006) and *Knocked Up* (2007), as well as in books such as Sally Koslow's *Slouching Towards Adulthood* (2012) and Gary Cross's *Men to Boys: The Making of Modern Immaturity* (2008), the opening years of the new millennium saw a resurgence of "men who continue to act like teenagers well into adulthood" (Abraham, par. 2). In comments that recall the observations in *The Peter Pan Syndrome*, these figures lament how the current generation continues to play video games, avoids getting married, and even lives with their parents. Cross refers to an individual who possesses these traits as a "boy-man," while Koslow deems them a "man-child"—the same term used in *The Peter Pan Syndrome*. Echoing another facet of Kiley, both Cross and Koslow see this trend as cause for alarm, not celebration. How can the United States remain a strong nation, they wonder, if its grown men—by which they primarily mean its white, middle-class, heterosexual, and cis-gendered ones—are little more than immature boys? Will anyone take these individuals seriously when they spend their time engaging in such "childish" activities as skateboarding, playing video games, and wearing T-shirts adorned with their favorite comic book characters?

As these and other examples make clear, Americans who defy the conventions of adulthood and engage in behavior that is more commonly associated with children are vilified at worst and regarded as a source of entertainment at best. From past examples such as the juvenile antics of the Three Stooges or the childish doddering of Charlie Chaplin's tramp to more contemporary incarnations like the immature stylings of Beavis and Butt-Head or the arrested development of the many on-screen characters played by Adam Sandler, silly, goofy, and puerile adults may be amusing, but they are not admirable. Dan Kiley made an observation during the early 1980s that still applies today: "society has little patience with adults who act like children" (25). Being viewed as childish or even as the less pejorative "childlike" causes individuals to be regarded as less culturally sophisticated, less socially significant, and, during some historical eras, even less fully human. In this way, the practice of establishing, maintaining, and policing the line separating children and adults is more than simply a method for distinguishing between different stages of the human life cycle; it is a means of social control. Condemning persons who defy the conventions of expected adult behavior protects existing power dynamics, thereby maintaining the status quo.

"I'm a Big Kid Now": Rethinking the "Childish Adult" with Rejuveniles, Grups, and Kidults

In the opening years of the twenty-first century, a now-familiar phenomenon began to occur in the United States. Individuals reached experiential milestones commonly associated with adulthood—moving out of their natal homes, obtaining full-time jobs, and getting married—but they did not embrace what is commonly considered an adult identity. Instead, they chose to retain a number of interests, activities, and attitudes associated with youth. As journalist Adam Sternbergh observed in 2006, "This cohort is not interested in putting away childish things. They are a generation or two . . . who are now happily sailing through their thirties and forties, and even *fifties*, clad in beat-up sneakers and cashmere hoodies" (par. 3; italics in original).

This phenomenon was particularly prevalent among middle-class whites, but a variety of cultural indicators pointed to its status as a nationwide phenomenon. "In Manhattan crowds cram bars for all-adult spelling bees," Christopher Noxon reported in 2006 (2). Along those same lines, kickball leagues for grown-ups became one of the biggest recreational sensations (Noxon 2). Likewise, classic board games like Operation, Pictionary, and Battleship made a comeback—not because children loved to play them, but because adults did (Garin 15). Meanwhile, Hello Kitty had become hugely popular among adults in general and women in particular; her likeness appeared on "toasters, taxicabs, and vibrators" (Noxon 3). Echoing this trend, by 2005, "Half of the visitors to Disney World are childless adults, making the Magic Kingdom the number-one adult vacation destination in the world" (Noxon 3). A few years later, articles in newspapers and magazines began documenting the latest development: the growing popularity of summer sleep-away camps for adults. While some of these camps had more adult-oriented themes like wine tasting (Kane, par. 2), many others were modeled directly after ones from childhood. As Thom Patterson reported for *CNN*, "Campers make friendship bracelets . . . they chow down in the mess hall" (Patterson, par. 4). Once again, middle-class whites constituted the primary demographic for these activities, but the phenomenon was not exclusively linked with this population. Instead, adult interest in spelling bees, cupcakes, kickball, Hello Kitty, and board games crossed lines of race, class, region, and ethnicity.

Both the breadth and depth of these events suggested that something much more significant was at work than merely a faddish trend. As Noxon asserted, "They constitute a new breed of adult, identified by a determination to remain playful, energetic, and flexible in the face of adult responsibilities" (2). Stern-bergh echoed this observation. As he made clear about this phenomenon, "It's about a brave new world whose citizens are radically rethinking what it means to be a grown-up and whether being a grown-up still requires, you know, actu-ally growing up" (par. 3). From baking cupcakes to playing Twister, "this new band of grown-ups refuses to give up things they never stopped loving, or rev-els in things they were denied or never got around to as children" (Noxon 2).

These events created a paradoxical situation in the United States. On one hand, by the dawn of the twenty-first century, young people were leaving childhood behind earlier and faster than ever before. As Susan Linn, Peggy Orenstein, and Neil Postman have documented, while boys and especially girls were still in early elementary school, they adopted the actions, attitudes, and accouterments commonly associated with those in adolescence and even adulthood. At the same time, though, a seemingly opposite trend occurred: their adult counterparts returned to and recaptured aspects of their youth. They partook in toys, games, and activities that were commonly connected with childhood.

These individuals were initially described in many of the same negative ways as earlier generations of adults who did not conform to prevailing expec-tations about "mature" behavior. Andrew Calcutt titled his book on the cur-rent trend of adults embracing youthful pastimes *Arrested Development*. Even critics who do not invoke the rhetoric of evolution still described this demo-graphic in pejorative ways. Journalist A. O. Scott, in a lengthy article that ap-peared in the *New York Times Magazine* in September 2014, was perhaps the most vocal critic. Pointing to examples such as the proliferation of 50-year-old men "riding skateboards" or the growing number of adult women who have "plastic butterfly barrettes in [their] hair," he lamented that millennium-era life has "killed off all the grown-ups" (pars. 7, 5). Scott even gave his essay the matter-of-fact moniker "The Death of Adulthood in American Culture." As he went on to assert, "nobody knows how to be a grown-up anymore. Adult-hood as we have known it has become conceptually untenable" (par. 10).

Contrary to the claims by critics like Scott and Calcutt, these individuals do not see themselves as having "killed off" adulthood. Instead, they regard their actions as working to reimagine, reinvent, and reinvigorate it. Even in the face of changing cultural conditions, Americans have largely believed "that there are some basic criteria that define 'true' maturity" (Cross 19). The new cadre seeks to challenge these longstanding viewpoints. These figures upend notions about what constitutes "appropriate" adult behavior, redefining it in a new way for a new millennium. In so doing, they differentiate themselves from their predecessors in a number of significant ways.

First, the current group is not recapturing their youth in an attempt to escape the responsibilities of adulthood. As journalist Kristoffer Garin has pointed out, unlike the men classified with having "Peter Pan Syndrome" a generation before them, these individuals "have a career, a home, and maybe even children, yet still prefer dodge ball to tennis, Monopoly to bridge" (15). In contrast to previous generations, they "feel unmoved by social pressure to give up childish pleasures simply because they're, well, childish" (Garin 15). Instead, these individuals openly and even enthusiastically retain them. In acts that would have been unthinkable even a decade ago, "Captains of industry are now appearing on the cover of *Business Week* with Super Soaker water pistols and Sea-Monkey executive sets" (Noxon 2).

For this reason, this new faction of adults can be described as childlike, but not as childish: "Most have busy lives and adult responsibilities. Many have children of their own. They are not stunted adults. They are something new" (Noxon 2). Noxon dubbed these individuals "rejuveniles" for the way that they revived their youth. However, this rapidly growing demographic is also known by an array of different designations. Adam Sternbergh, in his article that appeared in a March 2006 issue of *New York* magazine, deemed them "grups" (par. 5). The term was a contraction of the term "grown-up" and also, he confessed, a "nerdy reference to an old *Star Trek* episode in which Kirk and crew land on a planet run entirely by kids, who call grown-ups 'grups'" (par. 5). Meanwhile, others revived another and far earlier portmanteau—the "kidult"—to describe them (Barkham 8). Emerging initially during the 1960s to signify a "television programme, film, or other entertainment intended to appeal to both children and adults," the term had increasingly, according to the *OED*, come to signify "an adult with juvenile tastes." Finally, in this same linguistic vein, the neologism "adultescent" was born. In a telling indication of both the intellectual weight and cultural traction that this trend had generated, the word was added to the *Oxford English Dictionary* in December 2009 as a means to denote "An adult who has retained the interests, behavior, or lifestyle of adolescence."

Whatever the specific term used to describe them, grups, adultescents, and kidults make clear that their behavior is the product of a carefully considered decision to retain beloved aspects from their youth, not the result of a psychological or biological inability to relinquish them. Unlike generations before them who had been deemed inferior or, at least, incomplete adults because of their perceived childlike qualities, they see themselves as progressive for their possession of these exact traits. These individuals assert that they are improving upon and thus advancing adulthood, not eroding it and causing it to backslide. In the words of Sternbergh, "Being a Grup is . . . about rejecting a hand-me-down model of adulthood that asks, or even necessitates, that you let go of everything you ever felt passionate about. It's about reimagining adulthood as a period defined by promise, rather than compromise" (par. 54). Susan Barclay perhaps best articulated this belief when she made the following observation: "There is a perception that some things are for adults—*CNN*, chess, or opera—and others are for children. Why must this be? We can be both childlike in our wonder and joy and adult in our responsibilities" (A21).

Of course, not all of the forces fueling this trend are so positive. As Noxon reports, many adults who collect Legos or wear *Muppet Show* T-shirts "say their attraction to kiddie culture is at least in part a response to uncertain, anxious times—the terrorist attacks of 2001, followed by infectious disease scares, a convulsing stock market, war overseas, and natural calamities at home have generated a strain of free-floating anxiety that seems uniquely sated by childlike comforts" (10). Similar reasons are repeatedly cited as fueling the current coloring craze. Many popular coloring books for grown-ups have words like "relaxation," "calming," or "stress-relief" directly in their titles. Moreover, regardless of the specific coloring book they are using, many practitioners cite the therapeutic effect of the activity. As Julia Felsenthal has written, many "colorists," as devotees call themselves, report being "drawn to the activity as a low-tech antidote to the stress of our frenzied, increasingly digital, lives" (par. 3).

In this way, grups, adultescents, and kidults do not simply challenge conventional understandings of "being a grown-up" in the United States; they reinvent this period anew. While their behavior arises in part from a backward-looking form of nostalgia, it is also engages in a forward-looking form of futurism: that is, of redefining what it means to grow older and age. Whereas childhood and adulthood have long been regarded as separate and mutually exclusive phases of life, these individuals demonstrate that they could and even should be more permeable.

The recent emergence of the verb "adulting" embodies another powerful index of the transformations that have taken place to adulthood in the twenty-first century. The gerund refers to "the practice of behaving in a way characteristic of a responsible adult, especially the accomplishment of mundane but necessary tasks," such as making dinner, running errands, doing chores, paying bills, etc. Although "adulting" has yet to be added to the *Oxford English Dictionary*, it has moved out of the realm of niche slang and into the mainstream lexicon. Danielle

Tullo, in an article that appeared in *Cosmopolitan* magazine in 2016, noted: "In the past year, the term 'adulting' has increased in usage by 700 percent on Twitter" (par. 3). According to the *Merriam-Webster Dictionary* website, this new verb is not confined to social media; it also appears in book titles, is a popular search term on academic databases like LexisNexis, and adorns shirts, magnets, and coffee mugs ("Adulting: The Verb"). In the words of Tullo once again, "It's now so mainstream that brands like Reese's and Talenti are using it on social media to target to Millennial consumers" (par. 3). In the years since, the term has been deployed by an array of additional and vastly different companies, ranging from Target and TD Ameritrade to Post Foods (in the promotion of Fruity Pebbles) and Amazon ("Adulting: The Verb"). Given this situation, the *Merriam-Webster Dictionary* declared the word's "linguistic arrival."

Adulting is more than simply a clever neologism; it also signals a shift in the cultural understanding of this concept, especially for the current generation of grown-ups. In gerund form, the term moves from an identity to an action. Adulting is now a set of behaviors in which an individual engages rather than a period of life that one occupies. Consequently, in the same way that a person can decide to engage in adulting, they can also elect to refrain from it. Phrased in a different way, the advent of adulting "reduces being a grown-up to a hobby" (Tullo, par. 4). In a radical shift from early understandings about adulthood, it is now possible not to participate, to opt out, or to choose to do something else instead. As numerous individuals in the second decade of the twenty-first century have heard—and likely even said—"I just can't adult today." And, for perhaps the first time in history, they need not.

Taking the Children out of Children's Literature: Challenging the Boundaries of Age and Genre in Children's Literature for Adults

Discussions about the millennium-era phenomenon of grown-ups retaining various aspects of youth routinely focus on their interest in children's toys, clothes, and games. However, books for young people embody another powerful site of attraction. Julie Sinn Cassidy, for example, has written about the adult-targeted release of special "collector's editions" of various Little Golden Books. Spotlighting new editions of beloved classics such as *The Poky Little Puppy* and *The Saggy Baggy Elephant*, she comments on "the commercial repackaging of children's books for adult consumers and the 'manufacturing' of images from those same children's books as tattoos, T-shirt decals, stickers, collectables, or tchotchkes" (145).

A similar phenomenon has occurred with other texts and authors. Since the death of Dr. Seuss in 1991, and the subsequent lifting of his limitations on merchandising, a growing number of adult-oriented toys, clothes, and collectibles based on some of his famous picture books have appeared. These include T-shirts featuring Thing 1 and Thing 2, throw pillows adorned with the Lorax, and Halloween costumes that permit adults to dress up as the Cat in the Hat. In 1997, Jerry Griswold recognized this growing adult enthusiasm for the literature, culture, and material items of youth. The "dramatic increase in sales of children's books" during the previous few two decades, he explained, is largely attributed to "a considerable *adult* interest in children's books" (38; italics in original). As Griswold went on to elaborate: "In fact, several years ago, writer James Marshall told me that marketing studies done by publishers indicated that one-third of all illustrated children's books are purchased by adults who don't plan to pass them along to children" (38–39).

This trend expanded in the years following Griswold's discussion. The first book in J. K. Rowling's Harry Potter series was released in the United States in 1998 and became an immediate sensation with children and adults alike. Then, in the opening years of the twenty-first century, young adult (or, as it is commonly abbreviated, YA) literature likewise became incredibly popular both among its target audience of teenagers and with grown-ups, especially women. From the Twilight series and the Hunger Games trilogy to John Green's *The Fault in Our Stars* and Markus Zusak's *The Book Thief*, adults emerged as an enthusiastic readership of YA books. By 2014, this phenomenon had become so widespread that Ruth Graham commented in an article that appeared in *Slate*: "I'm surrounded by YA-loving adults, both in real life and online" (par. 3). Far from being limited to the journalist's own experience, this situation was national: "A 2012 survey by a market research firm found that 55 percent of these [YA] books are bought by people older than 18" (Graham, par. 2).

While the growing adult audience for young adult literature has been a boon for book sales, not everyone has seen it as a positive development. As Graham flatly stated in her *Slate* piece, "Adults *should* feel embarrassed about reading literature written for children" (par. 3; her emphasis). Instead of proudly declaring their fandom for YA literature, she argued that they ought to be ashamed of it. Joel Stein penned an opinion piece for the *New York Times* that echoed this sentiment. The article bore the matter-of-fact title "Adults Should Read Adult Books." "The only thing more embarrassing than catching a guy on the plane looking at pornography on his computer is seeing a guy on the plane reading 'The Hunger Games.' Or a Twilight book. Or Harry Potter," Stein asserted in the opening paragraph (par. 1).

Children's literature for adults can be seen paradoxically as a corrective to this perceived problem and also an exacerbation of it. After all, these picture books, bedtime stories, and board books are not simply co-opted and enjoyed by adults; they are created intentionally for them. And, in that way, children's literature for adults marks a new development both in what Griswold deemed the "adulteration" of children's literature and the rise of the rejuvenile in the twenty-first century. Whereas adults had previously enjoyed selected texts intended for young readers, they now claim at least partial ownership of this category as a whole. Instead of isolated titles crossing over to adult audiences, the entire genre is doing so. Even more significantly, whereas grown-ups had formerly appropriated narratives intended for adolescents, teens, and young adults, they are now doing so with formats associated with the youngest of children: coloring books, alphabet texts, board books, etc.

Children's literature for adults, however, is not merely a manifestation of this cultural trend in the nation's print culture. First, the genre predates the emergence of kidults and adultescents, appearing in mainstream American culture during the mid-1980s—as my discussion in chapter one examines. Second, and more importantly, it possesses some markedly different and thereby distinguishing characteristics. These books are silly as well as serious, whimsical and weighty, goofy but filled with gravitas. In filling opposing capacities, they go beyond simply trafficking in nostalgia. Titles like *Goodnight Bush*, *MA!*, and *Go the F**k to Sleep* demonstrate how literary styles and physical formats that have long been associated with storytelling for young readers can be effective platforms for engaging topics of interest to adults as well. Moreover, as my discussion in the chapters demonstrates, not only are picture books, bedtime stories, and alphabet texts suitable narrative forms for audiences of adults, but these modes can also give added richness, resonance, and complexity to the topics that they address. Literary critics have long discussed the interplay between form and content in texts. Children's literature for adults invites readers to engage with this issue in a whole new way.

This same observation applies to the current cadre of coloring books for adults. These items are not the same as their counterparts intended for young people. Coloring books for adults differentiate themselves from those intended for kids via their material format and their creative content. Generally speaking, coloring books for adults contain more pages; they use a higher quality of paper stock; they are assembled using more sophisticating bookbinding methods; they contain images that are more detailed and intricate; and, finally, they are more expensive. Moreover, many coloring books for adults feature subject matter that has limited appeal to young people. While some kids might enjoy Ming-Ju Sun's *Art Deco Fashions* (2014), A. G. Smith's *Victorian House Coloring Book* (2016), or Alphonse Marie Mucha Jr. and Ed Sibbett Jr.'s *Art Nouveau Design* (2015), the topics showcased in these titles seem far more compelling to adults.

In this way, children's literature for adults reveals itself as something different and more complicated than the mere appropriation of material forms, narrative styles, or literary schools associated with juvenile literature. Instead, the genre takes these elements and retools, recalibrates, or reimagines them for adult audiences. A picture book that is intended for pre-literate children has different aims, intents, and purposes than one that is geared for a readership of grown-ups. Likewise, a board book that is designed for a toddler serves different cultural as well as creative purposes than one that is produced for adults. As a result, children's literature for adults is simultaneously a throwback and a harbinger. The genre reconnects readers with schools, styles, and formats that they once loved. But it uses these elements as a vehicle for addressing subjects and storylines that are designed for adult audiences. These texts challenge their readers to reconsider what could and even should constitute narratives for grown-ups. Why can't picture books serve as a platform? What new kinds of stories could be told if the pop-up format were an option? What is the reason that bedtime stories have been historically excluded from the literary modes available to writers for adults? After all, don't adults also often wind down by reading a book when they go to bed? As a result, children's literature for adults echoes while it extends reconsiderations of the firm division between childhood and adulthood that is taking place in other cultural sites and material sources.

In some ways, the emergence of children's literature for adults can be viewed as an unavoidable or at least unsurprising phenomenon, not only because of the cultural circumstances in the twenty-first century, but also because of the nature of juvenile literature itself. As critics like Jacqueline Rose and, more recently, Perry Nodelman have commented, narratives for young readers have always possessed a powerful adult presence. After all, adults—not children—are the ones who commonly create, compose, edit, publish, select, and purchase books for young readers. For this reason, Rose asserts that there is a certain "impossibility" regarding children's literature. In spite of the longstanding belief that children's literature "represents the child, speaks to and for children" (Rose 1), this belief is untrue. In the words of Rose, "Children's fiction sets up a world in which the adult comes first (author, maker, giver) and the child comes after (reader, product, receiver)" (1–2). Nodelman builds on this observation. In his book by the same name, he discusses "the hidden adult" lurking in the background of all narratives for young readers. "The simple text implies an unspoken and more complex repertoire that amounts to a second, hidden text—what I call a 'shadow text,'" he asserts (8).

Children's literature for adults takes the long-acknowledged presence of grown-ups in narratives for young readers and makes it visible. Rather than attempting to deny the role that adults have played in the creation of juvenile-styled narratives, the genre embraces it. It calls added attention to a trait that has been present in these texts all along.

The picture books, bedtime stories, and board books profiled in this book can be regarded as taking this line of thinking to its logical conclusion. Books like *Goodnight Keith Moon, Go the F**k to Sleep,* or *MA!* take the "hidden adult" that Nodelman argues exists in the background of all juvenile-styled narratives and move it to the foreground. Rather than trying to resist the "impossibility" of children's literature, as Jacqueline Rose famously argued, these texts embrace it openly. As a consequence, children's literature for adults engages with ongoing considerations about the literary parameters and even generic limits of narratives for young people, while simultaneously pushing these conversations in new and unexplored directions. Children's literature for adults may seem like an oxymoronic and even nonsensical category, but it reveals how such unease and contradiction has always been the case. Children's literature—be it for young people or older individuals—has never been a stable, "pure," or uncomplicated category.

The advent of children's literature for adults raises a host of complex issues that call into question the composition, nature, and definition of the genre itself. In *The Hidden Adult,* Perry Nodelman remarks that children's literature is the only literary genre that is defined by its intended audience, not by its authorship, subject matter, or aesthetic features.[9] Given this trait, Nodelman wonders, what do books for young readers have in common beyond their intended audience? That is, what qualities, features, or characteristics do these narratives possess that unite them as a cohesive literary school or writing style beyond their shared readership? Accordingly, as the subtitle to *The Hidden Adult: Defining Children's Literature* indicates, Nodelman seeks answers to the question of how children's literature can be delineated as a genre.

Perry Nodelman is not the only critic to engage with this issue. Carrie Hintz and Eric Tribunella have pondered this question as well. "The history of children's literature," they assert, "cannot be fully understood without considering the history of childhood, and children's literature seems inextricably connected with audience" (14). As they go on to explain, the intended readership of these narratives greatly influences and often even dictates every other feature that they possess, from their subject matter and length to their tone and writing style (14).

This project is also interested in the relationship between audience and genre, but for different aesthetic purposes that have far different sociocultural ends. In it, I explore what happens to children's literature when arguably its most basic and fundamental characteristic is removed: a readership of children. Does children's literature lose its literary integrity or aesthetic validity as a distinct genre when it is created for a readership of adults, rather than kids? If we decouple children's literature from an audience of children, does this category cease to exist? If children's literature is able to endure being separated from children, what literary, artistic, and/or material transformations result from this condition—if any? What does the paradoxical genre of children's literature for adults reveal about both the possibilities and limitations of narrative taxonomies?

Methodology, Scope, and Chapter Summaries

Admittedly, the closing decades of the twentieth century were not the first time that juvenile-styled books had been created for a readership of adults in the United States. In the decades prior, texts written in genres traditionally associated with children's literature appeared for grown-ups.[10] Shel Silverstein's *Uncle Shelby's ABZ Book* (1961) forms a poignant example. Subtitled *A Primer for Adults Only*, the text offers an irreverent take on the traditional alphabet book, with entries such as "G is for Gigolo," "L is for Lye," and "Y is for Yell." Indeed, sections of Silverstein's text were originally published in *Playboy*. Two years later, a picture book echoed this same spirit: Louise Armstrong's *A Child's Guide to Freud* (1963). Although the narrative is ostensibly speaking to a youth reader—"This is Mommy"—the deadpan explanations of psychoanalytic theory reveal that it is directed at adults. For instance, as one page helpfully explains: "The feelings you have about Mommy and Daddy closing their door are called OEDIPAL." Meanwhile, another passage asserts: "If you paint a picture of a dragon and title it Daddy, this is called SUBLIMATION."[11]

However, such texts were unusual, appearing only occasionally in the United States. It was not until the mid-1980s that juvenile-styled narratives for adults began to be published with any cultural frequency and commercial force. Accordingly, this book profiles the period when juvenile-styled texts for adults moved from a sporadic novelty item to a full-fledged literary genre in its own right. At the same time, it is my hope that this book will inspire renewed attention to earlier titles, like *Uncle Shelby's ABZ Book* and *A Child's Guide to Freud*, that have been largely unexamined because reviewers lacked an aesthetic framework and critical vocabulary for discussing them.

In the same way that the existence of juvenile-styled books for adult readers is not limited to the closing decades of the twentieth century, it is also not limited to the United States. As my opening discussion about the British origins of the coloring book craze demonstrates, narratives of this nature can also be found throughout Europe. Alex Conway, in his blog post mentioned earlier, discusses the growing body of adult-audience parodies of classic children's books in Great Britain. As he writes, whole franchises have emerged around comedic retellings of Enid Blyton's Five Go series, along with the Ladybird Books for young readers. Titles include *Five Go Gluten Free* and *The Ladybird Book for Hipsters* (Conway). Meanwhile, Åse Marie Ommundsen has discussed a similar phenomenon in Norway. "Since the 1990s there has been a growing tendency in Scandinavia to publish not only crossover picturebooks but also picturebook-narratives exclusively for adults," she writes (17). To illustrate, she examines titles such as Erlend Loe's *Maria & José* (1994), Lars Elling's *Havet og kjærlighteten* (*Sea and Love*, 2002), and Gro Dahle's *Ikke gi opp håpet, Werner* (*Don't Give Up, Werner*, 2005). Given both the large number of such texts and their multi-decade history, Ommundsen considers this literary mode "something of a Nordic phenomenon" in many respects (17). Furthermore, Sandra Beckett, at various points in her books *Crossover Fiction: Global and Historical Perspectives* (2008) and *Crossover Picturebooks: A Genre for All Ages* (2011), mentions some additional examples from countries around Europe.[12] So, too, do various contributors to Beckett's edited collection *Transcending Boundaries: Writing for a Dual Audience of Children and Adults* (1999). Whether parodies or original texts, these titles possess a clear kinship with the books discussed in the chapters that follow. Texts such as Eva Eriksoon's *Titta Max grav!* (1991) from Sweden, Nick Bantock's *Griffin and Sabine: An Extraordinary Correspondence* (1991) from Canada, and Fam Ekman's *Tilberedning av hjerter* (1998) from Norway demonstrate that children's literature for adults is not limited to the United States, nor is it limited to English-language narratives.[13] Instead, it is a global phenomenon. Nonetheless, a discussion of juvenile-styled narratives for adult readers that have appeared in countries and cultures around the world is outside the scope of this project—as well as my own area of expertise. It is my hope that this book will inspire further research on this topic, including examinations of this phenomenon in other countries and from cross-cultural, as well as international, perspectives.

On a related note, with regard to methodology, the books featured in the following chapters were chosen not because they are the only examples of children's literature for adults in the United States during this period; rather, they were selected because they perform multiple literary, aesthetic, and cultural functions. First, all of these titles were popular and well-known. Each was commercially successful and, in many cases, also critically acclaimed. As a consequence, they embody a significant development in the emergence of children's literature for adults that helped to establish it as a cultural phenomenon in the United States. In addition, these books collectively work to provide a historical overview of the development of children's literature for adults over the decades. Beginning with Dr. Seuss's *You're Only Old Once!* in the mid-1980s and extending through the massive success of *Go the F**K to Sleep* in second decade of the twenty-first century, each chapter marks a different historical moment in the evolution of this phenomenon. Accordingly, the chapters are arranged chronologically, although they can be read out of order. Next, and just as importantly, the narratives featured in this book represent a cross-section of some of the most popular schools, styles, and types of books for young readers. From picture books and series novels to board books and bedtime stories, they document how children's literature for adults embodies a wide array of narratives. Please note that many of the children's books for adults that I analyze are unpaginated; page numbers are given whenever possible.

All of the titles featured in this study serve one final function: they demonstrate a different literary implication for, or cultural purpose of, children's literature for adults. Each chapter calls attention to an alternative aspect of the aesthetic construction, creative possibilities, and sociopolitical significance of the genre. From a literary standpoint, they ponder the role of narrative format (Seuss), popular characters (Maney), physical materiality (Spiegelman), authorship (Park), and well-known schools and literary styles (Mansbach; Origen and Golan). Meanwhile, from a sociopolitical perspective, they take up subject matters ranging from aging (*You're Only Old Once!*) and terrorism (*In the Shadow of No Towers*) to parenting (*MA!* and *Go the F**k to Sleep*) and partisan politics (*Goodnight Bush* and *Don't Let the Republican Drive the Bus!*). By engaging with a broad range of literary, aesthetic, and cultural issues, the texts allow me to explore children's literature for adults both on a mirco and a macro level. Each chapter offers a close reading of the feature text, but then it uses that analysis as a jumping off point to theorize about the larger phenomenon in which it is participating. As a result, this book serves a dual purpose. This project offers fresh, original analysis about an important example of children's literature for adults, while it also establishes the parameters and lays out the stakes of the genre as a whole. What new and different stories can be told when forms like the picture book, bedtime story, and board book become available to adult audiences? What is creatively, critically, and culturally gained, as well as potentially lost, by the existence of children's literature for adults? What happens to our understanding of both children's literature and books for adults by the creation of this category? What does it mean, both for literary taxonomies and for understandings of the human life cycle, when the line separating children and adults is blurred or even erased?

Chapter one spotlights the text that can be credited with inaugurating the millennium-era surge of children's literature for adults: Dr. Seuss's *You're Only Old Once!* (1986). Bearing the subtitle *A Book for Obsolete Children*, the text popularized the genre. Seuss's book demonstrated that not only could adult-audience works be released in literary schools, styles, or formats that had traditionally been associated with young people, but that such narratives would have powerful attraction and widespread appeal. Moreover, the elements of children's literature that were being utilized in these texts were not incidental. Instead, as the relationship between the form and the content of *Old Once!* reveals, these features allowed authors to tell more poignant and thus more powerful stories about adulthood. Viewing Seuss's 1986 text as a work of children's literature for adults calls attention to a powerful paradox concerning the human life cycle. Old age is the final phase of adulthood, the period that directly precedes death. Thus, it can be seen as the developmental state that is the farthest away from childhood. However, as the events that unfold in *Old Once!* reveal, the elderly are routinely infantilized. Rather than being the most removed from children, they ironically or paradoxically are treated like them. Viewed from this perspective, Seuss's use of the picture book format shifts from a seemingly irrelevant feature to one that is deeply symbolic.

Chapter two examines Mabel Maney's 1993 novel, *The Case of the Not-So-Nice Nurse*. A camp classic within the LGBTQ community, the narrative is an adult-audience retelling of two highly popular girls' mystery series: Nancy Drew and Cherry Ames. Maney's book adds a new facet to the emerging phenomenon of children's literature for adults in the closing decade of the twentieth century. Her text illustrates that adult readers need not leave behind any of their beloved protagonists simply because they have now reached the so-called age of maturity. Instead, characters like Nancy Drew can be pleasingly and successfully featured in texts written for adults. The literary implications and cultural significance of Maney's adult-audience retelling go far beyond this one isolated literary figure and book series. Her work can be placed at the forefront of a rich and rapidly growing source of children's literature for adults during the closing years of the twentieth century: fanfiction.

Chapter three examines Art Spiegelman's *In the Shadow of No Towers* (2004), a graphic narrative about the terrorist attacks in New York City on September 11, 2001. The narrative is a folio-sized text that is printed on heavy cardstock akin to the board books issued for infants and toddlers. Foregrounding the materiality of the book augments Spiegelman's exploration of both the logistical events of 9/11 and especially their emotional, psychological, and cultural aftermath. First and foremost, paying attention to the physicality of the book leads us back to the inherent physicality of the event it portrays: namely, the destruction of the World Trade Center. The terrorist attack graphically demonstrated how material structures that seemed strong, secure, and permanent were acutely vulnerable and ultimately ephemeral. Just as importantly, though, the appearance of *No Towers* as a board book also comments on the emotional impact of the day's physical destruction. Even the most cool-headed adults were left reeling: psychologically dazed, personally stunned, and emotionally in shock. As a result, they occupied positions of vulnerability and fear more commonly experienced by young children. *No Towers* meets its adult readers where they are, appearing in a physical format that can bear their grief, withstand their anger, and offer the sociopolitical lessons that they will need to learn in a post-9/11 world. The rich interplay between the content and the form of *No Towers* offers a compelling commentary about the relationship between childhood and adulthood amidst times of trauma, fear, and upheaval.

Chapter four spotlights Barbara Park's picture book *MA! There's Nothing to Do Here!: A Word from Your Baby-in-Waiting* (2008). Park, of course, is more commonly known as the author of the wildly popular Junie B. Jones books for young people. However, her 2008 picture book is directed at an adult audience. Since its release, the text, which is narrated by an unborn fetus in utero, has become a popular gift at baby showers. My chapter makes the case that *MA!* exemplifies the millennium-era shift toward what Lauren Berlant has termed "fetal citizenship." As she explains, the roles, rights, and responsibilities previously associated with adults are now being extended to the young. Whereas grown-ups were formerly regarded as the centerpiece and even the raison d'être of the nation, this position is now being occupied not simply by children but—as *MA!* demonstrates—the unborn. Park's book is purportedly "written" by not simply a child, but a fetus in utero. Together with upending a longstanding literary trend, this reversal adds a new element to the social significance and cultural impact of Park's text. While her picture book for adults might be seen as yet another example of the encroachment of grown-ups into the world of kids, the point of view that the text privileges points to the opposite phenomenon: it signals the growing power that the unborn have come to possess over adults in the United States. Together with serving as the narrative voice for their literature, children—including those who are still in utero—are also dictating the material, emotional, and psychological expectations for motherhood in the new millennium.

Chapter five spotlights four commercially successful adult-audience political parodies of popular picture books that have been released in the opening decades of the twenty-first century. Two of these texts emanate from the political left: *Goodnight Bush* (2008) and *Don't Let the Republications Drive the Bus!* (2012), both by Erich Origen and Gan Golan. Conversely, two are affiliated with the political right: *The Cat and the Mitt* (2012), by Dr. Truth, and *Dr. Paul* (2011), by Chris Ouellette. These narratives parody beloved picture books: Margaret Wise Brown's *Goodnight Moon* (1947), Mo Willems's *Don't Let the Pigeon Drive the Bus!* (2003), Dr. Seuss's *The Cat in the Hat* (1957), and Dr. Seuss's *Green Eggs and Ham* (1960), respectively. I make a case, however, that their true literary, ideological, and cultural kinship is with a far different genre: the broadside. Emerging in England in the fifteenth century and experiencing their heyday in the United States during the Federalist period, these single-sheet missives were easily disseminated and, thus, efficacious forms of print communication. My chapter argues that *Goodnight Bush, Dr. Paul, Don't Let the Republican Drive the Bus!,* and *The Cat and the Mitt* revive this once vibrant but now largely defunct print tradition for a new audience in a new era. An awareness of the broadside tradition that permeates these four books does more than simply complicate the mimesis that is operating within each text— it also reveals compelling new insights about the current state of political discourse in the United States, along with the possible role that print culture can play in participatory democracy during the twenty-first century. Released into a media-saturated environment where it is challenging for any message to get noticed, these parodies form an effective means to catch an individual's attention, bring pressing sociopolitical issues to light, and spark public de-bate. They embody a new venue by which to politically engage the citizenry. Political parodies of popular picture books call attention to the long, storied, and important role that print culture has historically played—and continues to exert—in American politics. At the same time, they add to ongoing dis-cussions about politics and children's literature. Rather than engaging with the longstanding question of what relationship books for young readers should have with political topics, these adult-audience parodies highlight the relationship that politics may choose to have with classic works of children's literature.

Chapter six makes visible the complex relationship that emerged between childhood and adulthood by the second decade of the twenty-first century. Whereas Christopher Noxon and Jerry Griswold cite such positive impulses as a happy longing for the carefree days of youth as fueling the recent growth of adults reclaiming beloved childhood toys, games, and activities, the experience of raising and being around actual children is often far different. Mothers and fathers feel profound love for their sons and daughters, but they also routinely feel frustrated, exhausted, and overwhelmed with them. A new subset of children's literature for adults provided a poignant cultural platform for these viewpoints. Appearing first in titles like *Safe Baby Handling Tips* (2005), ex-panding in books such as *If You Give a Kid a Cookie, Will He Shut the F**k Up?* (2011), and then reaching full fruition in narratives like *Go the F**k to Sleep* (2011), these narratives offered a new honesty about an aspect of adulthood that had previously been unspoken—or even silenced. The frustrations asso-ciated with parenting that are presented in these narratives make visible the simultaneously revered and reviled place that young people occupy in twenty-first-century American society as well as the powerfully mixed feelings that many adults have about children, especially their own. Parenthood has long been regarded as one of the major signposts of being an adult. The blunt hon-esty of *If You Give a Kid a Cookie* and *Go the F**k to Sleep* reveals how caring for children is so physically, emotionally, and logistically demanding that it engulfs and even eclipses parents' own lives. Having children simultaneously marks adulthood—and just as quickly erases it. Echoing the concept of the twisty, bendy, and even circular nature of the human lifespan that emerged by the opening decades of the twenty-first century, *Go the F**k* and *If You Give a Kid a Cookie* demonstrated how having and caring for children swallowed up adulthood—but the inverse was also true. Another work of children's lit-erature for adults that was released during this same period examined how childhood had been swallowed up by adulthood. The narrative was tellingly titled *The Littlest Bitch* (2010). Written by David Quinn and Michael Davis and illustrated by Devon Devereaux, it made a case that children are not simply growing up too fast—they are skipping childhood entirely.

Finally, the conclusion begins by recapping how each of the examples of children's literature for adults profiled in the previous chapters teases out a different way that the line between childhood and adulthood has blurred. Then, it contemplates what such blending means for this generation of readers and, even more importantly, for the next. The name of this new genre is paradoxical, and, perhaps appropriately, its social, cultural, and literary impact is paradoxical as well. On one hand, these books demonstrate that it is not merely our theoretical understandings of the human lifespan that are shifting, but our daily lived experiences. Formerly linear concepts of growing up and growing older are looping, leaping, and lurching back upon themselves in ways not previously acknowledged, discussed, or perhaps even realized. Moreover, these events are not abstract pie-in-the-sky potentialities, but actual current realities. Children's literature for adults provides a platform to represent such phenomena, while it also continues to push those boundaries, pointing out new developments and calling attention to new possibilities. At the same time, of course, these books are intended for an exclusively adult audience. Thus, the genre breaks down the barriers of age and audience in some regards and then ironically reinforces them in other ways.

One final note about methodology. As mentioned before, the narratives featured in the subsequent chapters provide an illuminating cross-section of children's literature for adults. However, they are not a comprehensive survey of books released from the 1980s to the 2010s. My goal is to spotlight some of the most socially significant, commercially successful, and culturally compelling examples of children's literature for adults, not to offer an exhaustive overview of them. This study uses a handful of key, provocative examples to develop a theoretical structure that can be used to examine not just these specific narratives, but a wider set of texts across what is a booming genre. Take, for example, Kathryn Petras and Ross Petras's *B is for Botox: An Alphabet Book for the Middle-Aged* (2009) and their follow-up text, *1, 2, Can't Reach My Shoe: A Counting Book for the Middle-Aged* (2010). Likewise, Christopher Behrens's popular board book *Penis Pokey* (2006) is another children's styled text that—as its title indicates—is intended for adult readers.[14] Along those same lines, pop-up books including Gary Greenberg and Matthew Reinhart's *The Pop-Up Book of Phobias* (1999) and *The Pop-Up Book of Nightmares* (2001), along with

Kathy Kelly's *Menopop: A Menopause Pop-Up and Activity Book* (2000), Sir Richard Burton and F. F. Arbuthnot's *The Pop-Up Kama Sutra* (2003), and Balvis Rubess and Kees Moerbeek's *The Pop-Up Book of Sex* (2006), can be grouped in this category.[15] Similarly, a bevy of paper doll books have appeared in recent decades, many of which were created by Tom Tierney. From the late 1970s until his death in 2014, the former fashion illustrator published over 400 paper doll books, which collectively sold more than 4 million copies (Bender, par. 6). As Margalit Fox said of his career, "Meticulously drawn and colored, and annotated with historical information, Mr. Tierney's paper-doll books are not just for children—and some are not for children at all" (B8). Examples include Tierney's *New Attitude: An Adult Paper Doll Book* (2008). Meanwhile, seek-and-find books, which ask readers to search for objects hidden in a highly detailed illustration and were made famous by the Where's Waldo? series, constitute one of the most recent literary categories to cross over. Titles like Sally Nixon's *Houseplants and Hot Sauce: An Adult Seek-and-Find Book* (2017) and Alexandre Clerisse's *Now Playing: A Seek-and-Find Book for Film Buffs* (2017) moved this genre which had formerly been the purview of kids to a readership of grown-ups. The 2016 presidential election and the inauguration of Donald J. Trump also inspired a variety of heavily partisan juvenile-styles narratives for adult audiences. Examples include Matt Maley's *Little Donny Trump Needs a Nap* (2016), Robert MacDonald's *Little Donnie Drumpf & the Magic Paintbrush* (2016), and Brad Herzog's *D is for Dump Trump: An Anti-Hate Alphabet* (2016).[16] It is my hope that this project will inspire additional work not simply on the growing new genre of children's literature for adults but on individual texts, titles, and taxonomies.

Patricia Buchanan Walsh once asserted: "the more life choices we are aware of and the more thoroughly we understand them, the more appropriately we can choose. We live in a social setting that offers a wide range of alternatives in how to conduct our lives; and the options, too, are continuously changing" (6). This book documents the presence of another transformation along these exact lines. In the same way that adults in the United States now have a myriad of options for how to experience adulthood, they also have an equally diverse array of literary schools or styles available to them. Whereas board books, bedtime stories, and picture books were formerly regarded as falling outside the confines of adulthood, the rise of children's literature for adults now brings them back within its purview. Millennium-era transformations to adulthood are not simply affecting grown-ups; they are having an equally profound impact on children and childhood. Both the presence and especially the popularity of narrative schools, styles, and formats that have long been associated with young people appearing in texts intended for adults destabilizes not simply the genre of children's literature, but the cultural conception of children and childhood as a whole. It raises questions about the purity, validity, and exclusivity of this category of identity and phase of the human life cycle. For this reason, children's literature for adults may be a linguistic paradox, but—as the following chapters demonstrate—it is also a culturally rich, aesthetically innovative, and politically potent phenomenon.

Benjamin Franklin, in the 1749 edition of *Poor Richard's Almanack*, speculated: "All would live long, but none would be old" (13). This project affirms the veracity of this prediction, while simultaneously expanding on it. This book reveals that not only can aging be separated from growing older, but even more radically, children's literature can now also be uncoupled from childhood.

CHAPTER 1

"A Book for Obsolete Children"

Dr. Seuss's *You're Only Old Once!* and the Rise of Children's
Literature for Adults

In early 1986, Theodore Geisel—better known by his pen name, Dr. Seuss—confounded his longtime editors at Random House when he submitted the manuscript for his latest picture book. Titled *You're Only Old Once!*, the narrative was unlike anything he had written before. Featuring an elderly narrator-protagonist who details his frustrations with the myriad medical ailments that accompany his aging body during a visit to a health clinic, the text was not one of Seuss's "Beginner Books." On the contrary, the narrative uses a formidable lexicon that includes words like "nasturtiums" and "anthracite," while the illustrations depict signs for medical departments with tongue-twisting names such as "Nooronoetics" and "Optoglymics." Additionally, the subject matter of Seuss's book worked against seeing it as a narrative intended for a youthful readership. As biographers Judith and Neil Morgan noted, "a newly arrived executive thought [the book] was 'a turn-off' and said, 'No one wants to think about being old,'" especially young children (263). For this reason, "Everyone around Random House agreed that *You're Only Old Once!* was not a children's book and should be handled by the adult division" (Morgan and Morgan 262). While Seuss himself pointed out "that his cartoon style and verse made it a Dr. Seuss book, whatever its subject," he concurred (Morgan and Morgan 262). Seuss worked with his regular editorial team on issues like page layout, color palette, and narrative pacing, but he allowed "the adult trade book department to market his book" (Morgan and Morgan 262–63).

When *Old Once!* made its debut on March 2, 1986, it did more than simply mark Geisel's forty-fifth published book to date; it also signaled the advent of an entirely new genre: children's literature for adults. Bearing the telling subtitle *A Book for Obsolete Children*, the text echoed the physical appearance of many narratives for adult readers. First, *Old Once!* is "the only Seuss book published by Random House with a dust jacket over a pictureless cover" (MacDonald 161). In addition, commentary that appears on the back cover "suggests to the unwary buyer that this is not a book for children" (MacDonald 161). More specifically, it read:

Is this a children's book?
Well . . . not immediately.
You buy a copy for your child now
and give it to him
on his 70th birthday.

Lest this caution is overlooked or not taken seriously, it is reiterated on the inside jacket flap.

As an adult-audience text that took the form of a child's picture book, Seuss's narrative puzzled critics. "In the often rigid world of book publishing," Morgan and Morgan observed, "*You're Only Old Once!* defied the most basic categorization" (264). As a consequence, reviewers did not know what to make of the text—or what to say about it. Discussions of the book in newspapers and magazines "were either cautiously polite or reticent, and some reviewed the author rather than his book" (Morgan and Morgan 264).

While reviewers may have been perplexed by *Old Once!*, readers were not. The picture book for adults sold well from the moment of its release. "[T]he first printing of two hundred thousand copies sold out promptly. . . . After five months and six hundred thousand copies, it was in its ninth printing, and within a year a million copies had sold" (Morgan and Morgan 263). The narrative continues to be popular among older Americans. It is a frequent sight at so-called milestone birthday parties, where the honoree celebrates their fortieth, fiftieth, or sixtieth year.

Of course, in this particular book, Dr. Seuss was not writing about the personal, social, and physical problems associated with aging from a purely abstract or theoretical standpoint. On the contrary, as past and present critics have pointed out, the book was highly autobiographical. In what has become an oft-repeated detail, *Old Once!* was released on Dr. Seuss's eighty-second birthday. Far from mere coincidence, this date was appropriate, for the narrative was exceedingly personal and intimately connected with Seuss's advancing age. In the years directly preceding the release of the picture book, the author-illustrator had experienced a variety of health problems. To pass the time in waiting rooms, Seuss began sketching hospital equipment and medical procedures. These drawings became the basis for *Old Once!* The narrative begins with an elderly male protagonist paying a visit to "the Golden Years Clinic." The remainder of the text chronicles the myriad tests that he endures over the course of his appointment. Predictably, most of them are as bizarre as they are humiliating: they involve Rube Goldberg–like contraptions, absurd processes, and varying degrees of humiliating undress. Moreover, the tests are seemingly interminable, with one coming right after the other without seeming rhyme, reason, or—routinely—consent.

This chapter takes a fresh look at Seuss's classic by viewing it as a landmark work of children's literature for adults. Seuss's text demonstrated that not only could adult-audience texts be released in literary schools, styles, or formats that had traditionally been associated with young people, but that such narratives would have powerful attraction and widespread appeal. Moreover, the elements of children's literature utilized in these texts were not incidental. As the relationship between the form and the content of *Old Once!* reveals, these features allowed authors to tell more poignant and, thus, more powerful stories about adulthood. Viewing Seuss's 1986 text as a work of children's literature for adults makes visible the ways in which it does more than simply lament the health travails that commonly accompany growing older. The narrative also calls attention to a powerful paradox concerning the human life cycle. Old age is the final phase of adulthood, the period that directly precedes death. Thus, it can be seen as the developmental state that is the farthest away from childhood. However, as the events that unfold in *Old Once!* reveal, the elderly are routinely infantilized. Rather than being the most removed from children, they ironically or paradoxically are treated like them. Viewed from this perspective, Seuss's use of the picture book format shifts from a seemingly irrelevant feature to one that is highly appropriate and deeply symbolic.

By presenting the human life cycle not as linear but more circular, the book invites us to pay attention to temporality and chronology more broadly. Doing so leads us to another and less commonly considered aspect of the text: the historical time period in which it was initially written and released. During the mid-1980s, the American public and especially its medical community was preoccupied with a health-related issue that was far removed from old age— the AIDS crisis. However unexpected and even unlikely, many of the events that the protagonist experiences in *Old Once!* have strong resonance with those suffering from this disease. Reading Seuss's book about aging in the context of the AIDS crisis introduces elements of queerness into the narrative, while it simultaneously embodies another facet to its commentary regarding the passage of time. The text suggests that the heteronormative lifespan might be circular, bringing the elderly back to a state of childlike dependence. A queer reading of the narrative in the context of the AIDS crisis further destabilizes our understanding of the human lifespan as linear by introducing notions of queer temporality.

"Obsolete Children" but Children Nevertheless: The Infantilization of the Ill, the Infirm, and the Elderly

From the time that *Old Once!* was released, critics have largely viewed the book's format as an incidental and even unimportant byproduct of the author-illustrator's standard literary platform. After all, picture books are Seuss's typical and, thus, most comfortable mode of artistic expression and narrative storytelling. As a result, even though he was addressing an audience of adults in this text rather than children, it was not surprising that he would continue to work in his standard and even preferred literary medium.

While the physical format for *Old Once!* can certainly be explained in this pragmatic way, Seuss's decision to tell this particular story using this specific mode can also be seen as being more deliberate and, thus, infused with cultural commentary. The fact that the author-illustrator's adult-audience story about the difficulties of growing older appears in a narrative form commonly associated with children can also be seen as engaging with a phenomenon that had taken root in American culture by the late twentieth century with regard to aging: the infantilization of the ill, the infirm, and especially the elderly. As Elaine H. Dolinsky and Herbert B. Dolinsky observed in 1984, "The comparison of old people with children, and old age with childhood, remains commonplace" (150). Many common stereotypes about being elderly "portray old age as a 'second childhood'" (Salari and Rich 116). In some respects, this connection arises from a variety of positive areas of overlap. After retiring, for example, older people have time once again to relax, engage in hobbies, and generally enjoy themselves. Freed from the responsibilities of going to work and raising children, they can—like kids themselves—focus on having fun. However, as Sonia Miner Salari and Melinda Rich point out, the likening of old age to childhood also emerges from an equally strong set of negative associations. This connection reveals the way in which "older persons are losing or have lost the developmental stages that a growing child gains" (Salari and Rich 116). For many, old age does not involve returning to a pleasurable state of childlike enjoyment; rather, it signals a time of increasing dependency wherein they experience cognitive decline and become increasingly unable to physically care for themselves. Accordingly, like children, they come to rely on others to help them manage even basic daily activities, such as dressing, eating, and bathing (Salari and Rich 116).

Whether growing older is associated with the more positive aspects of childhood or is linked with the more negative traits, the end result is the same: it infantilizes the elderly. As Stephen Marson and Rasby Powell explain, "Infantilization is a behavioral pattern in which a person of authority (social workers, medical personnel, etc.) interacts with, responds to, or treats an elderly person as if he or she were a child" (144). Infantilization can appear in a myriad of verbal, behavioral, and environmental forms. Danielle Brady, Andrew Clifton, Viv Burr, and Stephen Curran offer the following overview: "For example it could be the use of the phrase 'good girl' or 'who's being a naughty boy?', it could be the use of age-inappropriate environments such as decorations normally seen in a nursery or the use of children's toys, it could just be the tone of voice that somebody uses such as 'baby talk' . . . or it could be treating a person as though they are incapable of carrying out simple tasks and therefore threatening their independence" (22). Even when these behaviors are intended lovingly as signs of affection or endearment, they are demeaning. "The act of treating an adult who has lived an entire life—loved, worked, raised a family and made a home—as though they were a child just starting out in the world" is equal parts absurd and humiliating (Brady, Clifton, Burr, and Curran 23). As Randall Horton bluntly stated, "Age is not a sufficient reason to believe someone is stupid" (par. 9). Nor is it sufficient reason to deny someone their independence, their value, and their agency "as fully functioning adults" (Horton, par. 2). Whatever the motivation, treating the elderly like children robs them "of their dignity and personhood" (Horton, par. 2).

Old Once! engages with this phenomenon. Echoing the experiences of many older people not just inside of medical settings but outside of them as well, Seuss's narrator-protagonist loses his status as an agentic adult and instead is treated like a dependent child from the moment that he arrives at the Golden Years Clinic, where he is told where to go and what to do. Like a child, he laments how he has little control over where he is going next, how long he will have to wait once he gets there, or even whether he can keep his clothes on.

The cover image to *Old Once!* foreshadows this condition. The illustration shows the protagonist being pushed around in a wheelchair which—with its horizontal back handle and front caster wheel—resembles a stroller. The fact that Seuss relays these experiences within a picture book further comments on this condition. The juvenile format that the famed author-illustrator selected for this story signals the way in which his central character feels infantilized or treated like a dependent child as he ages. Seuss's use of the picture book format enhances his narrative, thereby demonstrating how literary

schools, styles, and modes that have long been associated with juvenile literature can be effectively harnessed to tell stories for adults.

In alluding to early childhood, *Old Once!* underscores how, by the closing
decades of the twentieth century, stages of human life were no longer regarded
as linear but instead could be seen as looping or twisting back onto themselves.
Seuss reinforces the notion that, once adults reach old age, they cycle back
around—either by choice or by force—to being children once again. The ill,
the infirm, and the elderly become infantilized from a cultural, social, intellectual, political, emotional, and physical standpoint. As the book's subtitle
reveals, Seuss's text may be *A Book for Obsolete Children*, but the adults it
targets remain de facto children nonetheless. The treatment that the narrator-
protagonist endures throughout the narrative demonstrates how individuals
who are older and especially who are unwell occupy a societal place that is akin
to that of young children once again.

Old Once! embodied a landmark moment in American print and popular
culture. The picture book for adults demonstrated that narratives which use
schools, styles, and formats commonly associated with kids but are intended
for a readership of grown-ups could be critically and commercially successful. The new genre of children's literature for adults was born.

In the years that followed, an ever-growing number of books and authors
would follow in the footsteps of *Old Once!* While these new works of children's
literature for adults addressed a myriad of themes and subject matters, they
adhered to the model established by Dr. Seuss. As his text made clear, children's
literature for adults did not signal an escape from adult issues, problems, and
concerns. On the contrary, these narratives could offer a direct engagement
with them. Furthermore, the elements of children's literature that were incor-
porated into these texts were not incidental. Rather, they could greatly con-
tribute to the text's content, message, and critique. Children's literature for
adults allowed authors to tell stories about adulthood that were even more
complex, rich, and meaningful.

From Period of Life to Historical Time Period: *You're Only Old Once!* and the AIDS Crisis

Old Once! is indisputably autobiographical. The picture book is undeniably a
meditation on the author-illustrator's failing health as he grew older. However,
the way in which the narrative contemplates the role of time—its importance,
influence, and instability—encourages readers to engage with issues of temporality more broadly. While the focus of *Old Once!* is largely inward—spotlighting

the experiences of its protagonist and those who are also in the same stage of life—the text's interactions with time can be directed outwardly as well: to the historical era in which it was initially written and released. As Dr. Seuss was chronicling his travails at the "Golden Years Clinic," the American public and its health-care industry were preoccupied with a different health-related issue—the AIDS crisis. Although the disease received scant media attention when it first began appearing in gay men in the early 1980s, Acquired Immune Deficiency Syndrome would become the subject of extensive coverage in newspapers, magazines, and television broadcasts by the middle of the decade. From statistics about growing infection rates and reports about promising medical breakthroughs to speculation about how the disease was transmitted and human interest stories about individual patients like Ryan White and Rock Hudson, AIDS was a topic of national concern and widespread awareness by 1986. As conservative political commentator Paul Weyrich observed, by the time Rock Hudson died in fall 1985, AIDS had become "the number one talked about issue in every household in America. You hear it on every talk show. It's on the front page of newspapers day after day" (qtd in Barnes 12).

Seuss's book was written and released against the backdrop of the AIDS crisis. It is difficult to imagine that either Dr. Seuss or all of the hundreds of thousands of individuals who comprised his initial readership could have examined his text about the problems of American health care system, the frustrations of going to the doctor, and the hassles of being ill and not have been reminded about ongoing discussions about AIDS. These associations are also powerfully evident to contemporaneous readers who have an awareness of the early days of the crisis. Many of the events that Seuss's protagonist experiences in *Old Once!* have strong resonance with those suffering from AIDS.

The second part of this chapter moves the original sociohistorical context of *Old Once!* from the background to the forefront of consideration. Doing so adds to our understanding of the role of time in the picture book, while it simultaneously demonstrates the type of fresh, new, and innovative interpretations that become possible by viewing this narrative through the lens of children's literature for adults. While Seuss's text has long been seen as addressing an experience that is universal—the aging process—the discussion that follows suggests that it can likewise be viewed in the context of a series of specific events that were occurring during the 1980s. While the picture book is, of course, not directly or explicitly about the AIDS crisis, many verbal and visual elements are applicable to it. Whether these suggestive echoes were intentional or unintentional, seen by the book's original readership or evident only now in the wake of historical distance, they suggest a new way of reading, viewing, and understanding the text. This alternative critical reading reveals the previously overlooked importance of the book's historical particularity. At the same time, it also ties back into the narrative's interest in tracing pathways of the human life cycle.

The points of correspondence between *Old Once!* and the AIDS crisis begin, ironically, with the element of the book that is also the most quintessentially autobiographical: its main character. As illustrations on the cover, front matter, and opening page convey, the narrator-protagonist is an elderly white gentleman. Since the book's publication, this figure has been seen as a thinly disguised rendering of the octogenarian author-illustrator himself (Smith, par. 5). While the physical likeness to Seuss himself is undeniable and surely embodies the primary referent, this character can also be placed in dialogue with a second and far different set of individuals: those who suffered from AIDS. During these early years of the epidemic, AIDS overwhelmingly affected not simply men but gay men. Seuss's protagonist can be viewed in a queerly suggestive way. The main character's clothing—a fussy suit, high-collar shirt, and bow tie—is more than merely the formal, antiquated attire associated with older men. Instead, it is suggestive of the unusual and even eccentric sartorial style that is a stereotype associated with gay men. Indeed, Seuss's narrator-protagonist has not simply chosen a bow tie over the more common (and, for many, more masculine) necktie, but he has selected one that is an effeminate color: pink.

The connections between Seuss's narrator-protagonist and the AIDS crisis go beyond simply his fashion choices. They also, paradoxically, extend to his age. While AIDS overwhelmingly affected young gay men during these early years of the epidemic, one of the effects of the illness was that it caused these individuals to look much older. Both G. Thomas Couser and Virginia Anderson have written about how a variety of physical factors contributed to this condition, and many of them mirror the symptoms of Seuss's elderly protagonist. Many AIDS patients' cheeks hollowed out, for instance; their hair rapidly thinned and grayed. They experienced a dramatic loss in muscle mass, and their bodies becoming more brittle and frail. These men went from being in the prime of their lives to looking haggard and far older than their actual age (Couser 149; Anderson 230). Indeed, when images of the ailing Rock Hudson first appeared in mainstream media in summer 1985, many were shocked by his sickly appearance—and especially by how much he appeared to have aged

(Miller, par. 9). Although Hudson was only fifty-nine years old at the time, he appeared, with his gaunt face and grizzled hair, to be in his seventies or beyond (Rudolph, par. 2).

Premature aging was only one of the oft-discussed effects of AIDS. Another equally common—and widely reported—condition was the development of purplish skin lesions known as Kaposi's Sarcoma. Forming yet another connection to Seuss's aged protagonist in *Old Once!*, this disease "was known as 'an old man's syndrome'" prior to the AIDS crisis (Shilts 36). Before the AIDS crisis, Kaposi's Sarcoma, or KS, was a rare form of cancer that "usually struck Jewish and Italian men in the fifth or sixth decade of their lives" (Shilts 37). For this reason, when young men in San Francisco and New York first began appearing in doctor's offices with KS lesions, they astounded dermatologists and baffled epidemiologists at the Centers for Disease Control. KS, after all, was "a bizarre skin cancer that hardly anybody got"—especially not men in their twenties and thirties (Shilts 22).

A final, but equally significant, feature about Seuss's protagonist is the fact that he is alone. Echoing the social ostracism and familial abandonment that many AIDS patients faced, the elderly man arrives at the Golden Years Clinic by himself. He endures the battery of medical tests by himself; he waits for the results by himself; and he leaves by himself. At no point is this character shown with a family member, friend, or spouse. He has no one there to keep him company during his travails or, even more importantly, to offer him any comfort. Instead, he has to face the tedium, fear, boredom, loneliness, and uncertainty of his day at the clinic alone. Far from a tacit feature of *Old Once!*, the picture book calls repeated attention to this situation as well as the emotional hardship that it imposes. Several illustrations throughout the book show the protagonist sitting in a chair by himself in the waiting area looking frightened and even forlorn: his eyes are sad, his demeanor is cowed, and even his mustache is droopy. Moreover, in a powerful indication of the protagonist's strong personal desire (and even psychological desperation) for some type of social contact, he befriends the fish in the waiting room aquarium, who is named Norval. On several pages, in fact, the main character talks with the aquarium animal. Furthermore, in another equally telling detail, these discussions are always ones in which the character is seeking some type of solace. Rather than merely making inane small talk to pass the time and stave off boredom, he reaches out to Norval for consolation, support, and even succor. Significantly, the narrator-protagonist is rebuffed each time. "Norval won't bring you / much comfort you know. / But he's quite sympathetic / as Clinic Fish go," Seuss's narrator relays after his first attempted conversation. Then, a few pages later: "So you'll find yourself talking to Norval once more. / And Norval will think you're a bit of a bore / because Norval has heard the same stories before. / To this fish you'll become a plain pain in the neck."[1] Even the name that Seuss chose for the fish echoes the sadness and distress of his isolated main character. "Norval" was the commercial name for the drug "mianserin," a prescription antidepressant during the late 1970s and early 1980s (Murphy and Bridgman 199).

The isolation and loneliness that the narrator-protagonist endures assumes added narrative significance since it diverges from Seuss's own experiences. The author-illustrator was not alone during his bouts with ill health. As biographers Judith and Neil Morgan have discussed, he had his wife, friends, neighbors, and colleagues around him. Seuss did not have to visit doctor's offices by himself, wait for test results alone, or endure troubling diagnoses on his own. Instead, he was surrounded by a large and supportive community. At times, in fact, Seuss felt that he had too many people around him. Morgan and Morgan report how the author-illustrator would grow annoyed by the constant stream of visitors who called or even stopped by to say hello, check on him, and see how he was doing. Seuss, who had always been a bit of an introvert, often just wanted to be left alone; he bristled when people repeatedly asked him how he was feeling or if they could do anything for him (Morgan and Morgan 273).

As *Old Once!* progresses and the plot of the book unfolds, the points of correspondence between it and the AIDS crisis continue. As readers learn on one of the opening pages, the book's main character comes to the doctor not because he has a specific physical ailment or medical problem, but because he is experiencing a general sense of poor health. As the narrator relays, "Just why are you here? / You're not feeling your best . . ." While this lack of physical vitality is certainly a facet of growing older, it also resonates with the progression of the AIDS virus. As Perry N. Halkitis, G. Thomas Couser, and Michael D. Quam have all documented, during the early years of the epidemic, many individuals who would later be diagnosed with the disease had a similar experience with its onset. Formerly healthy young men began arriving at their doctor's offices after weeks of not feeling like their usual energetic selves. They complained of being tired, having low-grade fevers, and losing weight "for no apparent reason" (Shilts 35).

To determine the possible cause of his ill health, Seuss's main character is given a variety of medical tests. The first one is humorously deemed "an Eyesight and Solvency Test." A double-page spread shows the gentleman's head strapped into a Rube Goldberg–like contraption. When Seuss's central character looks through the machine, however, he does not see the expected Snellen Eye Chart. Instead, he gazes at a sign on the wall that reads in all caps: "HAVE YOU ANY IDEA HOW MUCH MONEY THESE TESTS ARE COSTING YOU?" In both a humorous homage to the Snellen Eye Chart and an indication of the growing alarm that Seuss's character feels about the cost of his medical care, the letters grow increasingly larger, not smaller, as you move down the chart. Visually, this gag makes it obvious that the narrator-protagonist is also clearly concerned about his financial health.

In a further commentary on both the high cost of medical services and the manner in which this worry weighs on patients, this issue resurfaces at the end of the book. After the narrator-protagonist has completed his visit to the clinic, he learns that "a few paper forms / must be properly filled / so that you and your heirs / may be properly billed." The illustration that accompanies these lines shows the narrator-protagonist sitting in a chair as a seemingly endless line of documents pass by him on a conveyor belt. Indicating the sheer volume of paperwork that he must complete, he has a pen in both hands. Moreover, the orderly standing beside him has two additional pens waiting in reserve.

Of course, frustration with the bureaucracy of the American health care system and anxiety over the cost of medical treatment are common experiences for many patients, regardless of their age or ailment. Likewise, failing eyesight is an experience that routinely accompanies getting older. That said, all of features of the "Eyesight and Solvency Test" also have an especially powerful resonance when examined through the lens of the AIDS epidemic. As the mainstream media widely reported during the 1980s, problems with vision—and even total loss of eyesight—were common complications of the disease. A condition known as cytomegalovirus retinitis caused the retinas of AIDS patients to cloud over, impeding their vision (Halkitis x). As G. Thomas Couser has documented, the "deterioration and eventual loss of sight in both eyes" often bookended a patient's battle with the disease (133). Many individuals learned that they had contracted AIDS after going to their doctor because their "retina had clouded over for no apparent reason" (Shilts 95). Meanwhile, "the onset of blindness" was almost always a sign that the disease had progressed to its final, fatal stage (Couser 134).

Furthermore, echoing the worry of Seuss's protagonist about "how much these tests are costing you," the care and treatment of those who had AIDS was exorbitant. Ronald Bayer and Gerald M. Oppenheimer, for example, discuss how the medications alone used to treat AIDS during the 1980s were "very expensive, costing upwards of $10,000 per year" (134). Moreover, this figure did not include the many additional bills generated by doctor's visits, medical tests, and hospitalizations. For this reason, a variety of insurance companies during the first half of the 1980s refused to insure gay men or even dropped individuals who were diagnosed with AIDS, seeing them as an excessive drain on their resources and an unwarranted, or at least unwise, financial expenditure for a disease that was ultimately fatal (Shilts 239). As a result, the cost of treating AIDS patients was often passed on to the general public, as uninsured patients were compelled to visit an emergency room or—echoing the type of office patronized by Seuss's narrator-protagonist—a clinic for treatment.

After completing his eyesight exam, Seuss's protagonist is taken to a room where he meets a row of identical-looking physicians presiding over tall stacks of papers and talking simultaneously. "The Quiz-Docs will catch you! / They'll start questionnairing! / They'll ask you, point blank, how your parts are all faring," he tells readers. The barrage of personal questions, however, does not end there. As he relays, these doctors continue to pry further:

> ... And please try to recall
> if your grandma hurt most in the spring or the fall.
> Did your cousins have dreadful wild nightmares at night?
> Did they suffer such ailments as Bus Driver's Blight,
> Chimney Sweep's Stupor, or Prune Picker's Plight?
> And describe the main cause of your uncle's collapse.
> Too much alphabet soup? Or martinis, perhaps?

Of course, the need to give a full medical history and the often humiliating nature of the questions asked during this process are nearly universal experiences of visiting the doctor. That said, this process has particular resonance with the AIDS crisis. Especially during the first half of the 1980s, when the disease was new and doctors were struggling to learn about it, patients were subjected to a series of lengthy, detailed, and highly invasive questions about their pasts. In events that recall the experiences of Seuss's narrator-protagonist with the "Quiz-Docs," Randy Shilts relays the diagnostic queries that Dr. Mary Guinan, who worked on the disease for the Centers for Disease Control, made about AIDS patients in 1981: "She strained to consider every possible nuance of these people's lives. The CDC, she knew, needed to work every possible hypothesis imaginable into the case-control study. Had they been to Vietnam? Maybe this was a delayed effect of Agent Orange. Did their grandmother ever have cancer? Maybe this was some genetic fluke only appearing now. Or perhaps this was some health food gone awry" (83).

When readers turn the pages of *Old Once!*, the situation for Seuss's character worsens. As the narrator-protagonist anxiously cries: "Your escape plans
have melted! You haven't a chance." Gary D. Schmidt has written about the
"narrative quality" of many of Dr. Seuss's illustrations (42). Such drawings, he
explains, embody more than "mere replications of the text" (42). Instead, he
argues, they help to tell the story. This observation is true for nearly all of the
images in this particular text, but especially for the drawings that accompany
the various medical exams. In this scene, when the narrator-protagonist reports, "The Oglers have blossomed / like roses in May! / And, silently, grimly,
they ogle away," the illustration on the facing page offers much additional information. The character remains in the same blue barrel-like contraption as
on the previous page, but the number of experts examining him has multi-
plied. There is a new male doctor on his left, peering through a scope that is
aimed roughly at his buttocks. Even more humiliatingly, another female health
care worker has popped up through a hole in the floor and is peering through
a scope that is positioned between his legs; she is clearly looking at his groin.

Admittedly, this scenario is one that many male patients—regardless of
their age—would find not simply embarrassing but emasculating. This illustration traffics in the fear that many individuals—perhaps especially those who
are growing older—have about the loss of personal dignity as well as bodily
control that often accompanies medical treatment. That said, this scene also
reverberates with some key facets of the AIDS crisis. While much about the
disease baffled doctors during the first half of the 1980s, one aspect of its eti-
ology quickly became clear: the fact that it was transmitted by sexual contact
in general and anal intercourse especially. For this reason, asking about past
sexual activity, often via detailed, lengthy, and prying questions, became a
standard part of taking medical histories (Bayer and Oppenheimer 53–54).
While women had long been subjected to questions of this nature, they were
new to many male patients. As Dr. Alvin Friedman-Kien recalled, "I suddenly
began to take sexual histories, something nobody ever taught me in medical
school" (Bayer and Oppenheimer 53).

Seuss's book calls repeated attention to the way in which the protagonist's
medical examinations frequently involve the most private parts of his anatomy.
Not only does the illustration to this scene show an "Ogler" examining the
groin of the narrator-protagonist and another looking in the general direction
of his buttocks, but the text that accompanies this image calls attention to the
fact that the character is naked. "[B]oth your socks and your pants and your

drawers and your shoes / have been lost for the day," the passage on the facing page reads.

This scene is not the only one in which the main character is presented in manner that is sexually suggestive. A few pages later, he is met by an orderly who escorts him to all of his remaining appointments in a wheelchair. The passage used to describe the arrival of the wheelchair, the orderly, and his services are filled with gay innuendo:

> With great *swish* and great *swank*
> a wheelchair will come!
> You've gained status and rank!
> And Whelden the Wheeler will say with great *pride*:
>
> .   .   .   .
>
> "Through thin and through thick
> *I'll be at your back side*." (my italics)

Adding to the queer nature of this interaction, Seuss's character has an anxious expression on his face. Although he is facing forward in the wheelchair, his eyes are looking behind him at the orderly in a suspicious fashion, as though he does not trust this gentleman who is so eager to be "at [his] back side." The narrator-protagonist's body language likewise conveys unease: he is sitting in the Seussian wheelchair with his legs closed tightly and his arms placed securely in his lap, his elbows covering or even shielding his groin. By contrast, the orderly has a blissful look on his face: his eyes are closed and his mouth has a satisfied and somewhat dreamy smile. Moreover, he is walking in a manner that could be described as strutting, preening, or even prancing: his head is thrown slightly back, his right leg is fully extended, and his toes are pointed.[2]

The potentially queer relationship between Seuss's narrator-protagonist and Whelden the wheelchair driver continues on the following page. The orderly takes the narrator-protagonist to "Stethoscope Row" where he promptly tells him: "And I know that, like all our top patients, you're hoping / to get yourself stethed with *some fine first-class scoping*" (my italics). Far from merely embodying a funny Seussian rhyme, this passage alludes to a highly invasive medical procedure. According to the *OED*, an endoscope "is a device with a light attached that is used to look inside a body cavity or organ." While such a device can be inserted into a patient's mouth to examine the lungs, it is also commonly placed in the rectum to view the gastrointestinal tract. The resulting procedure is called an endoscopy. Given the recurring problems that people with AIDS experienced with intestinal infections, parasites, and diarrhea, they frequently were subjected to endoscopies.

Seuss's narrator-protagonist seems acutely aware what the orderly means by "first-class scoping." The illustration that appears in the foreground of the double-page spread shows him visibly startled and even alarmed. He has turned around in the wheelchair and is looking at the orderly in a manner that suggests he is highly distressed: his eyes are opened wide, his eyebrows are elevated high on his forehead, and his hands are raised in front of him. Finally, given the physical placement of the endoscope during the procedure, the scene is also imbued with some sexual overtones: namely, it seems to hint at the possibility of anal sex. Indeed, the mannerisms of the orderly have become even more fey. Although he is still gripping the wheelchair, he is now holding up the pinky finger on each of his hands—a gesture that has long been used in American books, television shows, and films as an indicator of male homosexuality. Similarly, being a patient has long been compared to a feminized state. However, it is significant that in this scene it is the orderly Whelden and not Seuss's narrator-protagonist who possesses effeminate traits.

The rest of the illustration can be read in an equally homoerotic way. Occupying the top potion of this double-page spread and spanning its full width, Seuss depicts "Stethoscope Row": it is a long yellow hallway housing a series of rooms with bright blue doors. Each room features a different doctor standing in the entrance with the door partially open.[3] The physical appearance of the physicians varies: some have facial hair and some do not, some look young while others seem much older, some appear angry while others seem confused. Nonetheless, they all share one key quality: the series of all-male doctors are standing in the doorways of rooms that are completely dark. This corridor draws to mind the gay bathhouses that were common features in cities like New York and San Francisco during the early 1980s. It was there, as the media commonly reported, where AIDS spread so rapidly through anonymous and usually promiscuous sexual contact (Shilts 305–7).

Enhancing the parallel, each one of Seuss's doctors already has inserted his stethoscope earpieces. Consequently, the long tubing that holds the chest piece and forms the main listening device hangs down their chests in what could be seen as a highly phallic manner. To be sure, not only are the stethoscopes inexplicably of varying lengths and widths, but they are also a shade of beige that is suggestively flesh-colored for Caucasian men.

Echoing this feature, all of the doctors on "Stethoscope Row"—along with all of the other characters in the book as a whole—are white. In 1965, librarian Nancy Larrick published what quickly became a landmark article: "The All-White World of Children's Literature." As the title implied, her discussion called attention to the problematic fact that the vast majority of authors who write for children are white, as are the bulk of the characters that they present. Although *Old Once!* is a picture book for adults and not children, it lamentably also presents an-all white world. In recent years, children's literature critics like Philip Nel have called attention to the problematic use of minstrelized elements in *The Cat in the Hat*, while scholars Katie Ishizuka and Ramón Stephens have discussed Seuss's reliance on racist caricature in titles like *If I Ran the Zoo*. These features reveal the ongoing presence of racism as well as white supremacy in Seuss's work, which has long been lauded for championing civil rights via titles like *Horton Hears a Who!* (1954) and *The Sneetches* (1961). *Old Once!* in many ways continues in this same vein. While the text has been praised for giving much-needed voice and visibility to the issue of aging, its commendable portrayal of growing older exists in the absence of racial and ethnicity diversity—a feature that, to my knowledge, has not been mentioned in previous analyses of the book. Moreover, the all-white cast of characters in *Old Once!* becomes even more problematic when it is read against the backdrop of the AIDS crisis. As findings published by the Centers for Disease Control have repeatedly demonstrated, the disease disproportionately impacted (and continues to impact) men of color.[4]

The scene on "Stethoscope Row" is not the only one that contains the possibility of sexually charged "scoping." A few pages later, the orderly tells the narrator-protagonist that he has an appointment with Dr. Ginns, an *"A and S Man* who does Antrums and Shins" (italics in original). Of course, when spoken aloud, the phrase "A and S" sounds roughly like the word "ass." Moreover, the abbreviation "A and S" recalls the more common expression "T and A," where the letter "A," of course, stands for "ass." Finally, although the word "Antrums" may strike readers as one of Seuss's nonsense words or neologisms, it is a legitimate biological concept: an "antrum" is a general term that refers to any bodily cavity or interior corporeal chamber. While a physician might refer to a nasal cavity or heart chamber as an "antrum," the more direct referent for the word in *Old Once!* given its context is the anus.

Luckily for Seuss's protagonist, Whelden the orderly decides that "we'll bypass this bunch" on "Stethoscope Row" since "[t]here is plenty of time to see *them* after lunch" (italics in original). However, the main character has not escaped being placed in a precarious physical predicament. Barbara Bader has observed about the picture book genre: "As an art form, it hinges on the

interdependence of pictures and words, on the simultaneous display of two facing pages and on the drama of turning the page" (1). *Old Once!* makes effective
use of all of these elements, but it especially capitalizes on the final feature—"the
drama of turning the page"—in the scene directly following "Stethoscope Row."
When readers turn the page, they are likely startled to see the situation in which
the narrator-protagonist now finds himself. The gentleman is being examined
by "Dr. Pollen, our Allergy Whiz." Even though this medical specialty sounds
relatively innocuous, it places him in a physically exposed and thus vulnerable position. The main character has lost the long fuzzy robe that he has been
wearing since the "Oglers" and is now clad only in his boxer shorts.

While Seuss's narrator-protagonist regains his robe after leaving Dr. Pollen's
office, he is stripped down to his boxer shorts one final time in *Old Once!* Near
the end of the picture book, the character visits a dietician who operates a contraption called "the Wuff-Whiffer." The written text provides a succinct overview of this machine. The "Diet-Devising Computerized Sniffer," readers learn,
has individuals "lie down in repose / and sniff at good food as it goes past your
nose." The illustration that appears on the facing page augments this description: it shows the main character lying facedown in a contraption that vaguely
resembles a CAT scan. Below him is a device that looks like a Ferris wheel ro-
tating platters of various foods past him; a mechanical arm pulls the lid off the
plate as it nears his nose.[5] Forming a final facet to the homoerotic overtones
permeating this scene, the food that the narrator-protagonist is currently being
asked to sniff is nothing other than a plump hot dog wiener on a bun.

From this point on, the frequency of tests increases exponentially. The orderly who has been pushing the narrator-protagonist around in the wheelchair explains the dizzying line-up of doctors awaiting him:

> And nextly we'll drop in on young Dr. Ginns
>
> . . . .
>
> and of course *he'll* refer us to Doctors McGrew,
> McGuire and McPherson and Blinn and Ballew
> and Timpkins and Tompkins and Diller and Drew,
> Fitzsimmons, Fitzgerald, and Fitzpatrick, too

Seuss's character is never informed of the medical specialties to which any of
these physicians belong nor of the health problem for which they will be testing. Instead, he is simply dragged from office to office for test after test.

Once again, while medical tests can be physically frustrating, psychologically disorientating, and intellectually bewildering for many patients, these

sentiments were particularly pervasive among people with AIDS in the 1980s. Especially during this era, before the antibody test for the disease was developed, most patients had to visit numerous doctors and receive multiple tests before learning what was wrong with them. As one person recalled, "I went from one doctor to another, and they never diagnosed it as AIDS, until my doctor finally gave up and sent me to an infectious disease specialist" (Barouh 24). Meanwhile, another person echoed this experience: "I went through the whole ream of testing" (Barouh 24). As a result, akin to Seuss's protagonist, most patients grew "tired of the poking and endless testing" (Shilts 6). Unfortunately, for many AIDS patients, all of the doctors' appointments and medical tests did not even yield helpful results. Randy Shilts describes the experiences of one man named Ken Horne in 1980: "He was angry that years of visiting doctors had not made him one bit better, or even told him what was wrong" (Shilts 47).

This exact experience, of course, also happens to the main character in *Old Once!* After having his stomach, chest, and nether regions examined while standing in the barrel-like contraption, Seuss's narrator-protagonist does not even learn what any of the physicians saw, thought, or diagnosed. Instead, he is sent out to the reception area to wait. "What those Oglers have learned/ they're not ready to tell./ Clinicians don't spout/ their opinions pell-mell./ So you're back/ with the vestibule fish for a spell," he laments to readers. The illustration on the facing page only amplifies his sense of disappointment, his experience of isolation, and even his feeling of defeat. The drawing shows the elderly gentleman wearing his fuzzy bathrobe and sitting by himself in a high-back chair. His eyelids are downcast and his mustache is sagging. Moreover, his body language also conveys his mental state: his hands are folded on his lap, and his feet are flat on the floor beside each other. Even Norval, the goldfish in the aquarium beside him, is forlorn: his mouth is shaped into a frown and his fins are all droopy. To further underscore the amount of time spent waiting for test results, the character is sent into the lobby several more times over the course of the narrative. "We'll study your symptoms. We'll give you a call./ In the meantime, go back and sit down the hall," he had remarked earlier in the narrative. Then, a following page features him doing just that: sitting in a chair in the waiting area with Norval once again. As he informs readers: "There you'll sit several hours, growing tenser each second,/ fearing your fate will be worse than you reckoned,/ till finally Miss Becker, your beckoner, beckons . . ."

Near the end of *Old Once!*, Seuss's protagonist finally finishes all of the medical appointments and accompanying tests. As a result, he receives a plethora of prescriptions. A double-page spread shows him standing in front of a table covered with pills of varying sizes, shapes, and colors. In the text that accompanies this image, the central character explains what ailment many of the pills address:

> These loganberry-colored pills
> I take for early morning chills.
> I take the pill with zebra stripes
> to cure my early evening gripes.
> These orange-tinted ones, of course,
> I take to cure my charley horse.
> I take three blues at a half past eight
> to slow my exhalation rate.
>
> .   .   .   .
>
> The speckled browns are what I keep
> beside my bed to help me sleep.

Yet again, while many patients—and especially those who are already of advanced age—receive an abundance of prescriptions to treat their ailments, this experience has special resonance with the AIDS crisis. G. Thomas Couser has discussed "the staggering number of medications" used to treat the disease during the 1980s (134). "Before the discovery of HIV," Ronald M. Bayer and Gerald M. Oppenheimer noted in their book *AIDS Doctors*, "physicians had no alternative but to search for a way to treat the cascade of diseases they encountered with AIDS" (119). Given that AIDS attacked the immune system and made the person susceptible to a variety of maladies often in different parts of the body simultaneously, patients were almost always taking what the cover story to *Life* magazine from 1985 called "a desperate battery of drugs" (Barnes and Hollister, par. 9). Ronald Bayer and Gerald M. Oppenheimer document, for example, that it was not uncommon for patients in the 1980s to be taking a dozen different medications each day (119, 135).

When *Old Once!* is viewed through the lens of the AIDS crisis, many other facets of the book take on a new meaning, allowing them to be read in queerly suggestive ways. For example, the opening prologue to the text, which describes a utopian world of jubilant fun where no one is ever ill, is reminiscent of the halcyon days for the queer community after the gains made by the gay liberation movement but prior to the onset of AIDS. As Ronald Bayer and Gerald M. Oppenheimer have discussed, "For many gay men, a lifestyle involving the broad acceptance of multiple sexual partners and the thrill of sexual abandon was part of a precious and newly won freedom" (23). Seuss describes his world before old age set in as being one "with nary a care," much in same way that many gay men remember life in the bathhouses during the 1970s: as times of carefree pleasure. Randy Shilts, for example, offers the following portrait of the gay pride parade in San Francisco in summer 1980, just before the disease made its impact on the community: "The crowd cheered the parade again when the Bulldog Baths float came rolling into the Civic Center. The young musclemen, in black leather harnesses . . . [t]hat night they would be at the huge Cellblock Party at the bathhouse, one of a panoply of celebrations sponsored that day by San Francisco's thriving sex industry" (19). Furthermore, the locale that Seuss presents is not only immune from illness, but—echoing stereotypes about the gay community's obsession with youth— without any ill effects of aging. "In those green-pastured mountains / of Fotta-fa-Zee / everybody feels fine / at a hundred and three." The community's method for attaining this condition is equally sexually suggestive. Although Seuss's narrator-protagonist notes that they remain so healthy and vibrant "'cause the air that they breathe / is potassium-free," this quality is also accredited to the fact that "they chew nuts / from the Tutt-a-Tutt Tree."

The drawing that accompanies these lines only furthers their potential link to the queer community. The figures are engaged in boisterous dancing, and they are also wearing lavish costumes that can be placed in dialogue with the flamboyant fashions typically associated with gay men in general and drag performance in particular. To be sure, the double-page spread could be a scene from a gay pride parade. The figure on the left is wearing puffy knickerbocker pants and elfin shoes with long, pointed toes. Additionally, he is sitting on a throne that is suspended atop a camel. The animal itself is wearing a fez and has a series of bells around its neck. The figures on the right side of the page are equally flamboyant: a bearded fellow, who is wearing fuzzy purple tights and a jester's shirt, is clicking castanets, while the other individual, whose gender is ambiguous, is wearing ruffled pants and a crown. Completing this queerly charged scene, the figure on the left is feeding the one on the right Tutt-a-Tutt nuts.

The final page of *Old Once!* shows the narrator-protagonist getting ready to leave the clinic. But the building does not have the standard red-and-white sign indicating the exit. Instead, forming another facet to the gay subtext that permeates the book, there is a large pink placard bearing lavender-colored letters which read: "OUT." More than three decades after the initial release of Dr. Seuss's picture book, the time has come to bring the various visual as well as verbal elements that recall the AIDS crisis out of the closet and into the open as well.

Out of Time: *You're Only Old Once!* and Queer Temporalities

Reading *Old Once!* as a coded commentary on the AIDS crisis seems to move the text far afield from its avowed subject matter: aging. This alternative interpretation does more than simply offer a different way of viewing the events in Seuss's text; it competes with and even contradicts them. At the very least, examining the picture book through the lens of the epidemic forms a shadow text that haunts its primary focus.

Old Once! contains one final twist, loop, and reversal. Rather than moving readers further away from the issue of aging, a queer reading of the narrative actually brings them back to it. Viewing Seuss's picture book for adults in the context of AIDS further destabilizes our understanding of the human lifespan as linear by introducing notions of queer temporality.

While the field of LGBTQ studies has long examined the interplay between the passage of time and the construction of nonheteronormative sexualities, the opening decades of the twenty-first century saw this issue assume new importance. As Elizabeth Freeman observed, during this period, queer theory took "a turn toward time" (117). A bevy of books—including Lee Edelman's *No Future* (2004), J. Jack Halberstam's *In a Queer Time and Place* (2005), and Elizabeth Freeman's *Time Binds: Queer Temporalities, Queer Histories* (2010)—"examined not simply how queer might be understood in relation to time, but the relationship that queer itself has to temporality" (Abate 32). As I have written elsewhere on this subject, "conceptions of time in Western culture have long been regarded as both linear and teleological" (Abate 32). The events of a person's life are "expected to follow a certain ineluctable order, namely 'the conventional forward-moving narratives of birth, marriage, reproduction and death'" (Abate 32). This sequence, however, "is predicated on heterocentric understandings of the human life cycle" (Abate 32). As Jodie Taylor has written, "Dominant heteronormative temporalities operate under the assumption that a life course is (or should respectably be) conducted in a linear, sequential progression—that is, birth, childhood, adolescence, early adulthood, marriage, reproduction, child rearing, retirement, old age, death and kinship inheritance" (894). The steps along this pathway are both predetermined and unidirectional.

LGBTQ individuals have historically been unable to participate in this process. Until recently, they have been forbidden to marry, barred from adopting, and unable to have children on their own. As a result, their relationships have "existed outside of the typical progression narrative embodied in paradigmatic examples of heterosexual romance—first courtship, then marriage, then procreation" (Abate 32). For this reason, they can be connected with nonlinearity. A slogan that adorned T-shirts and appeared on buttons throughout the 1990s encapsulated this sentiment. "I Can't Even Think Straight!" it declared. This expression invited individuals to consider the ways "in which nonlinear storytelling is a queer act, and *vice versa*" (Abate 32).

Queer temporalities explore the unique relationship that LGBTQ individuals have with chronology. The concept signifies what Maria Mulvaney has characterized as an "existence outside of the heterocentric chronormative time" (159). Because members of LGBTQ community are excluded from the expected teleology of life, they embody "the potentiality of a life unscripted by the conventions of family, inheritance, and child rearing" (Halberstam 2). For this reason, queer temporalities represent "forms of interruption" as well as "points of resistance to this temporal order" (Freeman xxii).

Old Once! presents a presumptively heteronormative life cycle. However, by calling attention to the ways in which the elderly often return to a state of childlike dependency, the narrative suggests that this process might be more circular than linear. The human lifespan, rather than being unidirectional, might loop back around to the beginning when individuals reach old age. In making this suggestion, Seuss's text can be placed in dialogue with queer temporalities. LGBTQ individuals are not the only ones for whom the progress through life's stages of development may not be entirely, well, straight. This same observation may also apply to heterosexual ones as well. The title of Seuss's picture book for adults may be *You're Only Old Once!*, but its message is that—if you reach old age—you will be infantilized twice. Given this situation, the 1986 narrative reveals the appropriateness and even the necessity of children's literature for adults. To more fully and accurately document this experience, a format associated with young people is not merely helpful but illuminating.

The next chapter demonstrates continuity as well as change in the evolution of children's literature for adults. It spotlights a text that takes another popular literary format for young readers—girls' detective fiction—and reimagines it as a story for adult audiences *and* one that is inherently queer. Mabel Maney's *The Case of the Not-So-Nice Nurse*, I argue, also adds a new facet to the origin, function, and impact of children's literature for adults. Maney's queer parody of the Nancy Drew mystery series reveals more than simply that the characters, plots, and conventions of books for young readers can be marshalled to tell interesting, fun, and effective stories for adults. In another and arguably even more important implication that pushes the genre beyond the operations of *Old Once!*, it also demonstrates how this process can reveal compelling new insights about the books for young people on which they are based. Echoing the way in which stages of the human life cycle began looping, leaping, and lurching back upon themselves as the twentieth century neared its end, so too did children's literature for adults.

CHAPTER 2

Off to Camp

Mabel Maney's *The Case of the Not-So-Nice Nurse*, the Nancy
Drew Mystery Stories, and Fanfiction

In 1993, San Francisco–based writer Mabel Maney released *The Case of the Not-So-Nice Nurse*. The book offered a comedic retelling of classic girls' series fiction in general and the popular postwar narratives featuring nurse Cherry Ames and sleuth Nancy Drew in particular. In Maney's book, the former character is humorously reimagined as "Cherry Aimless"; meanwhile, the latter protagonist is wittily dubbed "Nancy Clue." Together with mimicking the central characters, *Not-So-Nice Nurse* also mimics the writing style and storylines of these narratives. The text features a variety of Dickensian coincidences, a plot that unfolds rapidly in a linear way, and a bumbling villain who is all too eager to confess his maniacal scheme to the protagonists. Forming one of the many tongue-in-cheek passages in the book, for instance, Maney's narrator reminds readers about Nancy's knack for getting out of tight spots in the following way: "in *The Case of the Twice-Burnt Toast* she had overpowered a gang of criminals using just the contents of her purse" (140).

In spite of all of the ways in which Maney's text lovingly lampooned classic girls' detective fiction, *Not-So-Nice Nurse* was intended for an audience of adults. This designation arose from the book's content. Maney's narrative did not simply offer a parodic retelling of the Nancy Drew and Cherry Ames novels; it openly queered them. As Kathleen Chamberlain has written, *Not-So-Nice Nurse* "brings to the fore the underlying homoerotic content of many juvenile mysteries by showing a loving lesbian affair between Nancy and 'Cherry Aimless'" (9). Accordingly, the text is filled with tongue-in-cheek references to queer female culture, community, and especially camp. For instance, Cherry's boss in the Seattle hospital, Nurse Margaret Marstad, is never without her signature "lavender handkerchief" (18).[1] Likewise, when the perky protagonist inquires about the whereabouts of one of her coworkers, she receives the follow reply: "Nurse Rooney is very much alive and well and living in Key West with Nurse Greta Green. I should know. I was her roommate until the day Nurse Green showed up" (21). Meanwhile, after the book's central mystery is solved, Cherry, Nancy, and their pals celebrate with a rousing soft-ball game (169).

While much of the queer content in *Not-So-Nice Nurse* arises from winky references to lesbian culture, some scenes are more sexually explicit or, at least, suggestive. An excerpt from the book that is featured on the back cover provides a telling example:

> The night air cut through her silk dress. She pulled her wrap closer.
> "Don't do that," her companion whispered. "I like looking at you."
> The girl surveyed Cherry, looking her up and down. She whistled a long, low appreciative whistle.
> Cherry dropped her coat.
> "It's a full moon," the girl said. "You never know what will happen."
> A shiver went down Cherry's back, for she was having the very same thought.
> Cherry began to wish that she had worn panties. She had decided against them to preserve the line of her dress, but they would be a big help now.

Although *Not-So-Nice Nurse* never enters into the realm of pornography, passages such as this one caused it to be seen as "unsuitable" for children. Echoing this viewpoint, the publisher categorized Maney's book, first and foremost, as a work of "Lesbian Studies." Meanwhile, upon its release, *Not-So-Nice Nurse* was reviewed in a variety of venues—including *The Advocate*, *Armchair Detective*, and *Lambda Book Report*—but none that specialized in books for younger readers. Likewise, none of the reviews recommended the narrative for a juvenile readership. On the contrary, all of these assessments discussed *Not-So-Nice Nurse* as a parody for adults. Kevin Burton Smith, for example, called Maney's novel "a hilarious, pitch-perfect, sexed-up send-up of girls' fiction of the past, this time squarely aimed at adult readers" (par. 3).

Maney's novel was a commercial and a critical success. *Not-So-Nice Nurse* quickly became a bestseller in the category of gay and lesbian fiction, and it was also nominated for a Lambda Literary Award (Brownworth 59). Based on the favorable public reception and accompanying strong sales of *Not-So-Nice Nurse*, two sequels followed. Maney released *The Case of the Good-for-Nothing Girlfriend* in 1994 and *A Ghost in the Closet* in 1995. In the apt words of one reviewer, *Girlfriend* embodied "another sly and lusty lampoon with the two dyke dicks rushing home to River Depths, Illinois to investigate the murder of attorney Carson Clue, Nancy's father, apparently done in by his maid of thirty-odd years" (Smith, par. 5). *Good-for-Nothing Girlfriend* was even more popular than Maney's first title. As Victoria A. Brownworth discussed, the text "sold out of its advance printing before it even hit bookstores" (59). When the narrative was finally released, it embodied the press's largest printing (Brownworth 59).

A Ghost in the Closet offered a slight variation on Maney's previous literary formula. The narrative follows Nancy Clue once again, but this time she joins forces with characters from another popular juvenile detective series, the Hardy Boys. Mirroring Maney's treatment of Nancy Drew, the protagonist brothers are reimagined as queer. In keeping with the campy humor of the series, Frank and Joe are redubbed "The Hardly Boys." In addition, whereas the duo hailed from the small town of "Bayport" in the original novels, they reside in the suggestively named town of "Feyport" in Maney's retelling.

Akin to *Not-So-Nice Nurse*, both *The Case of the Good-for-Nothing Girlfriend* and *A Ghost in the Closet* were intended for an audience of adults. Once again, this designation arose from the fact that the narratives introduced not simply sexual content, but elements of queerness into classic children's series books. Kathyne Bryne called the series "a snappy send-up of 'girl detective' stories that turns white-bread America on its head. The 50s meet the 90s, and they're both in the gay bar around the corner" (par. 2). Similarly, Marie Kuda deemed the texts "shriekingly funny" largely because of the inability of Maney's central characters "to distinguish drag queens and dykes from ordinary mortals" (257). Given these features, reviews that appeared in LGBTQ-themed publications and in those catering to fans of the detective genre touted Maney's trilogy as "shrewd, dead-on parodies of some of the most popular mystery series ever to be marketed to kids. Except these parodies are definitely not aimed at kids" (Smith, pars. 1–2).

The queer-infused nature of Maney's series places it in dialogue with what Alexander Doty has called "making things perfectly queer" or uncovering and reclaiming "queer cultural and political spaces" by transforming "what has been for the most part publicly invisible and silent visible and vocal" (4). Indeed, the *Encyclopedia of Gay, Lesbian, Bisexual, Transexual, and Queer Culture* heralds Maney as a satirist who "spins lesbian adventure tales out of perky feminine archetypes from the 1950s and 1960s" (Pettis, par. 1).

Maney's work adds a new facet to the emerging phenomenon of children's literature for adults in the closing decade of the twentieth century. Her narratives not only constitute another significant signpost in the commercial success and cultural visibility of the genre, but they also expand its aesthetic construction. Dr. Seuss's *You're Only Old Once!* demonstrated how literary formats that are commonly associated with young readers can be productively used to create books intended for adults. Meanwhile, in *Not-So-Nice Nurse*, Maney adds another possible point of origin for such narratives: the central characters of children's literature. Her text illustrates that adult readers need not leave behind any of their beloved protagonists simply because they are now adults rather than children. Instead, protagonists like Nancy Drew can be pleasingly and successfully featured in texts written for grown-ups.

The literary implications and cultural significance of Maney's adult-audience retelling go far beyond this one isolated character and book series. Her work can be placed at the forefront of a rich and rapidly growing source of children's literature for adults during the closing years of the twentieth century: fanfiction. As the name implies, "fanfiction" is an umbrella term that is used to denote material that has been written by readers or fans of a book, television, or movie series, rather than its official author. The word first emerged in the mid-1940s in response to changes taking place in science fiction magazines, but it quickly spread to other genres and mediums. *The Case of the Not-So-Nice Nurse* predates the internet-fueled explosion of fan-authored retellings on the eve of the new millennium, while it also calls attention to the important role that this phenomenon would specifically play in the realm of children's literature for adults. Adult-audience fanfiction based on popular narratives for young people would embody a popular and prolific source of children's literature for adults, as well as one that was often insightful and astute. Narratives like *Not-So-Nice Nurse* demonstrate how retellings of texts by fans and fandom cultures can reveal aspects about the original source material that mainstream critics and extant interpretations have overlooked. Given the way that fanfiction upends notions of professional authorship and challenges beliefs in literary ownership, it is known for its inversions and disruptions. *Not-So-Nice Nurse* adds another facet to these reversals and, in so doing, illuminates an additional aspect of the creative potential and cultural purpose of children's literature for adults. In the same way that children's literature can represent new narrative possibilities for adult texts, adult-audience retellings of children's books can shed new light on stories intended for young people.

How Nancy Clue Reveals What Nancy Knew: The Creative Pleasures and Literary Insights of Fanfiction

Maney's adult-audience parodies do more than simply expand the literary parameters of books intended for adult readers; they also engage in a process that is recursive. The queer elements that fuel the Nancy Clue trilogy cause it to loop back around to its literary origins in books for young readers. *Not-So-Nice Nurse* makes visible the lesbian subtext that permeates classic girls' detective fiction. In so doing, it offers a compelling commentary about popular conceptions concerning both children's literature and American childhood. Given that Maney's parody queers the characters, plots, and even premise of beloved protagonists Nancy Drew and Cherry Aims, it challenges a divide that is commonly seen as separating the period of youth from that of adulthood: sexuality.

In the apt words of Steven Bruhm and Nat Hurley: "There is currently a dominant narrative about children: children are (and should stay) innocent of sexual desires and intentions" (ix). Young people are regarded as not merely devoid of, but oblivious to, erotic thoughts, feelings, and desires. As James Kincaid has written, for centuries now, Western society has subscribed to the following axioms: "the child is that species which is free of sexual feeling or response; the adult is that species which has crossed over into sexuality" (*Child-Loving* 6–7). For this reason, erotic content has long been regarded as inappropriate in books for young readers. Discussion of any aspect of human sexuality is viewed as confusing and even corrupting to boys and girls. In the words of Kincaid once again, material of this nature violates "the doctrine of asexuality in children" (*Erotic* 55). Consequently, books for young readers that engage with sexual subject matter in any way have been subjected to challenges and even outright bans. Examples range from Maurice Sendak's picture book *In the Night Kitchen*, which depicts the fantastical nighttime adventures of a young male protagonist who is naked, to Judy Blume's young adult novel *Forever*, which discusses a teenage girl's first sexual experiences. Both texts are routinely viewed as including information that young people do not need to have—information that might even be harmful to them.

The relationship that children have to sexuality is more complicated than mere innocence. As Bruhm and Hurley have discussed, a powerful paradox exists: at the same time that young people are seen as being blissfully unaware of sexuality, they are "also officially, tacitly assumed to be heterosexual" (ix). Boys and girls are expected and even presumed to grow up and be attracted to the opposite sex. Thus, while young people are regarded as being asexual, they are also simultaneously viewed as heterosexual. Not only are such beliefs contradictory,[2] they also foreclose the possibility that young people might possess an erotic identity that does not conform to these views. "If society is unwilling to imagine the sexual nature of young people more generally," I have written with Kenneth Kidd on this topic, "then it is surely not ready to consider their tendencies toward nonnormative sexualities" (13). Numerous concrete examples of this abstract ideological viewpoint permeate American society. For example, conservatives have long accused LGBTQ teachers, same-sex parents, and queer youth leaders of wanting to "indoctrinate" or even "recruit" young people (Abate and Kidd 13). Comments of this nature position childhood and queer identity as mutually exclusive. This cultural conception, of course, influences the books created for children. Because children are thought to be wholly unaware of LGBTQ impulses and identities, the narratives intended for them are expected to reflect this state as well (Abate and Kidd 13). In this way, children's literature has long been typified not simply by a prevailing erotophobia, but by an even stronger homophobia (Abate and Kidd 1).

Mabel Maney's Nancy Clue series disrupts both of these elements and thereby disrupts longstanding assumptions about childhood and children's literature in the United States. *Not-So-Nice Nurse* demonstrates the literary, aesthetic, and cultural value of fan-created material. As figures like Henry Jenkins, Matt Hills, and Anne Jamison have discussed, beginning in the late twentieth century and accelerating rapidly in the opening decade of the new millennium, the reappropriation, repurposing, and even wholesale reimagining of characters and plots from books, movies, and television shows in new creative works composed by audiences became a global phenomenon. Often called fanfiction (or referred to by the abbreviation "fanfic"), these narratives emerged as one of the most popular and prolific new genres in the twenty-first century. Not only does fanfiction call into question who creatively controls or imaginatively owns characters and plots after they have been released to the public, it also raises interesting issues about what texts can reveal to audiences—or, conversely, what audiences can discover or decode within texts (Jenkins 86–91). For example, when J. K. Rowling revealed in October 2007 that she had always imaged her character Albus Dumbledore as gay, this disclosure confirmed something that writers of fanfiction had long known. As sites like Fanfiction.net revealed, fan-authored stories had been appearing for years that presented Dumbledore as a homosexual. Rowling's disclosure gave mainstream legitimacy along with authorial credence to what had formerly been mere speculative conjecture and even a rogue form of reading.

Mabel Maney's *The Case of the Not-So-Nice Nurse* was released just before the internet-fueled explosion of fanfiction. Nonetheless, the book can be placed in dialogue not simply with this general phenomenon but with a particular subset of it, known as slash fiction. This specialized type of fanfic, first embodied by the popular pairing of James T. Kirk and Spock, features romantic relationships between same-sex characters—either within the same book, television show, or film or across different ones. The name comes from the convention of placing a slash (/) between the names of the characters who are being erotically entangled. Akin to the early fanfiction treatment of J. K. Rowling's character of Dumbledore, Maney's retelling reveals aspects about girls' detective fiction that have been overlooked in extant readings and official criticism: namely, the lesbianism that permeates both the Cherry Ames and Nancy Drew series.

While *Not-So-Nice Nurse* would be classified as a work of fanfiction today, when it was originally published in 1993, it was simply deemed a parody text. Parodies, of course, have long been seen as largely imitating their source text. Maney's book, however, reveals that parodies do not simply satirically mimic material. Rather, these works can also reveal compelling new critical insights about it. *The Case of Not-So-Nice Nurse* has long been seen as offering a comedic monologue about the Nancy Drew series, but the narrative is also engaging in a fresh interpretive dialogue with it. Her parody series defies the "prohibition against the representation of any sexuality, much less queer sexuality, in early childhood" (Abate and Kidd, Introduction 6). Maney's books reveal how classic girls' fiction is not devoid of sexually suggestive material. Even more radically, of course, her lesbian-themed spoofs demonstrate that the eroticism embedded in the original works for young readers exists outside the realm of heteronormativity.

In this way, *Not-So-Nice Nurse* and its sequels challenge the asexuality along with the presumed heterosexuality of children and children's literature. Contrary to longstanding assumptions, not all young people are innocently unaware of the erotic. Furthermore, not all children currently are, nor will they grow up to become, interested in the opposite sex. Instead, as Maney's queer spoofs attest, some young people will identify as homosexual. As the author herself recalled about her experience of reading these books as a girl, "I always thought the nurses in those Cherry Ames books were so sexy in their snug white uniforms and their all-female world" (qtd in Brownworth 59). The success of Maney's books affirms that she was not alone in such sentiments. The campy humor of her texts arises from the way that they bring an aspect of classic girls' detective fiction that LGBTQ readers already knew to the forefront: its queer-infused content. In the *Lambda Book Report*, for example, Kanani Kauka begins her review of *Not-So-Nice Nurse* with the statement: "We always knew she was . . . we knew Nancy Drew was One Of Us" (36). As these comments attest, the adult-audience parody is not introducing new elements of queerness into the classic girls' detective series. Rather, it is amplifying ones that queer female readers had long recognized as already permeating these texts. In a further indication of the centrality of this feature to the attraction and appeal of Maney's narrative, Kauka ends her review by repeating this sentiment. "It's what we've been waiting for: Nancy goes butch. We always knew she was," she says of *Not-So-Nice Nurse* (36). Contrary to longstanding beliefs that children are disinterested in, and even oblivious to, elements of eroticism, Maney's parody exposes the fact that young readers not only detect but even delight in the queer overtones that can be located in the originals. *Not-So-Nice Nurse* is intended for an adult audience, but the book traffics in the childhood remembrances—both by the author and by her readers—of the lesbian subtext pervading Nancy Drew and Cherry Ames. Maney's book raises the possibility that young people not only might be aware of sexuality, but—in a detail that is even more radical given societal assumptions about children's presumed heterosexuality—unconventional and even iconoclastic erotic identities as well.

In this way, *The Case of the Not-So-Nice Nurse* demonstrates how children's literature for adults can shed new critical light both on books intended for grown-ups and those aimed at kids. Her spoof reveals how literary plots, premises, and characters that are intended for young people can be appropriated to create engaging and enjoyable narratives for adults. At the same time, Maney's text offers a powerful demonstration of how these adult-audience books can provide new understandings about the function, presence, and use of this narrative style in its original form for juvenile audiences. *Not-So-Nice Nurse* calls attention to a facet of girls' detective fiction that had gone overlooked or, at least, unacknowledged by generations of mainstream critics. By reimagining, retooling, or reappropriating classic girls' detective fiction for adults, Maney is able to make the lesbianism that pervades the characters, scenes, and plots visible. Mabel Maney based Nancy Clue on Nancy Drew. However, she also brought to light what many past and present young readers of the original Nancy knew.

"Jeepers! . . . It's the Body of Christ!": From Secular to Sacred Mysteries in *Not-So-Nice Nurse*

Homoeroticism is not the only element of classic girls' detective fiction that Mabel Maney moves from the background to the forefront in her work of fanfiction. In another, unexplored detail about the first book of the trilogy, *The Case of the Not-So-Nice Nurse* also unpacks the complex meanings of an element that forms a cornerstone to the Nancy Drew Mystery Stories series: the concept of mystery. Although this term is commonly regarded as secular today, it has a long, rich, and complicated history as a word that embodies the sacred. For centuries, "mystery" referred to ideas, individuals, or events that possessed a religious significance or a spiritual essence. More specifically, it was commonly used to denote facets of Christian belief and those associated with the Roman Catholic Church in particular, ranging from divine rights and sacraments to the Holy Trinity and the resurrection.

The Case of the Not-So-Nice Nurse takes place against the backdrop of a clandestine convent and features a plot involving the abduction of an entire order of nuns. During the course of telling this story, the book recoups the etymological history of the word "mystery," weaving faith-based meanings back into an otherwise secular narrative. Indeed, in a telling portent of the significance that Judeo-Christianity in general and Roman Catholicism in particular will play in *Not-So-Nice Nurse*, these elements appear in the opening chapter. In a development that evokes the past sacred meanings of the term "mystery" and its more contemporaneous secular ones, the unexpected appearance of a nun sitting at the bedside of nurse Cherry's most recent patient sets the detective case that drives the narrative in motion. A few chapters later, references to Roman Catholicism prove to be more significant. Cherry's boss asks her to deliver a package to a friend in Oregon while she is on her way to San Francisco. Although Nurse Marstad says that the package contains "a special experimental medication" (20), Cherry discovers that it is actually a copy of a book, *The Lost Secrets of the Sisters of Mercy* (29).

Not surprisingly, during the course of solving the mystery, Cherry and her pals encounter a variety of facets of the Roman Catholic faith, traditions, worship spaces. After learning about the disappearance of the order of nuns, for example, the group travels to the convent to investigate. As they explore the grounds, Maney's book shifts from simply referencing occasional facets of Roman Catholicism to systematically educating its readers about this faith tradition. Upon arriving at the abbey, for instance, Lauren explains the symbolic significance of the landscaping: "The building is ringed with old rose bushes, which have really big thorns. It's an allusion to Christ's crown of thorns. . . . It's a medieval practice" (117). Likewise, another character shares the following tidbit from *The Secrets of the Sisters of Mercy*: "The heart of every convent is the chapel" (120). A few moments later, Midge adds to this information, noting that chapels often "contain a relic" (121). In a passage that could have appeared in a factual book about the religious history of the Church rather than a fictional parody of a girls' detective novel, Lauren explains that a relic is "a bone or a fragment from a saint with a shrine built around it. Sometimes they have a statue made that looks like the saint—only dead—and put the bone in that" (121).

Maney's characters complete their exploration of the convent chapel, quite appropriately, by encountering the most sacred object of all: the Holy Eucharist. While the text never directly discusses transubstantiation—or, as the *Oxford English Dictionary* puts it, "the conversion of the Eucharist of the whole substance of the bread into the body" of Jesus Christ during holy mass—this central tenet of Catholicism is embedded within this scene. When one of the girls puts a host in her mouth out of curiosity, Lauren is horrified: "Jeepers! . . . Spit it out!" (122). She goes on to explain to Midge that the wafer is not a dry cracker: "It's the body of Christ!" (122).

Even after the group exits the scared space, their religious encounters and education continue. While walking through the hallways of the convent, for example, Lauren is startled by a large stone figure: "'It's just a statue,' Midge said, examining the bulky white stone figure. 'You only thought it was a real body because it's dressed in real clothes. Catholics dress up their statues sometimes'" (122). Unlike previous explanations about the Roman Catholic Church, which had no immediate bearing on the plot, this information quickly becomes relevant. As Midge gets closer to the stone figure, she discovers that Lauren's concerns are valid: the statue is made from a real body. With the corpse of an unknown person entombed within the stone sculpture, the detective case that Cherry and her friends seek to solve has not only morphed into a murder mystery, it also has become even further imbricated with the mysteries of the Catholic Church.

All of these various secular and sacred threads culminate in the book's climax: Cherry and her pals discover the abduction of the Sisters of Mercy was not a senseless act of random violence. Instead, it was the work of a money-hungry priest, Farther Helms, who sought to take possession of "the convent from the good sisters and develop the land into a retirement home" (Maney 115–16). Together with engaging in a mass kidnapping to carry out his plan, Helms has also committed murder, killing "that nosy accountant from the Catholic Men's Club" who discovered his financial improprieties and entombing his corpse in a church statue (138). In typical Nancy Drew fashion, however, Cherry Aimless and her pals save the day: they free the nuns, escape the clutches of the priest, and stop the bomb from detonating that he set to blow up the convent if he his plans were discovered—all without breaking a nail or mussing their hair (141–48).

Since the initial appearance of *The Case of the Not-So-Nice Nurse* in 1993, the text's inclusion of elements from Roman Catholicism has been read through the lens of female homosexuality. As historians Judith C. Brown and Sherry Marie Velasco have written, nuns have long been a locus of queer female identity and even erotic activity in the West. For centuries, joining a convent was one of the few socially acceptable choices for queer women who sought a life outside of the institutions of marriage and motherhood. Likewise, after becoming part of a religious order, some otherwise heterosexually identified women became involved in erotic relationships with other nuns in what has been termed "situational homosexuality"—or "sexual behavior limited to circumstances in which members of the same gender are generally deprived of contact with the other gender" (Greenberg, Bruess, and Conklin 355).

Maney's decision to feature Roman Catholicism in *Not-So-Nice Nurse* can be seen as arising from this history. The author draws on the longstanding association of nuns with lesbianism to accentuate the codes of queer female culture and especially camp in *Not-So-Nice Nurse*. Maney herself has acknowledged this link. In an article that appeared in *The Advocate*, for example, she made the following observation about both the sartorial uniform and homosocial environment of the nurses that populate the Cherry Ames novels: "They're like nuns, and I'm Catholic, so I guess that explains why I find them so attractive" (qtd in Brownworth 59). Moreover, later in that same piece, she uttered another remark along these same lines that has since become her tagline. Discussing her childhood, Maney quipped: "For a long time I thought I wanted to be a nun. Then I realized what I really wanted to be was a lesbian" (qtd in Brownworth 60). In this way, Maney's choice of Roman Catholicism imbues the book with a preexisting element of lesbianism that it would not possess if it were focusing on a different faith tradition. In other words, secular and sacred forms of mystery do more than simply co-exist throughout the book; they are co-dependent.

From the Mysteries of Religion to Religious Mysteries: Nancy Drew and the Case of the Missing Spirituality

The way in which *The Case of the Not-So-Nice Nurse* weaves together secular and sacred understandings of the concept of "mystery" demonstrates the literary richness and cultural complexity of children's literature for adults. The book offers a nuanced, important, and commonly overlooked perspective on the detective genre. That said, the significance of religion in *Not-So-Nice Nurse* has implications that go beyond simply the specific plot of this one book.

Because Maney's text is a retelling of a beloved girls' detective series, the narrative invites its audience to read these details back into the original volumes of Nancy Drew. Since the release of the first text about the girl sleuth in 1930, the books have commonly been viewed from the perspectives of race, class, and gender. The second portion of this chapter illuminates the critical rewards that can emerge with children's literature for adults by demonstrating how *The Case of the Not-So-Nice Nurse* uncovers the presence of another important but largely unexplored facet to Nancy Drew: religion. Doing so complicates conventional understandings of the classic mystery series as largely ahistorical. At the same time, the religious facets of *Not-So-Nice Nurse* incite a reconsideration of the elements of spirituality which influence the shape, structure, and style of a key set of Nancy Drew novels.

However, the way in which Maney's text revives the forgotten theological components to the concept of mystery is not entirely divorced from its interest in highlighting the latent lesbianism within Nancy Drew. At repeated points, *Not-So-Nice Nurse* calls attention to the intersection of queerness and spirituality. Consequently, a complex feedback loop emerges between children's literature for adults and the narratives for youth on which they are based. As Mabel Maney's narrative reveals, the former is not simply inspired by the latter, it also helps to illuminate it.

Even though Cherry Aimless and not Nancy Clue is the main protagonist of *The Case of the Not-So-Nice Nurse*, the book is patterned far more closely after narratives featuring the famed girl sleuth than those concerning the popular wartime nurse. As Stephanie Foote has pointed out, "The covers lovingly borrow the lurid elements of the classic Nancy Drew book covers, the prose mimics the breathless excitability of the mysteries, and perhaps most importantly, the texts pick up on some of the strangeness of the Nancy Drew cast of characters" (525).

Contrary to analyses by Foote and other critics, *The Case of Not-So-Nice Nurse* does not lampoon Nancy Drew Mystery Stories in a broad or general way. Rather, it can be seen as focusing on a particular time period within the series. Although Maney's text was written and released in the early 1990s, it takes place in the late 1950s, during the heyday of the original series about the girl sleuth. More specifically, two particular years recur in *Not-So-Nice Nurse*: 1957, when character Cherry Aimless graduates from nursing school; and 1959, when the action of the book occurs. The narrator calls repeated attention to these dates, as do Maney's characters themselves. The first reference, in fact, appears on the opening page of *Not-So-Nice Nurse*, when readers learn that

Cherry "graduated from Stencer Nursing School, class of 1957" (7). In the following chapter, Maney establishes the current time period for her narrative. Her narrator notes how "Just a year ago, [Cherry] had sat in this very spot, convincing Nurse Marstad that she was probation nurse material" (18). Then, on the following page, they are informed that Cherry was hired on "July 5, 1958" (19), a detail that places the current narrative action in 1959.

The years 1957 and 1959 are not inconsequential ones in the history of Nancy Drew; they denote important milestones within the series. The year 1957 marks the release of the first Nancy Drew novel written under Harriet Stratemeyer Adams' new editorial guidelines. With the series about the girl sleuth approaching its thirtieth anniversary, Adams wanted to ensure that the books appealed to a new generation of young readers (Nash 468). Thus, she altered the formula that the novels had been following for decades. As Carolyn G. Heilbrun, Carolyn Stewart Dyer, and Nancy Tillman Romalov have all documented, new Nancy Drew novels would have simpler plots: they would contain fewer tangential storylines and extraneous characters. Likewise, the books would be shorter in length, possessing only twenty chapters instead of the previous twenty-five. In addition, the age of the girl sleuth would be raised from sixteen to eighteen, to reflect the new national standard for obtaining a driver's license. Finally, the new books would avoid negative portrayals of individuals from racial and ethnic minority groups as well as the working class (see Heilbrun 11; Dyer and Romalov 92–93). Adams felt so strongly about this new approach that she hired a bevy of editors to overhaul all of the previous books so that they would conform to it. The first of these revisions appeared in 1959, when new versions of *The Secret of the Old Clock* and *The Hidden Staircase* appeared on bookstore shelves, replacing their 1930s originals (Nash 468).

The timespan highlighted in *Not-So-Nice Nurse* calls attention to this important period in the history of Nancy Drew. More specifically, given the prominence of the years 1957 and 1959 in Maney's text, the novel invites readers to reexamine the first two original narratives that were released under the new editorial guidelines: *The Haunted Showboat* (1957, #35) and *The Secret of the Golden Pavilion* (1959, #36). Doing so turns a much-deserved spotlight on two compelling but widely overlooked books in the Nancy Drew series. Moreover, given the importance of organized religion in *Not-So-Nice* Nurse, it also calls attention to the role that faith plays in these original stories. Whereas previous Nancy Drew books like *The Hidden Staircase* (1930, #2), *The Secret of Red Gate Farm* (1931, #6) and *The Mystery of the Ivory Charm* (1936, #13) contained many facets of the supernatural—as ghosts, cults, and curses abounded—*The Haunted Showboat* and *The Secret of the Golden Pavilion* demonstrate a new interest in questions of spirituality. In a detail that *The Case of the Not-So-Nice Nurse* recognizes and reverberates, these two books merge elements from the original religious meaning of the term "mystery" back into their otherwise secular detective mysteries. Moreover, in a further reflection of Maney's narrative, they do so by drawing on religious traditions that exist outside of mainstream forms of American Protestantism.

The original editorial formula used from 1930 to 1957 to create the Nancy Drew Mystery Stories makes use of many vectors of identity—from gender, race, and ethnicity to class, region, and age—in the construction of their characters and plots, but religious beliefs are not among them. In fact, of the thirty-four novels that were created using this ethos, only a few contain scenes that involve explicitly religious people or places. In *The Witch Tree Symbol* (1955, #33), for example, Nancy's attempt to stop a cunning thief takes her to an Amish community in rural Pennsylvania. Even so, the Pennsylvania Dutch people and especially their particular form of Christianity do not play a significant role in the narrative. While the novel does explain some of the rudiments of Amish culture—including foods like "*fasnachts*" (99), community events like barn-raisings (186), and the faith-healing practice known as "pow-wowing" (33, 72)—it does not discuss the Anabaptist faith that forms the cornerstone to the way of life for this community.

In an even more interesting feature of the first thirty-four Nancy Drew novels, while the stories about the girl sleuth are set against the backdrop of many different kinds of social institutions—ranging from farms, cottages, and summer camps to inns, ranches, and restaurants—places of worship are not among them. Nancy, her father, and her friends are never shown attending religious services, and they only rarely befriend individuals who do so. Similarly, Drew and her companions eat many meals together, as well as in the company of various individuals that they meet in the course of the mystery, but rarely do any characters say a blessing. Likewise, few individuals ever quote from sacred books like the Bible or, more astoundingly, even seem to possess them. These details seem even more surprising given that the action in many of the books occurs on Fridays, Saturdays, and Sundays—days of special religious observance for each of the three major world religions: Islam, Judaism, and Christianity, respectively.

The lack of reference to religious beliefs or practice in the first thirty-four Nancy Drew narratives is an especially notable absence given the longstanding Judeo-Christian tradition within American culture in general and the time that these books were written and released in particular. The decades encompassing the 1930s through the 1950s witnessed a renewed national interest in organized religion and especially in Christianity. Church membership in all denominations increased, and the proliferation of radio gave rise to broadcast evangelism which brought religious sermons, discussions of scripture, and faith-based music into countless numbers of homes, offices, and businesses around the United States ("Religion," par. 1). Indeed, Father Charles Coughlin, a Roman Catholic priest, attained nationwide celebrity in the 1930s with his weekly broadcasts, which reached 30 million people during the height of their popularity (Severin and Tankard 106).

Not surprisingly, the national fervor for faith during the 1930s, 1940s, and 1950s was reflected in its literature for young readers. Some of the most commercially successful and critically acclaimed books for children in the United States from this period contained either explicit or implicit Judeo-Christian values, characters or messages. Examples range from the books in Laura Ingalls Wilder's Little House series (the first of these, *Little House in the Big Woods*, was published in 1932) to C. S. Lewis' *The Lion, the Witch and the Wardrobe* (1950). Not only are these books now considered classics of children's literature, but they are also—akin to the Nancy Drew books—works of series fiction.

But the presence of faith in mystery fiction is more complicated. On one hand, as Lawrence Frank, Bill Phillips, and Carole Cusack have all discussed, these elements are not common features of the genre. As Phillips matter-of-factly states: "Detective fiction emerged as a result of the increasing secularisation of society" (139). Carole Cusack goes on to provide a more detailed explanation of this phenomenon. "As organized religion retreated," she writes, "it became more difficult to believe the theologically charged notion that good and evil do not go unpunished, and that human life is ultimately meaningful, even when random violence threatens to destabilize both individual and community" (161). Detective fiction emerged to serve this role and provide this structure. "The detective provides the rational replacement" for a member of the clergy (Phillips 140). The protagonist sleuth is a man capable of "ascribing meaning to the otherwise random *minutiae* of existence" (Cusack 161). He is also a figure committed to punishing wrongdoing and thereby maintaining the distinction between good and evil. "Conan Doyle's Sherlock Holmes is archetypal: rational, scientific, calculating and infallible," Phillips remarks (140). Of course, over the years, Christian-themed detective stories, arguably originating with G. K. Chesterton's Father Brown series (1911–1936), have been released. But the fact that these narratives are categorized separately only further underscores that most whodunits are secular in nature. Indeed, the mid-twentieth century saw the release of many now-classic titles of detective fiction—Agatha Christie's *Murder on the Orient Express* (1934), Dashiell Hammett's *The Thin Man* (1934), and Mickey Spillane's Mike Hammer series (beginning in 1947). While the plots, characters, and narrative happenings of these books varied widely, they shared one common feature: they lacked any significant engagement with mainstream religions or religious issues.[3]

While traditional faith is consistently absent from classic works of detective fiction, unconventional and even iconoclastic ones have often played a role in the genre. As Carole Cusack has discussed, minority religions—ranging from New Age cults and nature sects to marginalized faiths like Mormonism—appear with some regularity (159). When one of these spiritual traditions is introduced into a detective novel, it is not for the purpose of promoting religious diversity or fostering interfaith understanding. Instead, it is commonly used to help paint a portrait of evil. As Cusack has documented, "From as early as Conan Doyle's seminal *A Study in Scarlet* (1887), new religious movements have provided detective and crime novelists with fertile subject matter for exploring deviance and anti-social motivations" (159). If a character is identified as being a member of a cult, sect, or non-mainstream form of Protestantism, this figure is likely the book's villain or associated with the villain's nefarious machinations in some way. In the words of Cusack once again: "The conservative nature of much detective fiction demands that the values of mainstream society are reaffirmed in the plot's resolution; this frequently results in the demonization and punishment of the minority religion featured" (159). Given this situation, the role that spirituality has historically played in the detective genre can be described as contradictory, hierarchical, and heavily biased. As Bill Phillips has aptly said about this phenomenon: "There is, then, an absence of mainstream religion in the works of writers such as Dashiell Hammett, Raymond Chandler, Ross MacDonald and Robert B. Parker, though they may well . . . pit their heroes—or heroines—against insidious sects" (141).

The Nancy Drew mystery series reflects these features of the detective genre. The novels are devoid of any engagement with mainstream religious traditions like Protestant Christianity, but they do draw on unconventional and iconoclastic forms of spirituality to create their plots and, especially, to construct their villains. *The Secret of Red Gate Farm* (1931, #6) forms an early and representative example. In the book, a mysterious "nature cult" turns out to be a group of counterfeiters who don robes and recite fake chants in an attempt to scare away the locals and obfuscate their activities to the authorities. Episodes along these same lines recur in a variety of subsequent novels, so much so that they could be regarded as an unofficial facet or secondary feature to the narrative formula used to create the series.

Mabel Maney's *The Case of the Not-So-Nice Nurse* with its focus on Roman Catholicism, its blending of sacred and secular uses of the term "mystery," and its emphasis on the years 1957 and 1959, calls attention to a shift in the way that faith in general and non-mainstream forms of spirituality in particular are employed in the Nancy Drew novels released after the change in editorial practices. In a departure from previous narratives in the detective series, religion-infused people, places, and events appear in *The Haunted Showboat* (1957, #35) and *The Secret of the Golden Pavilion* (1959, #36). These features exist not only outside of conventional American Protestantism—with the former novel showcasing Roman Catholicism and the latter the beliefs of indigenous Hawaiians—but, perhaps even more surprisingly, they also exist outside of the literary construction of villainy. Akin to *Not-So-Nice Nurse*, *The Haunted Showboat* and *The Secret of the Golden Pavilion* provide an opportunity to educate readers about faith traditions with which they are presumed to be unfamiliar. At the same time, these details also constitute important plot points in solving the mystery. These Nancy Drew narratives demonstrate the desire, as Maney's book spotlights, of reuniting past sacred uses of the concept of mystery with more current secular ones. Akin to *Not-So-Nice Nurse*, the solution to the mystery in these two Nancy Drew books does not result in demonizing or even disparaging the faith that is being profiled. Instead, the presentation of this non-mainstream religious tradition in these texts strives to promote greater understanding, appreciation, and even empathy for it.

An interest in religious belief appears early in *The Haunted Showboat*. The book follows Nancy Drew and her longtime gal pals Bess Marvin and George Fayne as they travel to New Orleans to work on a new case: strange noises, bizarre occurrences, and even spooky ghosts have been emanating from an old showboat that has been abandoned in the bayou swamp for many years. The vessel belongs to Bess's aunt and uncle, who hope to tow the boat back to their estate, restore it to its former glory, and hold a party on board in honor of their daughter's engagement. Although this plotline doesn't possess any obvious similarities to *Not-So-Nice*, numerous details connect it. First, akin to the adventures of Maney's protagonist, the opening chapters of *The Haunted Showboat* are comprised of a road trip. Nancy, Bess, and George spend over four chapters—and a total of 40 pages of a 184 page text—driving from River Heights, Illinois to Bess's relative's house in New Orleans. Although the distance between the two locales is substantial, it takes the girl sleuth and her companions so long because—echoing the experiences of Maney's characters—they are pursued by villainous men driving a convertible whose various machinations delay their progress. As Bess relays at one point, "I have an awful feeling that thief doesn't want you to reach New Orleans, Nancy. . . . he put a bomb in this car and now he's following us!" (20).

Next, in an even more persuasive link between the texts, the color of Nancy's car matches that of her queer counterpart in Maney's book. In *The Haunted Showboat*, the girl sleuth does not have her signature blue roadster. The automobile is stolen by one of the book's villains in the opening pages, and so her father buys a replacement: "Presently a stunning new yellow convertible entered the Drews' driveway" (11). In a detail that seems more than a mere coincidence given the importance of the roadster to her identity, in *Not-So-Nice Nurse*, Maney's Nancy Clue possesses the exact same type and color of vehicle: "It was almost noon by the time they backed Nancy's sporty yellow convertible out of garage and headed toward the convent" (114).

The links between *The Haunted Showboat* and *Not-So-Nice Nurse* continue after Nancy and her companions arrive in New Orleans, when the story develops an unexpected interest in various forms of spirituality. First, the mystery takes place in the days leading up to a celebration that has clear ties not simply to religious belief in general but to the Roman Catholic Church in particular: Mardi Gras. Moreover, this event is far from an inconsequential backdrop for *The Haunted Showboat*; it factors prominently throughout the narrative, with characters making costumes, participating in the parade, and partaking in all manner of the revelries. In fact, the climax of the novel occurs directly on Shrove Tuesday (177).

The spiritual aspects of *The Haunted Showboat* are not limited to elements of Roman Catholicism. Uncle Rufus, the black man that Bess's uncle hires to guide the girls through the bayou, is also a local voodoo doctor. Although Rufus is a relatively minor character, an entire chapter is dedicated to him. The segment does not spotlight his knowledge of the bayou but highlights his work as a spiritual leader; the chapter is titled "A Voodoo Preacher" (68).

Akin to many previous Nancy Drew novels featuring characters who possess nontraditional interests or engage in activities that exist outside of the status quo, Uncle Rufus's work as a voodoo doctor at first seems like a ruse. When Nancy initially visits the abandoned showboat, she wonders if a group of voodoo practitioners in general and Rufus in particular are responsible for its "haunting" (75). "From the cabin came the sounds of doleful chanting and the rise and fall of a wailing voice, evidently praying," the text reads (74). "Sounds like a voodoo session," George confidently speculates (74). The girl sleuth agrees: "'Do you suppose Uncle Rufus could head a group of voodoo believers who hold secret meetings on the showboat?' George said it was very likely. 'And perhaps they're deliberately haunting it so the boat won't be moved!' she suggested" (75).

In a significant departure from the outcome of many previous Nancy Drew novels, the elements of voodoo in the book are not a hoax—or, rather, not entirely. While the villains who are "haunting" the *River Princess* are, indeed, mimicking various chants and ceremonies of voodoo in an attempt to "frighten" people away so that they can search the showboat for its hidden cache of pirate treasure, Uncle Rufus is not among them. In a marked change from the fictional formula employed in earlier narratives like *The Secret of Red Gate Farm* (1931, #6), Rufus is a legitimate and even highly respected voodoo doctor. For example, he tells Nancy and her companions of a time when a woman who had been limping came to visit him: "A radiant expression spread over the old man's face when he added, 'Now through prayer she's cured. We sang an' we prayed together" (75). Although the girls are skeptical, they remain respectful of his beliefs, choosing to remain silent rather than say something that might be discourteous (75).

At numerous other points in *The Haunted Showboat*, the narrative takes time away from its main mystery plot to provide information—however rudimentary—about the practices, beliefs, and symbols of voodoo. While paddling the girls through the bayou, for example, Uncle Rufus explains the meanings associated with various animals: "'Take spiders,' he said. 'They represents the devil on this earth. They pi-son folks, an' snakes do, too.' Uncle Rufus said that on the other hand the turtle represented great patience" (76).

Perhaps the most significant and certainly the most memorable reference to voodoo appears near the end of the novel, when Nancy finds Uncle Rufus in the midst of making a medicinal tonic: "As the young sleuth rounded the corner of the house, she stood still in amazement. In the center of the yard a large tripod had been erected over a log fire. Swinging from the tripod was a huge iron caldron. Back of it stood Uncle Rufus, waving his arm back and forth slowly and muttering to himself" (152). Although neither Nancy nor any of her companions become converts to this belief system, they do hold it in some esteem—and they encourage the book's readers to do so as well. As the narrator notes: "Nancy hesitated about interrupting the voodoo preacher-doctor. He was probably brewing a potion from herbs and uttering prayers for its success and efficacy whenever it might be used by his patients" (152). To be sure, the girl sleuth opts to wait until he is finished to speak with him. A few pages later, Bess's cousin confirms the wisdom of this decision, remarking on Uncle Rufus' reputation as a voodoo doctor: "It's said that Uncle Rufus has brought about many good cures " (155).

Whereas *The Haunted Showboat* shows a passing interest in questions of spirituality, the novel that was released directly after it, *The Secret of the Golden Pavilion* (1959, #35), makes this issue its central focus. Capitalizing on the widespread public interest in Hawaii given recent efforts for it to be granted statehood, Nancy is invited to Honolulu by Mr. Kamuela Sakamaki to solve a mystery connected to the estate of his recently deceased grandfather. From the beginning, the case is intimately connected with the indigenous culture of Hawaii in general and religious beliefs in particular. Echoing the plot of *Not-So-Nice Nurse* once again, the secular mystery in the novel is inextricably connected to sacred ones. In fact, the first clues that Mr. Sakamaki gives the protagonist about the mystery at Kaluakua are two Polynesian hieroglyphs (20). Several of the traditional Hawaiian gods and goddesses are offered as possible referents for these symbols—or, at least, important clues about their potential meaning. Mr. Sakamaki, for example, offers a long explanation about Pele, "the Sleeping Goddess of the Volcano" (32–33). His description occupies two pages and—akin to segments of *Not-So-Nice Nurse*—it reads more like an entry from an encyclopedia than a passage in a novel.

Such informational passages increase exponentially after Nancy and her companions arrive in Honolulu. When giving the girls a tour of the city, for example, Mr. Armstrong points to a statue and informs them: "That is a likeness of King Kamehameha, first king of all the Hawaiian Islands" (63). King Kamehameha is not just a legendary political figure in Hawaii; he was also an important one from a religious standpoint. The monarch was the last indigenous ruler to adhere to the traditional religious system of the islands, known as *kapu*. Stephanie Seto Levin has explained that, under this system, "Persons belonging to the *ali'i* stratum derived their high status by virtue of the fact that they were direct descendents of the gods" (408). Consequently, the king's political power was derived from his spiritual prowess. As Levin details: "The main duty of the paramount chief was to initiate and participate in religious rituals, the efficacy of which was needed for the well-being of society" (416). So, if crops failed, poor weather dominated or fishing yields were low, the king was seen as failing to appease the gods. This duty was regarded as such a paramount one for the king that being unable to satisfy it could lead to dethronement. "It was firmly believed that if religious affairs of the society were not given proper attention . . . , political authority would pass into the hands of another chief under whom religious rituals would be strictly and correctly performed" (Levin 416).

When Nancy begins investigating the mystery at Kaluakua, such coded references to the Hawaiian *kapu* system and its various gods—or *akua* (Kashay 18)—become more overt. After seeing the Golden Pavilion, Bess remarks that the structure is so beautiful that "Somebody *must* be buried beneath it" (74)—a detail that would account for why a vandal recently "hacked in a few places down to its concrete subfloor" (73) in search of valuables. Kiyabu, the caretaker of the estate, has another theory about the Golden Pavilion. He agrees that a figure is likely entombed beneath the structure, but, he adds, "not anyone human" (74). Instead, Kiyabu suggests "it might be a grave of one of the helpers of the Queen of Sharks" (74). Nancy and her friends—along, presumably, with the book's readers—are unfamiliar with this figure and her legend, so he explains it to them: "Her name was Kaahupahau. . . . She loved the human race and ordered her shark people never to attack them" (74).

The solution to the mystery likewise involves the island's ancient religious beliefs, myths, and legends. When Nancy flies over the Golden Pavilion in a helicopter, she spots an important clue: "Ned, look! I never noticed that the flower bed down there is in the shape of a plumiera flower. Also, one petal is a little longer than the others. It points directly to the secret doorway under the pavilion" (160). Ned is unsure about the significance of this clue, but the girl sleuth has a theory: "'I believe,' said Nancy, her eyes sparkling, 'that some treasure belonging to an ancient Hawaiian king is hidden at the center of the golden plumiera'" (161–62). Of course, Nancy's hunch proves correct. "I have the king's treasure!" Ned announces after searching under a portion of the roof. "Over his arm he was carrying a long, varicolored cape made of feathers. . . . 'Why, this is one of those ceremonial capes made from the extinct o-o bird!,' Nancy exclaimed softly. 'A museum piece!'" (168). Although the cape is briefly stolen from Ned and Nancy when they are ambushed, knocked unconscious, and then tied up beneath the pavilion in a final exciting plot twist, they recover the garment in the following chapter. Upon doing so, they learn more about the cape from a note written in the hand of Grandfather Sakamaki: "It . . . explained that the garment was a duplicate of a king's feather cape which had been given to one of his wife's ancestors as a special mark of favor. Since a king's cape was always buried with him, this duplicate was very valuable and had been hidden by the family, so that neither thieves nor conquerors from foreign lands would take it" (176). Once again, the fact that the garment belonged to "an ancient Hawaiian king" infuses it with not merely a political but a religious significance. As Jennifer Fish Kashay points out, "Prior to the arrival of Captain Cook, the Hawaiian people lived by a religio-political belief system known as *aikapu* (sacred eating). The *kapus* or taboos made the Sandwich Island chiefs gods on earth" (19).

In this way, *The Secret of the Golden Pavilion* follows a narrative arc that closely matches that of *Not-So-Nice Nurse*. While the precise faiths profiled differ, the overall message remains the same: the key to solving the secular mystery in both books is rooted in solving various religious mysteries. More specifically, the cases in each text are cracked when the central characters develop a greater understanding of a faith to which they do not belong: Roman Catholicism in the case of Maney's text and the indigenous *kapu*-based spirituality of Hawaii in Nancy Drew.

Of course, this new interest in exploring various forms of spirituality does not eliminate or even compensate for the various negative comments regarding race, class, gender, and ethnicity that still permeate the Nancy Drew Mystery Stories. In *The Haunted Showboat*, for example, Uncle Rufus may be respected for his status as a knowledgeable voodoo doctor, but he is still presented in a highly stereotypical manner. From his physical appearance and his personality to his speech patterns and mannerisms, he is patterned after antebellum images of plantation blacks and especially the figure of Uncle Remus, whom his surname strongly recalls.[4] When Uncle Rufus is first introduced, for example, the narrators notes: "A white-haired Negro immediately stood up. He was tall and slender, and his face had the look of a trustworthy, helpful person . . . 'I got my ka-noo outside,' he said. 'When you all is ready, Uncle Rufus will paddle you upstream'" (65).[5]

Unfortunately, analogous elements permeate *The Secret of the Golden Pavilion*. Even though the book is interested in educating its readers about the religious traditions of ancient Hawaii, many problematic comments are still made about the islands' people, history, and culture. Before leaving for Honolulu, for instance, Nancy receives a hula lesson from Mr. and Mrs. Sakamaki. Echoing the longstanding colonialist practice of white Anglo-Europeans co-opting the culture of native peoples, she becomes nearly as proficient a hula dancer in one afternoon as native Hawaiians who have been practicing the art for generations: "They said that with a little practice and a proper costume, she could easily join a Hawaiian group" (45). Then, even more problematically, in the closing lines of the book, Mr. Sakamaki proposes having a *luau* to celebrate the girl sleuth solving the mystery. Although he suggests hiring a professional

and, presumably, native Hawaiian troupe, George has an alternative suggestion: "'Let's have our own entertainment,' she suggested. 'And Drew will dance
the hula for us and [Ned] Nickerson will be crowned king and wearer the
feathered cape!'" (184).

Such problematic and disappointing features notwithstanding, *The Secret
of the Golden Pavilion* and *The Haunted Showboat* follow a narrative arc that
closely matches that of *Not-So-Nice Nurse*. Furthermore, the insights about
spirituality in the Nancy Drew series that are revealed via Mabel Maney's *The
Case of the Not-So-Nice Nurse* do serve at least one progressive purpose: they
highlight the benefits of considering the books about the girl sleuth as individual entities rather than a monolith. *The Haunted Showboat* and *The Secret
of the Golden Pavilion* do not contain the same approach to individual faith
and organized religion as their previous counterparts. Maney's book calls attention to this difference and reminds us to take a cue from the detective in-
stallments of Nancy Drew herself by viewing the books on a case-by-case basis rather than lumping them together as if they were a uniform aggregate.

I Retold You So: Adult-Audience Retellings as a Fertile (In More Ways Than One) Source of Children's Literature for Adults

While Mabel Maney's Nancy Clue series was an adult-audience retelling of a
classic children's book series that called attention to some of the tacit themes,
subtextual messages, and implicit ideologies in the original, it was not the first
narrative to engage in this practice. On the contrary, the book joined a variety of other titles that employed the same strategy. In 1982, for example, Benjamin Hoff released *The Tao of Pooh*. The text, which was published by the
adult division of Dutton, used A. A. Milne's Winnie-the-Pooh series as a vehicle for introducing the Chinese philosophy of Taoism to Western readers.
As Hoff demonstrates, the characters, plots, and premise of Milne's original
classic embed many of these concepts; his reworking merely amplifies what is
already powerfully present. According to his own website, Hoff's book was a
massive success, appearing on the *New York Times* bestseller list for 49 weeks.
It sparked a sequel or companion text, *The Te of Piglet* (1992). As the title revealed, the narrative uses Milne's character of Piglet as a means to convey the
Chinese concept of "Te" or "virtue—of the small" (back cover). *The Te of Piglet* was likewise a commercial success, spending 37 weeks on the *New York
Times* bestseller list, according to Hoff's author website.[6]

Echoing Mabel Maney's Nancy Clue series, some of the adult-audience retellings that have been released over the years have showcased the sexual

dynamics lurking in the source text. In 1979, Angela Carter released *The Bloody Chamber*, a feminist reimagining of a variety of classic fairy tales.[7] A passage from the title story demonstrates Carter's interest in exploring the eroticism that permeates many of these tales. "Off comes the skirt; and next, the dress of apricot linen that cost more than the dress I had for first communion," she writes. "He stripped me, gourmand that he was, as if he were stripping the leaves off an artichoke" (Carter 11). A few pages later, Carter's tale becomes even more explicit: "I had heard him shriek and blaspheme at the orgasm; I had bled" (15).

Eric Tribunella, in a recent essay, examines narratives of this nature in more detail. As he writes, a variety of reworkings of children's stories from the closing years of twentieth century and opening decades of the new millennium have been "adult" in a literal sense, meaning they have been erotic and even pornographic (136). For example, Tribunella cites Alan Moore and Melinda Gebbie's *Lost Girls* series (1991), "a three-volume set of graphic novels that revisits Carroll's *Alice* books, Baum's *Oz*, and Barrie's *Peter and Wendy* (1911)" (136). As he explains, Moore and Gebbie have embraced the label 'pornography' for *Lost Girls* and have discussed it as an effort to reunite artistic and pornographic endeavors" (Tribunella 136).

A few years later, novelist Chris Kent continued in this vein when he began releasing adult-audience retellings of some classic nineteenth-century school stories. His book *Coral Island Boys* (1998) reimagined R. M. Ballantyne's *The Coral Island* (1857). Meanwhile, Kent's text *The Real Tom Brown's Schooldays* (2002) reworked Thomas Hughes's *Tom Brown's Schooldays* (1857). Akin to the Nancy Clue/Cherry Aimless series, both narratives brought the homoeroticism that permeated these stories set in all-boys educational institutions to the forefront. Additionally, in a further echo of Maney's work, *Coral Island Boys* and *The Real Tom Brown's Schooldays* are marketed as parodies of the original texts (Tribunella 137). However, they differ from the Nancy Clue series in a significant way. As Tribunella discusses, "they include extremely graphic depictions of sexual acts on nearly every page" (137). Sexually explicit retellings of children's books like *Lost Girls*, *Coral Island Boys*, and *The Real Tom Brown's Schooldays* do more than simply represent a new vehicle for the creation of erotica. As Tribunella asserts, they also "represent adult reclamation of an element of children's culture" (136).

This phenomenon would only increase as the 1990s gave way to the 2000s. In the new millennium, individual characters, specific plots, and overall premises from well-known children's books being reimaged for adult readers, often with the introduction of erotic elements, grew exponentially. As discussed in one of the opening sections of this chapter, however, these materials were increasingly written by amateur fans, not professional authors. Additionally, they more commonly appeared as online posts on websites for fanfiction and slash fiction, not as physical books released by a publisher. Regardless, the end result was the same. Adult-audience retellings of children's stories demonstrate the creative possibilities and readerly pleasures of having our favorite characters from childhood populate books we encounter in adulthood. Furthermore, beyond simply allowing grown-ups to continue to enjoy their favorite stories, fanfiction and slash fiction also enables them to view these plots, characters, and books in new ways—or, as in the case of *Not-So-Nice Nurse*, in ways that they had long suspected. Just as importantly, the sheer number and the mass popularity of fan-authored stories would further blur the lines between readers and writers, novices and professionals, and children and adults in the United States. These narratives demonstrated that beloved childhood characters could and even should circulate in books written for adults. They likewise revealed how so-called "adult" issues like sexuality were powerfully present in children's literature and, by extension, in childhood. Echoing the name of a popular mode of fanfiction, the formerly solid barrier separating childhood and adult was slashed open by this phenomenon.

The rise of prose-based fanfiction online did not mean that either printed books that engaged in this practice or ones that also included visual components disappeared. On the contrary, the second decade of the twenty-first century saw the release of a bevy of physical picture books that engaged with sex and sexuality. In keeping with the looping, lurching, and leaping relationship between childhood and adulthood by this period, though, the "adult" treatment of sex in these narratives could ironically be regarded as "juvenile" in many ways. The picture book *Do You Want to Play with My Balls?* (2012) by the Cifaldi Brothers is an early example that exemplifies this phenomenon. The title of the text notwithstanding, the text is not pornographic; it is comedic. The book traffics in the humorous double entendre that arises from this noun simultaneously referencing bouncy balls being enjoyed by young people and as a slang term for scrotum. To that end, representative passages include: "I can hold your ball sack so it won't drag on the ground" and "Wow! Your balls are so big, I can't even fit them in my mouth!" The child characters in *Do You Want to Play with My Balls?* are wholly unaware of the slang connotation for the word "ball," an assumption that the book extends to the young people who exist outside of its pages as well. Indeed, the humor of the book arises from the adult belief that the young people in the text, along with those out-side of it, are completely oblivious to the sexualized way in which what they are saying can be interpreted. As Eric Tribunella has written about *Coral Is-land Boys* and *The Real Tom Brown's Schooldays*, the fact that these erotically charged comments are uttered by child characters for the amusement of adult readers might "set off alarms about the threat of pedophilia" (137). However, *Do You Want to Play With My Balls?* is not seeking to eroticize its young pro-tagonists. Instead, it is capitalizing on comedic puns and word play. It is lan-guage that is being exploited here, not young children.

Four years later, in 2016, creator Matt Williams, writer Bimisi Tayanita, and illustrator Sumguyen Bangladesh collaborated on a series of narratives along these same lines. As the publisher's blurb revealed, the books they released re-lied on "the timeless power of double entendre." Far from false advertising, the texts—which are written in the style of simple children's picture books and include cartoonish-style illustrations—had the following titles: *Brenda's Bea-ver Needs a Barber*; *Spank the Monkey Lends a Hand*; *Put Tony's Nuts in Your Mouth!*; *Come Swing with Us!*; and—in a powerful echo of the previous title by the Cifaldi Brothers—*Suzy Likes to Look at Balls!* Once again, the humor in the book is predicated on the belief that the children both inside and out-side of the narrative are too naïve or innocent to understand why it is funny.

While none of the passages or images in any of the books are sexually ex-plicit, they clearly traffic in aspects of the pornographic. One year later, in 2017, Gary Galvin published two books that continued this trend: *Would You Like to Play with My Ass?*, which is about a farm girl and her pet donkey; and *Would You Like to Play with My Pussy?*, a story about the same young woman and her beloved house cat. While all of these books can ostensibly be read to a child—once again, none of them contain any overtly explicit content—they are clearly directed at an audience of adults.

To this point, this study has explored the role that literary format and nar-rative style can play in the creation of children's literature for adults. Chapter one examined the use of the picture book format as an effective medium to discuss the topics of aging and growing older. Meanwhile, this chapter revealed how series books, detective fiction, and girls' novels constitute a rich site for adult-audience retellings of classic children's books, thereby acting as a power-ful source for the new genre as a whole. The next chapter expands on the range and repertoire of children's literature for adults. It examines Art Spiegel-man's *In the Shadow of No Towers* (2004), a graphic memoir that documents the Pulitzer Prize–winning cartoonist's experience of living in New York City during the terrorist attacks of September 11, 2001. Although *No Towers* is commonly viewed as a work of comics, I argue that it can also be categorized in a different way: as a board book. Spiegelman's series of cartoons are printed on heavy cardstock akin to the sturdy books given to babies and toddlers. In light of these features, *No Towers* invites us to consider a new aspect in the creation of children's literature for adults: physical materiality.

CHAPTER 3

Material Matters

Art Spiegelman's *In the Shadow of No Towers* as a Board Book

The public has been infantilized by the press.

—Art Spiegelman, *The Nation*, February 2006

In 2004, Pulitzer Prize–winning cartoonist Art Spiegelman released his latest book, *In the Shadow of No Towers*. The graphic narrative examined the terrorist attacks in New York City on September 11, 2001. A longtime resident of Lower Manhattan, Spiegelman was an eyewitness to the events. Accordingly, *In the Shadow of No Towers* is equal-parts personal memoir and political commentary. Scott Thill, in his review for *Salon*, called the book "dark," "troubling," and "sharply satirical" (par. 1). As a result, even though the text comprises a series of comics—a genre that has historically had a strong connection with youth readers—none of the reviews suggested that it either was or could potentially be reading material for children. Affirming this viewpoint, the *School Library Journal* profiled the book soon after it was released, but in an article titled "Great Reads for Grown-Ups" (Genco 54–55).

Over the years, *In the Shadow of No Towers* has been viewed from a variety of critical perspectives. Gillian Whitlock, in an essay titled "Autobiographics," reads the text largely as a memoir. Meanwhile, Mary Louise Penaz, in her article "Drawing History," examines the narrative as a documentary work of nonfiction. Finally, Kristiaan Versluys, Martha Kuhlman, and Katalin Orbán have all explored *No Towers* in scholarly discussions through the lens of trauma writing.

This chapter pushes the critical conversation about Spiegelman's text and, by extension, children's literature for adults in a different direction. I examine *No Towers* not simply in the context of its subject matter but also from the standpoint of its physical materiality. The 2004 narrative is a folio-sized text printed on heavy card stock that is used frequently for board books produced for babies, infants, and toddlers. Indeed, major online bookseller Amazon classifies Spiegelman's title not as a hardcover narrative but as a board book.

The discussion that follows explores what happens when we foreground the materiality of *In the Shadow of No Towers*. What new interpretative insights do we gain if we view this element as a key facet of the text rather than as an incidental feature of its physicality? How do we reconcile the juxtaposition of violent, macabre, and politically charged subject matter for adult readers in the text with the employment of a physical form that is used for some of the most playful, didactic, and seemingly innocuous books for preliterate youth? How does the material being discussed in Spiegelman's narrative interact with its materiality? Finally, but far from insignificantly, what do the answers to these questions tell us about children's literature for adults? What role does the physicality of a text play in the construction of this genre?

Literary critics have long recognized that the writing style of a text influences its content. It makes a difference whether a story is told as a work of prose or poetry, fiction or non-fiction, realism or sci-fi. Bill Brown, building on the work of scholars like Jerome McGann and D. F. McKenzie, has taken this observation one step further by making the same argument about the materiality of a text. Brown has asserted that the physical form of a book—its size, its weight, and so forth—impacts the way that it is viewed, read, and even interpreted. A narrative that is published as a calfskin hardcover is approached, examined, and regarded much differently than one that is issued as a pulp paperback. For this reason, Brown, in *A Sense of Things*, contemplates the ideological, metaphysical, and ontological ramifications that would occur if critics made "the effort to think with or through the physical object world" that exists inside, outside, and through printed texts (3). This chapter heeds this advice. The presentation of *No Towers* as a board book is far from an inconsequential feature or a purely pragmatic choice; rather, it forms an important and overlooked facet of the experience of reading and interpreting Spiegelman's text. The events of September 11, 2001 were devastating. The death and destruction that unfolded in New York City on that day caused many adults to feel shocked, numb, and even traumatized. In the wake of the attacks, many Americans no longer felt like capable, competent, and in-control adults. Instead, they felt more like frightened and helpless little children.

Foregrounding the materiality of *In the Shadow of No Towers* augments Spiegelman's exploration of the logistical events of 9/11 and especially their emotional, psychological, and cultural aftermath. First and foremost, paying attention to the physicality of the book leads us back to the inherent physicality of the events: namely, the destruction of the World Trade Center. The terrorist attack graphically demonstrated how material structures that seemed strong, secure, and permanent were actually highly vulnerable and ultimately ephemeral. Just as importantly, though, the appearance of *No Towers* as a board book also comments on the emotional impact of the day's physical destruction. Even the most cool-headed adults were left reeling: psychologically dazed, personally stunned, and emotionally in shock. As a result, they occupied positions of vulnerability and fear more commonly experienced by young children. *In the Shadow of No Towers* meets its adult readers where they are, appearing in a physical format that can bear their grief, withstand their anger, and offer the sociopolitical lessons that they will need to learn in a post-9/11 world.

For these reasons, Spiegelman's book also constitutes a compelling coordinate for mapping children's literature for adults. *No Towers* demonstrates how the material modes utilized by books for young people remain not simply relevant to adults, but necessary for them. In the same way that young readers need sturdy books printed on thick card stock that can withstand being treated roughly, so too do audiences who are older. While grown-ups know how to properly handle and carefully treat books, there are some experiences, events, and subject matters that are so upsetting that they no longer want—or are even able—to do so. When children's literature of adults adopts the materiality of the board book, it serves this function and satisfies this need. In so doing, texts like *In the Shadow of No Towers* add a new facet to the literary aim, cultural impact, and psychological purpose of the genre. Board books for young people often teach early literacy skills, such as letters, numbers, and colors. *In the Shadow of No Towers* serves a similar function for its adult audience. In the wake of the terrorist attacks of 9/11, Spiegelman's comics offer his readers what he regards as much-needed literacy in US politics.

"I Tend to Be Easily Unhinged": *No Towers* and Traumatized Post-9/11 Adults

Ironically, *In the Shadow of No Towers* was not initially released as a physical book or even intended as one. As Spiegelman explains in an essay that prefaces the text, the ten large-size comics that form the core of the narrative were composed for the newspaper *Die Zeit* and released serially ("Sky Is Falling").[1] *Die Zeit*—which means "The Time" in German—is not a US-based publication. Instead, it is a national newspaper in Germany that is published weekly. Spiegelman's comics were first printed in *Die Zeit* and then were picked up by a variety of other newspapers around Europe: France, Italy, the Netherlands, and England (Spiegelman, "Sky Is Falling"). Of course, Spiegelman is a cartoonist living and working in the United States. Moreover, he is writing about an event that occurred in New York City. Nonetheless, the fact that the cartoons which comprise *In the Shadow of No Towers* initially appeared in Europe call further attention to the international nature of children's literature for adults. As Spiegelman has commented in various articles and interviews, he agreed to the publication offer by *Die Zeit* in large part because it afforded him the creative freedom to write and draw what he wanted (Spiegelman, "Sky Is Falling"). The terrorist attacks of September 11 were then and remain now an intensely inflammatory issue. Any discussion of the event and its aftermath that criticizes the US government, military, or media is often met with opprobrium. Such views are seen as unpatriotic, un-American, and even treasonous. Indeed, as Spiegelman noted, "mainstream publications that had actively solicited work from me . . . fled when I offered these pages or excerpts from the series" (Spiegelman, "Sky Is Falling"). By having his cartoons appear in Europe, Spiegelman was able to comment on 9/11 without fear of censure: by editors, readers, reviewers, and public leaders.

Spiegelman's decision also underscores the way in which children's literature for adults is inherently global in its roots and its reach. Akin to the events of 9/11 themselves, which all took place on American soil but whose impact was felt around the world, this new genre is not geographically isolated or culturally contained. On the contrary, from the standpoint of its origins, existence, evolution, and certainly impact, it is inherently transnational and cross-cultural.

The format of *Die Zeit* newspaper accounts for the physical dimensions of Spiegelman's *No Towers*. Each comic appeared as a full-page spread in a broadsheet-style newspaper. *In the Shadow of No Towers* reprints the series in its original size. Accordingly, the 2004 text is big: it measures 14.5 inches tall and 10 inches wide. This almost folio size renders Spiegelman's text more of a coffee-table book than a collection of comics. Furthermore, each cartoon occupies a double-page spread. To read them, *No Towers* needs to be rotated from a vertical position where the spine runs up and down to a horizontal one in which the spine extends left to right.

While the initial appearance of Spiegelman's comics in a broadsheet-sized newspaper might account for the physical dimensions of *No Towers*, it does not account for the choice to reprint them on thick card stock. In fact, this detail seems entirely antithetical to the medium. If Spiegelman made *No Towers* a large book to preserve the dimensions of the newspaper pages in which his work first appeared, then it would have been more appropriate to reprint them on newsprint or at least on paper of conventional thickness.

The oversized format and the card-stock paper of *No Towers* lack any clear connection to one another, and they also make for an exceedingly clunky text. As Michael Joseph rightly notes, these two elements combine to create "the overwhelming physical awkwardness of *In the Shadow of No Towers*" (460). To be sure, Spiegelman's volume violates many of the oft-cited edicts from William Morris's landmark essay "The Ideal Book": "You may want a book to turn over easily and lie quiet, while you are reading it," Morris writes, and its pages ought to be "peaceful and give no trouble of body." *No Towers* is anything but an easy, peaceful, or comfortable book. It is awkward to hold, cumbersome to read, and generally too big and bulky to "give no trouble of body." In this way, Spiegelman's narrative actively resists what Bill Brown has described as the process by which texts typically try to make their own "object qua object" disappear (11). Most narratives downplay their own physicality, striving to get their audience to forget that they are holding a tangible object and instead to lose themselves in the process of reading. As Georges Poulet has said about this phenomenon: "You are inside [the book]; it is inside you; there is no longer either outside or inside" (56). Joseph views the choice of heavy card stock for *No Towers* as an extension of Spiegelman's message. As he notes, the thick paper "cautions against the dubious *weightiness* of the book as the warrant of religious, governmental, and scholastic authority" (460). Other critics have been far less poetic—and far less generous—in their assessments. Michael Lewis, for instance, speculates that Spiegelman not only includes reprints of old comics at the end of *No Towers* but also publishes the entire book on heavy cardboard, "evidently as a way of filling out what would otherwise be an exceptionally skimpy volume" (74).

Building on the work of Michael Joseph, I contend that the thick card stock used for *No Towers* is anything but an incidental feature of the text. Rather, it calls attention to key facets of the book's subject matter as well as the psychological condition of its audience. The shock, horror, and tragedy of September 11 left many Americans grasping—literally and figuratively—for something solid and sturdy once again. The appearance of *In the Shadow of No Towers* as a board book reflects this condition. The thick card stock brings issues of physicality to the forefront, inviting readers to consider the ways that material objects protect us, fail us, and weigh on us. Many adults were traumatized by the events of 9/11. Because *No Towers* appears on thick card stock, it is physically strong enough to withstand their expressions of outrage, grief, and bewilderment. Akin to board books for babies and toddlers, though, Spiegelman's text is designed to do more than simply bear mistreatment; it is also intended to be instructive. The United States was forever changed on September 11. In the wake of the attacks, Americans needed to learn an array of new and often difficult lessons. *In the Shadow of No Towers* addresses these sociopolitical issues, offering insight that Spiegelman believes is essential. Ultimately, the rich interplay between the content and the form of *No Towers* offers a compelling commentary about the relationship between childhood and adulthood amidst times of trauma, fear, and upheaval.

At its core, 9/11 was a day of profound physical loss: the death of nearly 3,000 people and the destruction of the two tallest skyscrapers in New York City. Of course, these events also carried with them tremendous emotional weight. As Brad Schmidt and Jeffrey Winters wrote, "On September 11, terrorists did more than destroy buildings; they scarred the American psyche" (par. 3). They go on to cite a variety of studies to support this claim. "In the weeks immediately after the attacks," Schmidt and Winters write, "a survey of 668 Americans by the Institute of Social Research in Ann Arbor, Michigan, reported that 49 percent of participants felt their sense of safety and security had been shaken" (par. 4). In addition, Schmidt and Winters continue, "some 62 percent of respondents said they had difficulty sleeping" (par. 4). Given these statistics, the duo rightly notes, "We are having difficulty grappling with our sudden loss of security" (par. 4).

Spiegelman foregrounds the importance that materiality will play in *No Towers* even before readers open the text and see the first comic: the cover image features a silhouette of the World Trade Center. The graphic narrative will be about the loss of these two massive physical structures. That Spiegelman's book is also large and rectangular shaped—not unlike each of the Twin Towers—only furthers this association. Unsurprisingly, the physical presence and especially the tangible weight of objects are preoccupations throughout *No Towers*. On the one hand, the cartoonist-narrator routinely seeks solace in the material, such as in a panel that appears on the seventh double-page spread where he dives under an American flag for protection. On the other, he is just as commonly assaulted by physical objects, as in the panels on page ten where a piece of 9/11 kitsch blows up in his face and a multitude of George W. Bush–style cowboy boots rain down on his head. Through these sequences, *No Towers* demonstrates Richard Terdiman's observation about "the brute and often brutal difficulty of materiality" (14). Spiegelman would like nothing more than to escape from or, at least, to transcend the material, but he cannot. His traumas originated in and are being perpetuated by physical objects: television sets, newspapers, American flags. The presentation of *No Towers* as a board book both echoes and extends this interest in physicality. The heavy card stock used to construct the text calls attention to itself. Because the thick cardboard is an unconventional choice that makes interacting with the book awkward, it reminds readers with every turn of the page that *No Towers* is itself a material object.

The significance of *No Towers* as a board book extends beyond simply calling attention to physical items that appear inside the text, that exist outside of the text, and that are embodied by the text itself. Because Spiegelman's text uses the same thick card stock as items for babies and toddlers, it invites readers to consider the emotional, temperamental, and developmental links between very young children and post-9/11 adults. *In the Shadow of No Towers* begins with an introductory essay by Spiegelman, entitled "The Sky Is Falling! The Sky Is Falling!" This two-page prose commentary describes the cartoonist's experiences of living in Lower Manhattan on 9/11. The essay opens with Spiegelman's confession: "I tend to be easily unhinged. Minor mishaps—a clogged drain, running late for an appointment—send me into a sky-is-falling tizzy." Consequently, the cartoonist says, he was grossly "ill-equipped for coping" when the sky actually fell on September 11, 2001. "Before 9/11 my traumas were all more or less self-inflicted," he tells readers, but hearing the planes crash into the towers, smelling the smoke from the fires, and witnessing the giant buildings collapse "left me reeling" (Spiegelman, "Sky Is Falling").

This sense of being "unhinged" forms an apt metaphor for the comics that follow. In numerous panels throughout these pages, Spiegelman presents himself as losing control of his physical, emotional, and psychological faculties. This message is vividly conveyed in the series that runs across the top of the second double-page spread. "DOOMED!" the speech balloon for Spiegelman's cartoon avatar announces. "Doomed to drag this damned albatross around my neck, and compulsively retell the calamities of September 11 to anyone who'll listen!" (2). The drawing that accompanies these lines presents the cartoonist-narrator with his hands raised in exasperation, his eyes opened wide in alarm, and beads of sweat emanating from his brow. The albatross to which he refers is a bald eagle wearing a red, white, and blue top hat. In the three panels that follow, Spiegelman's presentation of himself as anxious and unnerved intensifies. "I insist the sky is falling," the cartoonist-narrator tells readers (2). His comics persona is depicted in greater close-up to showcase his anxiety: his hands are raised even higher to convey the urgency of his message and the drops of sweat radiating from his brow have doubled. A mere two panels later, the eyes of Spiegelman's cartoon avatar have been replaced by red swirls, suggesting that he has—to borrow the term from his opening essay—become completely "unhinged" (2).

The loss of control that Spiegelman's cartoon avatar experiences in this scene evokes a common experience for young children. Throughout childhood, young people are placed in a subordinated position to adults and compelled to defer to their rules, decisions, and authority. *No Towers* demonstrates repeatedly that 9/11 placed adults in an analogous situation. Like young people, adults felt a profound sense of helplessness. The terrorist attacks caused them to feel that they were no longer in control over either their individual lives or the world at large. As Spiegelman's cartoon avatar reveals, this new subject position caused many adults not simply to experience childlike frustration but also to become wholly "unhinged." After all, adults are supposed to be calm, competent, and in control at all times.

Such characterizations continue. In the fifth comic, for example, the cartoonist-narrator rants about the Bush administration: "Trauma piles on trauma! Over half the country was already doubled over in pain after the *coup d'etat* [sic] in 2000. . . . Now everyone's too scared, stupefied or demoralized to stop you." In fact, Spiegelman refers to himself and his fellow Americans as "basket cases" in the wake of 9/11 (5). Perhaps not surprisingly given this portrait, the eighth comic shows another swirly eyed rendering of the cartoonist-narrator driving a jackhammer into his own brain. By the ninth comic, Spiegelman has become so enraged that his cartoon avatar throws an adorable kitten off his lap. "**Shit!** This gang in power gets me so mad I could **scream!**" he erupts as the fuzzy animal goes flying across the living room and out of the panel's frame (9).

As even these brief descriptions indicate, the attacks of 9/11 and especially the Bush administration's response to them have left Spiegelman feeling frustrated and even angry. The heavy card-stock paper used for *No Towers* recognizes and accommodates for this state. Akin to the babies and toddlers for whom board books traditionally are intended, the cartoonist-narrator finds that he cannot be trusted to treat a conventional book gently and to handle it carefully. He assumes that his readers cannot be trusted to do so, either. Because Spiegelman has become emotionally, physically, and psychologically "unhinged," he needs the thick card stock to withstand his rage, rants, and outbursts. Presumably, his readers might respond in the same way to *No Towers*. The heavy cardboard anticipates their mental state and their possible physical responses: they can throw, tear, or gnaw *No Towers* without harming it. As a consequence, a powerful but tacit irony pervades Spiegelman's text: the sturdy materiality of *No Towers* is designed to withstand the expressions of stress and anxiety that are responses to the failure of materiality at the World Trade Center on 9/11.

Of course, Spiegelman does more than simply present himself in *No Towers* as losing what we might call an adult sense of self-control and reverting to a more impulsive state associated conventionally with babies and toddlers. In addition, he often casts himself as a child. The ten comics that Spiegelman originally composed for *Die Zeit* and that are collected in *No Towers* are followed by seven plates that reproduce a variety of classic comics from the opening decades of the twentieth century. More than simply being historically significant artifacts from the past, these comics also have a powerful geographical resonance for the present day. In a later essay in *No Towers* entitled "The Comic Supplement," Spiegelman explains that the newspapers in which these strips appeared were created just "two blocks away from Ground Zero." As the cartoonist-narrator tells readers earlier in *No Towers*: "The blast that disintegrated those Lower Manhattan Towers also disinterred the ghosts of some Sunday Supplement stars born on nearby Park Row about a century earlier. They came back to haunt one denizen of the neighborhood addled by all that's happened since" (8).

Spiegelman identifies seven strips that he finds both aesthetically significant and sociopolitically resonant: Lyonel Feininger's *The Kin-der-Kids*, Richard Outcault's *Hogan's Alley*, Gustave Verbeek's *The Upside Downs of Little Lady Lovekins and Old Man Muffaroo*, Rudolph Dirks's *The Katzenjammer Kids*, Frederick Burr Opper's *Happy Hooligan*, Winsor McCay's *Little Nemo in Slumberland*, and George McManus's *Bringing Up Father*. The second section of *No Towers* reprints one installment from each strip. As James Campbell has aptly noted about the choices that the cartoonist made,

> The latter comics all in some way reflect the themes of Spiegelman's own drawings in the "first Tower." One, dated 1902, shows "Foxy Grandpa" reading the Declaration of Independence on the fourth of July and being interrupted by an explosion, while another depicts Happy Hooligan, a popular idiot, assuming the guise of "Abdullah, the Arab Chief," and coming to grief with a 1,000lb weight dropped on his head. (par. 6)

The last reprinted plate in *No Towers* is perhaps the most resonant, as Campbell suggests: "In a 1921 cartoon from the *New York American*, a character visits Pisa and, like Spiegelman after September 11, is kept awake by thoughts of the famous tower falling on him" (par. 6).

In a detail that has been overlooked in discussions about Spiegelman's inclusion of these strips in *No Towers*, many of these early comics feature children as their central characters. *Hogan's Alley, The Katzenjammer Kids, Little Nemo in Slumberland,* and *The Kin-der-Kids* all contain young people as protagonists. Spiegelman not only pays homage to the aesthetic style of these comics in many of his panels, but he also depicts himself as many of these juvenile characters. This tendency extends the interest in the materiality of the book by calling into question the stable physicality of the human body. Such messages appear in the very first double-page spread in *No Towers*. After hearing the plane crash into the North Tower, Spiegelman and his wife race to their daughter's school in Lower Manhattan. As they do so, they transform from cartoon likenesses of themselves to renderings of the Katzenjammer brothers, Hans and Fritz. Instead of being called the Katzenjammer Kids, as in Rudolph Dirk's strip, Spiegelman renames them the Tower Twins. The two look identical to their early twentieth-century incarnations, except that they each wear a small-sized replica of one of the World Trade Center towers on their head (fig. 1).

The Katzenjammer-inspired Tower Twins appear in several other sequences. These characters play an especially significant role on page five. In multiple panels at the top of this spread, the cartoonist presents a ghostly outline of one of the twins superimposed over the fiery glowing skeleton of one of the World Trade Center towers. Meanwhile, at the bottom of the page, an eight-panel series entitled "Remember Those Dead and Cuddly . . . Tower Twins" depicts the duo catching on fire and being doused with a barrel of oil by their "Uncle Screwloose," who is wearing the red, white, and blue colors of the American flag (5). Afterwards, Uncle Screwloose recklessly declares war against an insect with Saddam Hussein's face labeled "Iraknid" (5).

The cartoonist's depiction of himself as one of the Katzenjammer Kids in these and other sequences furthers the conceit of Spiegelman as child while it also augments the link between *No Towers* and the board book. In the cartoonist's prefatory essay, "The Comic Supplement," he remarks that one of the details that fascinated him about early comics was their "disposability." The "Sunday Funnies," he notes, were "vital, unpretentious, ephemera from the optimistic dawn of the 20th century." As he goes on to explain, "That they were made with so much skill and verve but never intended to last past the day they appeared in the newspaper gave them poignancy; they were just right for an end-of-the-world moment."

Board books, for all of their sturdy toughness, are also ephemeral objects. Designed both for a specific stage in a baby or a toddler's life and to be treated

Figure 1. In the bottom right panel, the artist reimagines the title characters from Rudolph Dirk's *Katzenjammer Kids* as the "Tower Twins." Detail from Art Spiegelman's *In the Shadow of No Towers.*

roughly, these texts are not generally considered keepsake items that will be passed down from generation to generation. Instead, as Barbara Bader, Alison G. Kaplan, and Susan Gregory Thomas have all documented, board books are "disposable": they are used and then generally discarded, either because the child has outgrown them intellectually or because they have become so gnawed, torn, and beaten up that the standards of good hygiene dictate that they be discarded. In fact, Kaplan has written that one of the reasons why researching the history of board books is so challenging is that these objects have always been "throw away" items (44). Given their utilitarian function and their rough treatment, few examples typically survive for posterity.

Of course, political cartoons—a genre to which *No Towers* clearly belongs—are also ephemeral. As Spiegelman himself notes in his opening essay to *No*

Towers, "[N]othing has a shorter shelf life than angry caricatures of politicians" ("Sky Is Falling"). While *No Towers* obviously is not offering instruction in letters, numbers, or colors as in a traditional board book for young readers, it is offering its adult readership a different kind of instruction in literacy: namely, one in American politics in general and the cartoonist's specific viewpoint in particular. In the wake of 9/11, Spiegelman repeatedly suggests, this subject is just as essential as learning to read. Furthermore, it is not enough for individuals simply to be knowledgeable about American politics; they must also possess the knowledge to critique it. As the cartoonist asserts in this introductory essay, "I hadn't anticipated that the hijackings of September 11 would themselves be hijacked by the Bush cabal that reduced it all to a war recruitment poster"("Sky Is Falling"). If conventional board books are intended for a specific developmental period in a baby or a toddler's life, then *No Towers* similarly is intended for a specific period in the life of its adult readers, namely the one in which they are developing a geopolitical consciousness. The graphic narrative offers lessons that adult Americans will need to know in a post-9/11 world.

Comix Meets Comics: *No Towers* and the Politicization of Children and Childhood

Rereading *In the Shadow of No Towers* as a board book does more than simply call attention to the way in which many adults felt like they had returned to a social, psychological, and educational state akin to babies and toddlers by the events of September 11. Given the way in which board books have long been connected with young people, the physical format also brings the concept of "the child" and the social construction of childhood to the forefront of thematic concerns in the text. Although *No Towers* is intended for an audience of adults, children play a significant role in and to the text. They appear as beloved sons and daughters, as prized future citizens, and as tragic innocent victims to current events. When these depictions are viewed collectively, they add another piece to the book's engagement with children as well as its exploration of childhood. Together with offering a critique about the politicization of 9/11, Spiegelman's text offers an analysis about the politicization of young people in the United States. In a paradoxical detail that is wholly in keeping with topsy-turvy temporality that permeates Spiegelman's text, *No Towers* then uses those exact elements to reflect back on adulthood.

Even though many early twentieth-century comics like *Little Nemo in Slumberland*, *Hogan's Alley*, and *The Katzenjammer Kids* featured child protagonists, they were not intended for a child audience exclusively. As Spiegelman notes in "The Comic Supplement," these strips were by-products of the fierce circulation war between newspaper moguls Joseph Pulitzer and William Randolph Hearst. The amusing comics were printed in the then eye-popping novelty of full color and were intended to appeal to what Spiegelman calls the "often uneducated immigrant readership" ("Comic Supplement"). Individuals who may not have had either the interest or the literacy skills to read the newspaper could enjoy the comics page and, as a result, become new customers (Santi 193).

Of course, as Avi Santi has documented, Sunday comics "were read by many children as well" (194). In fact, many early twentieth-century newspaper strips were deliberately "child-friendly," depicting stories and characters that appealed to adults and young people alike (193). This move was driven by commercial and cultural impulses. "In this manner," Santi notes, "comic strips drew upon ambivalences in 'modernist sensibilities' by using the bad behavior and 'innocent' insights of their child character to poke at consumer culture and to allow adult readers to vicariously rebel against its constraints through their refusal to conform to the rules" (193). Within a few decades, this medium would be associated primarily with children. By the mid-twentieth century, the passage of the Comics Code, the rise of television, and the advent of pulp fiction all conspired to make comics synonymous with "the very unserious, unsacred world of Loonytoons" (Gordon 84). Indeed, as Bradford W. Wright has discussed, beginning in the mid-1950s, comics were viewed by mainstream America largely as light fare for young children (179–81).

Spiegelman has a long, complicated relationship with comics as a medium associated with children. On the one hand, the cartoonist has participated in and thereby perpetuated this link. In a commonly cited detail about Spiegelman's career, he worked as a creative consultant for Topps from 1966 to 1986, "designing novelty stickers for 'Garbage Pail Kids' and other products" for young people (Gussow). On the other hand, the cartoonist also recognized that comics need not be solely for young readers; they had been an effective storytelling vehicle for adults in the past and they should remain so in the present as well. Spiegelman was part of the underground comics scene throughout the 1960s and 1970s that challenged the long-standing artistic appearance of comics and the typical audience for this medium. In texts like *Breakdowns: Portrait of the Artist as a Young %@&·*!*, Spiegelman used an experimental aesthetic style to shine a spotlight on decidedly adult subject matters and address a variety of taboo issues in defiance of the Comics Code. As James Young has commented, "Spiegelman prefers the word 'comix' to 'comics' [to describe this work] because it alludes to the co-mixture of image and text, and it distances the medium from 'funny' comics or children's comics" (672). Given that *No Towers* likewise is intended for an adult audience, Spiegelman refers to it as a work of "comix" and not "comics" throughout his introductory essay.

This designation notwithstanding, Spiegelman's 2004 text is intimately concerned with children and childhood. The cartoonist may appear to be distancing *No Towers* from youth and youth culture by calling it "comix," but its content frequently contradicts this designation. Together with the cartoonist's presentation of himself as the child protagonist from various early newspaper strips, young people play a recurring and instrumental role throughout the text. In the sequence on the opening page, for example, a young girl sits on the couch watching television with her parents: the first panel is dated September 10, the next one is labeled September 11, and the third one bears no specific day but, given its placement in the sequence, clearly takes place sometime afterward (fig. 2). The inclusion of the young girl in this scene, coupled with the fact that she is just as shocked, shaken, and panicked as her parents are as they view the television coverage of the terrorist attacks, demonstrates the impact of 9/11 on children.

On the next page, Spiegelman's reference to generalized children becomes more specific: the cartoonist and his wife race through Lower Manhattan on September 11—thereby becoming eyewitnesses to the explosions, fires, and building collapses—because they are trying to retrieve their daughter Nadja from her school. Moreover, Nadja and several of her classmates appear at various points in the text. On page four, for example, Spiegelman shows two high school boys callously giving each other high-fives after hearing that the Pentagon has been attacked (fig. 3). Meanwhile, one of Nadja's peers cries inconsolably in the school lobby because her parents work in the World Trade Center. Finally, the young daughter of tourists joins her parents in calmly watching the disaster unfold from the esplanade above the Hudson River as if it were a sightseeing stop on the Big Apple bus tour. In these sequences, Spiegelman demonstrates that, far from existing offstage from the events of 9/11, young people were directly involved: as eyewitnesses, as victims, and as analysts.

Children also appear in symbolic ways. Beside a sequence on the third double-page spread in which the cartoonist-narrator rants about the poor air quality in Lower Manhattan after 9/11 in general and inside his daughter's

Figure 2. This sequence documents the tremendous impact that the terrorist attacks of 9/11 had on individuals, including (and perhaps especially) children. Detail from Art Spiegelman's *In the Shadow of No Towers*.

Figure 3. Various reactions that the classmates of the cartoonist's daughter had to news of the 9/11 attack are depicted in this sequence. Detail from Art Spiegelman's *In the Shadow of No Towers*.

school in particular—"They never even cleaned the air ducts at Nadja's school"—Spiegelman includes a 1950s-style poster showing a young boy and a young girl wearing gas masks. Above them, in big, bold white letters, the heading reads: "NYC TO KIDS: DON'T BREATHE!"[2] Here, children serve as a metaphor or even as a metonym for all the residents of New York (fig. 4).

The reprinted plates in the second half of *No Towers* reveal that children occupied a similarly politicized place and served an equally socially charged function in early twentieth-century comics. The young characters that appeared in strips like *Hogan's Alley*, *The Kin-der-Kids*, *Little Nemo in Slumberland*, and *The Katzenjammer Kids* often operated as a screen that reflected the nation's hopes and dreams along with its fears and nightmares. Nearly all the comics reprinted in the closing section of *No Towers* illustrate this phenomenon. Plate one, a double-page image from *Kin-der-Kids* in 1906, shows the title characters setting sail from New York Harbor in a bathtub. The crowded composition—filled with people arriving, departing, and generally jostling for position—illustrates the chaos, overcrowding, and unruliness within American cities in general and amid the flood of immigrants arriving to its shores

Figure 4. The welfare of the city's young people was not a priority for adult officials in the wake of the attack, as shown in this mock poster. Detail from Art Spiegelman's *In the Shadow of No Towers.*

in particular. Indeed, as small boats packed with individuals who are Asian, Irish, and "Pilgrim" fight for space on the water with a large steamer of passengers arriving from the "City of Podunk," it is not difficult to imagine why the Kin-der-Kids are eager to leave. New York City and, by extension, the United States is presented as already overcrowded.

The second plate, "The War Scare in Hogan's Alley," is even more blatant in its use of child characters as mouthpieces for larger sociopolitical concerns. Released on the eve of the Spanish-American War, the large-sized panel shows the juvenile residents lined up for a military-style inspection. Several of the youngsters are holding up placards that state their position (in language that is part working-class slang and part juvenile diction) on current domestic debates and foreign controversies. "Why Dont England Turn De X Rays Onto Der Monroe Doctoring An Dey Kin See Wots In It," reads one. Meanwhile, another says: "We Dont Know Venezuela But We Are Wit Him Troo Tick and Troo Tin All Right."

Finally, but far from insignificantly, Spiegelman's own childhood deeply informs *No Towers*. In the first paragraph of his opening essay to the graphic text, he remarks that the terrorist attacks on September 11 highlighted the "faultline where World History and Personal History collide" ("Sky Is Falling"). In an oft-cited detail about the cartoonist's biography, his parents were Holocaust survivors. Their experience in Nazi-occupied Poland and then in the concentration camp at Auschwitz was the subject of the graphic narratives for which Spiegelman is best known, the Pulitzer Prize–winning *Maus I: A Survivor's Tale: My Father Bleeds History* and *Maus II: A Survivor's Tale: And Here My Troubles Began*.

The traumas that Spiegelman experienced during 9/11 mix and merge with the traumas that his parents experienced during the Second World War. Together with linking these events in the opening paragraph of his prefatory essay, the cartoonist also calls repeated attention to them in the comics that follow. In two separate panels that appear on the second full-page spread, Spiegelman presents himself in what Martha Kuhlman has described as "*Maus*-face" (850)—or in the style of the anthropomorphized mouse characters that he used to represent himself, his parents, and all European Jews in *Maus I* and *Maus II*.

These likenesses recur throughout the remainder of *No Towers*. In two long strips on page three, for example, Spiegelman again depicts himself as a mouse from *Maus*, and he makes a direct connection between past and present historical calamities. "I remember my father trying to describe what the smoke in Auschwitz smelled like," the *Maus*-version of the cartoonist tells readers in the opening panel. He continues: "The closest he got was telling me it was . . . 'indescribable' . . . That's exactly what the air in Lower Manhattan smelled like after Sept. 11!"

Spiegelman appears again in *Maus*-face in a series called "Weapons of Mass Displacement" on page nine. This visage is the final one that his cartoon avatar assumes while ranting about American domestic and foreign policy. Finally, and most significantly, a rendering of himself as a figure from *Maus* is the closing image that the cartoonist elects to leave with readers. The drawing presents Spiegelman, along with his wife and two children, as rodentine figures.

These *Maus*-style renderings not only create what Thierry Groensteen has termed *tressage* or the "manner of looping" or "braiding" recurring images to bind a comics text together (30), but they also link *No Towers* with the cartoonist's own childhood. These images bring the 2004 narrative back to the time—which is well documented throughout *Maus*—when Spiegelman was growing up and listening to his parents' stories about the Nazis, World War II, and the Holocaust. Thus, even though the cartoonist renders himself as an anthropomorphized adult mouse in many of these panels, they are inextricably connected with and even evocative of his childhood.

Spiegelman's invocation of his past comics narratives addressing his family's history is not entirely separate from his interest in the history of American comics. In multiple places in *No Towers*, the cartoonist presents himself in *Maus*-face alongside or embedded within renditions of early newspaper comic strips. This confluence, in fact, bookends the text: a panel in the first double-page spread shows the cartoonist-as-*Maus* lying with his head down on his drawing table; diminutive-sized versions of the Yellow Kid, Jiggs, and Happy Hooligan stand on his desk. Then, in one of the closing panels of the book, where Spiegelman presents himself in *Maus* style walking the city streets with his family, the crowd behind him is comprised of comics characters that span the full range of the twentieth century: Little Orphan Annie, Albert Alligator, Walt from *Gasoline Alley*, Mammy Yokum from *Li'l Abner*, Jiggs from *Binging Up Father*, Wimpy from *Popeye*, Charlie Brown from *Peanuts*, Der Captain from the *Katzenjammer Kids*, and Mike Doonesbury from the *Doonesbury* comic strip.

Pastiches of this nature appear on multiple other pages. In a single panel cameo within the eighth comic, for example, Spiegelman-as-*Maus* appears alongside Krazy Kat. Meanwhile, in two other single-panel inserts, the cartoonist presents himself in this rodentine fashion but in drawings that are rendered in the same artistic style and adopt much of the same subject matter as *Little Nemo in Slumberland*. In both images, Spiegelman is a child mouse who has fallen out of bed after having a nightmare. "Then John Ashcroft pulled off his burka and shoved me out the window," he tells his gas mask–wearing mother while sitting on the floor in the drawing that appears on page six.

Taken collectively, these elements reveal that, in addition to being a meditation on the adult cartoonist's efforts to cope with the traumatic events of 9/11, *No Towers* is also a meditation on the cultural construction of children and the political uses of childhood in the United States. Given that the text is printed on paper stock that is most commonly used for children's board books, its materiality points to one of its recurring concerns: the ways in which young people have served paradoxically but consistently as victims, pawns, and rallying points in times of national crisis. Children are exploited in political propaganda—usually as the "innocents" needing protection from whatever threat is being faced—but they can also be summoned as soldiers in geopolitical conflicts. A panel that appears on page seven of *No Towers* makes this connection explicit. The image reveals the centrality that children play in seemingly "adult" issues like partisan politics, foreign policy, and especially war. Near the middle of the page (but on the left side of the panel), Spiegelman presents a diminutive-sized figure who could easily be read as a meek young boy holding a protest sign that states, "IF YOU AREN'T OUTRAGED, YOU AREN'T PAYING ATTENTION!" (7) (fig. 5). Behind him, symbolic blue doves and red hawks tussle with each other as the Grim Reaper looks on. The presence of this child in the foreground of the composition reminds readers that, when a nation goes to war, it sends its young people. The elementary-aged boy is a stand-in for war participants who are old enough for conscription into the military, but still young enough to be considered youths. Middle-aged men like the cartoonist are not the ones who populate the nation's army nor are they the ones subjected to conscription; instead, these roles and responsibilities are shouldered by individuals who are not much older than Nadja and her high school classmates. In the same way that children existed on the front lines of the physical devastation from 9/11—attending schools contaminated by toxic dust—arguably they have the greatest stake in their nation's sociopolitical response to the attacks. It is members of the younger generation who will be asked to fight and even to die in the wars in Afghanistan and Iraq that were started in the wake of 9/11. Lower on this same page of *No Towers*, Spiegelman reveals that he has a second child, a boy. "My 11-year-old son woke up dreaming he was in Baghdad and bombs were falling on him," the cartoonist writes (7). The sequence ends with an upside-down panel inset that

Figure 5. On the far left, the protest sign reading "IF YOU AREN'T OUTRAGED, YOU AREN'T PAYING ATTENTION!" appears to be held by a young boy. Detail from Art Spiegelman's *In the Shadow of No Towers*.

is drawn in the style of *Little Nemo* and that presents a young boy, presumably Spiegelman's son, in *Maus*-face. Echoing the finale to many *Little Nemo* comics, the boy mouse has fallen out of bed, likely after having a nightmare. As he sits on the floor crying, an adult-sized creature wearing a military-style hat gruffly tells him in language that is highly reminiscent of American war operations in Afghanistan and Iraq: "You *disembedded* again, young man—now hush before Mama *liberates* you!" These panels take the previous abstract inference about how it is children who ultimately fight the wars that adults declare and make it far more concrete and, of course, more personal.

Viewing the board-book format of *No Towers* as an essential rather than as an extraneous facet adds a new critical perspective to the narrative. Engaging with Spiegelman's text from the standpoint of its materiality invites readers to examine it through the alternative lens of childhood studies. Anna Mae Duane, in the introduction to her landmark volume *The Children's Table: Childhood Studies and the Humanities*, argues that "to include the child in any field of study is to realign the very structure of that field, changing the terms of inquiry and forcing a different set of questions" (1). This observation certainly holds true for *No Towers*. Heeding the cue provided by its material presentation as a board book moves children and childhood from the margins to the center of Spiegelman's text. This new perspective reveals that, together with offering a sharp critique about the politicization of 9/11, the text contains an illuminating analysis about the politicization of young people.

Comics critics and creators have sought to differentiate adult-audience comix from their counterparts intended for young people over the past few decades. Reading *No Towers* from the perspective of materiality highlights the benefits of keeping these two forms linked. At the same time, Spiegelman's narrative offers a vivid demonstration of the cultural evolution and artistic uses of the board book in the twenty-first century. This literary format, which has long been associated with the presentation of rudimentary subjects for children, offers a rich and compelling platform for the examination of complex issues for adults. *No Towers* harnesses form and content, or physical materiality and narrative material, to present a compelling commentary on the past function as well as current uses of childhood both inside and outside of graphic-based texts.

Getting Physical: The Weight of Reading

Quite appropriately, the lessons offered by *In the Shadow of No Towers* can be seen as ending where they began: with materiality. The experience of reading Spiegelman's book sheds light on a different facet of the aesthetic innovations and cultural insights embodied by children's literature for adults. The text encourages its adult audience to pay attention to the physicality of texts in ways that they are unaccustomed. When it comes to narratives for young people, material format is routinely a central consideration. After all, the audience for a picture book, prose novel, and board book differs greatly. Thus, when parents, teachers, and librarians—along with children themselves—choose a book, they pay close attention to its physicality: how thick is the book, how sturdy is it, how many pages does it have, how comfortably could the child hold and handle it, etc. In light of these and other concerns, materiality is a key facet in the realm of books for children.

This issue, however, does not possess the same importance in books for adults. The physicality of texts intended for grown-ups is routinely given only minimal consideration, when it is considered at all. Beyond perhaps paying attention to whether a narrative takes the form of a hardback or paperback, few adults give much thought to a text's materiality. Details such as the book's physical dimensions, the way that it has been assembled, or the paper stock that it uses are generally overlooked or even wholly ignored.

In the Shadow of No Towers moves the issue of physicality from the background to forefront of consideration once again. The narrative reminds its audience that the ostensibly visual practice of reading has an inexorable tactile component. We do not simply look at the words and images on a page, we also touch the paper, handle the covers, and hold the binding in which these elements appear. Spiegelman's text documents the ongoing symbolic, psychological, and political presence of two buildings that are now physically absent. In so doing, it likewise calls attention another influential presence: the physicality of books. By bringing a common literary format for children into the realm of narratives for adults, *In the Shadow of No Towers* reminds us of the literal weight of reading. The matter of materiality in Spiegelman's text reveals how materiality matters.

The chapter that follows on Barbara Park's *MA! There's Nothing to Do Here!* revisits one of the most popular formats in children's literature: the picture book. In many ways, in fact, narratives of this nature are arguably the most emblematic or representative of the genre. When individuals think about works of children's literature, picture books routinely come to mind. From author-illustrators like Dr. Seuss to titles like *Where the Wild Things Are*, picture books are synonymous with narratives for young readers. As an article that appeared in the publication *Papers* asserted, "The picture book has, since its creation, been considered the prerogative of the young child. It will take much persuasion to destroy this image" ("Comments" 2). Given the large role that books of this nature occupy in children's literature, it seems only fitting for them to play a significant role in children's literature for adults. But Park's *MA! There's Nothing to Do Here!* does more than simply embody another example of how this literary format can be effectively used to tell stories for adults. On the contrary, the 2008 text expands on the adult-audience uses of this narrative platform by harnessing a far different textual element than Dr. Seuss in *You're Only Old Once!* more than twenty years earlier: that of narrative voice. Bearing the subtitle *A Word from Your Baby-To-Be*, Park's picture book is written from the perspective of an unborn fetus. While the possession of a narrator-protagonist who is a baby-in-utero might seem to align *MA! There's Nothing to Do Here!* with a work of children's literature, the book is addressing an audience of expecting parents in general and mothers specifically. Park's picture book extends our examination of the construction of

children's literature for adults by calling attention to a new facet of the leaping, looping, and lurching relationship that emerged between childhood and
adulthood at the dawn of the twenty-first century. *MA! There's Nothing to Do
Here!* demonstrates not merely the way in which adulthood is encroaching on
facets formerly reserved to childhood, such as picture books. With its possession of a narrator-protagonist who is critical of his mother's parenting skills
before he has even left the womb, Park's text also reveals the tremendous power
that even unborn children have come to assume over adults in the twenty-first
century.

CHAPTER 4

Baby Talk

Barbara Park's *MA! There's Nothing to Do Here!*, Fetal Personhood, and Child Authorship

In the apt words of Lizzie Skurnick: "Women have always written about motherhood" (par. 6). From getting pregnant and giving birth to being a parent and adjusting to an empty nest, having children—or opting not to do so—has been a longstanding topic in narratives by women.

In 2008, Barbara Park released a picture book that continued this tradition: *MA! There's Nothing to Do Here!* The author was far from a novice who knew little about parenting or children. On the contrary, Park was not only the mother of two grown sons, she was also a successful writer for young people. Her Junie B. Jones series, which originated in 1992 and continued until her death in 2013, was critically acclaimed as well as commercially successful. The books quickly became "the darling of the young-reader set" ("About the Series," par. 2) and earned Park fame and considerable fortune. Over her career, the author "won multiple children's choice awards and [was] featured on the *Today Show* and in the *New York Times*, *USA Today*, and *Time* magazine" ("About the Series," par. 2).

The new picture book that Park released in 2008, however, was not another children's narrative. Amy Lilien-Harper, in a review of *MA! There's Nothing to Do Here!* that appeared in the *School Library Journal*, commented on this issue: "This humorous story may work while discussing where babies come from with preschoolers or for pregnant moms to read to older siblings. However, its best audience seems to be the expectant mothers themselves, and it is likely to appeal more as a shower gift than as a children's book" (174). Readers agreed. Although *MA! There's Nothing to Do Here!* is sometimes shelved in the children's section with the other picture books, its primary appeal has been, in the words of one reviewer, as a "Clever Gift for Expectant Moms!" (Warren). In sentiments that are echoed by many others on Amazon, one customer touted: "I gave this book to a few friends who are first time pregnant moms and they LOVED it!" (Blakely, par. 1).

The reputation of *MA! There's Nothing to Do Here!* as an excellent gift for baby showers notwithstanding, the narrative does not present a woman's experiences with the reproductive process. Instead, it showcases those of her unborn baby. Expectant mothers often find it difficult to wait the long nine months for the arrival of their infant and, in Park's book, the baby is equally eager to enter the world. Although the period of gestation is seemingly filled with spectacular amounts of growth, change, and development, the narrator-protagonist finds it dull and uneventful. The title of Park's book—*"MA! There's Nothing To Do Here!"*—serves as both the narrator-protagonist's unwavering viewpoint and his refrain. Although the youngster is never officially identified as male or female, his interests, his appearance, and all of the toys that he desires are stereotypically associated with boys.

The basic premise for Park's text is not an anomaly. Rather, *MA!* is part of a small but growing subgenre of books written in the voice of a Caucasian male fetus and intended for a readership of expectant parents in general and mothers in particular.[1] Fueled in part by advances in sonogram technology that permit parents-to-be unprecedented ability to see—and, thus, bond with—their unborn babies, these narratives feature both sedate and silly tones. Some titles, such as Kathleen Blease's picture book *I Can't Wait to Meet My Daddy* (1996), are directed at fathers-to-be. The introduction to Blease's text provides an apt overview of its tone and content. "You're about to become a father. A daddy," it reads. "The word *innocent* finally has meaning . . . Those sweet eyes will be looking to you for what the world is, or what it's supposed to be" (Blease 1; italics in original). In both the lines of written text and in the artistic style of the illustrations that accompany them, the pages that follow offer an equally inspirational and emotional take on becoming a father. "I can't wait to meet my Daddy," a representative passage near the end of the book begins. "He'll love to hold me and comfort me and even sing to me (no matter how off key he may be), and he'll show me how to be brave and kind, and how to build all of the things I need inside of me" (Blease 23). The illustrations by Bruce Fackenthal amplify such sentiments. Utilizing pastel colors and often appearing in soft focus, they add to the dreaminess, gentleness, and emotionalism of this landmark life event.

Other examples of fetus fiction, such as Regina Doman's picture book *Angel in the Waters* (2004) and David Javerbaum's parody *What to Expect When You're Expected: A Fetus's Guide to the First Three Trimesters* (2009), differ from *I Can't Wait to Meet My Daddy*.[2] Rather than being directed at fathers-to-be, they are geared for a general readership of parents. That said, each book offers an alternative approach, perspective, or treatment of this issue. As the title of Regina Doman's narrative implies, *Angel in the Waters* is spiritual in nature. Although it does not reference any specific religion, it is predicated on the belief that life is created and even controlled by a higher power. The opening passage, for example, documents the time before the fetus had even been conceived—affirming that it existed in the cosmos nonetheless. "In the beginning, I was. I was for a long time," it reads.[3] Then, the rest of the text documents the angel who shares the womb with the developing fetus, helping it, guiding it, and loving it as it grows. "'Who are you?' / I asked my angel. / 'You will know,' said / my angel. 'Eat now'." The angel parts ways with the gestating fetus soon after it is born. However, in the same way the book affirms that the baby's spirit existed before birth, it also affirms that the two will be reunited in the afterlife. "[T]here is another, / bigger world outside this one / Someday I will take you there," the angel tells the newborn baby just before departing. "'When?' I asked my angel. 'When it is time,' said my angel."

By contrast, David Javerbaum's *What to Expect When You're Expected: A Fetus's Guide to the First Three Trimesters*, takes a completely different tack from its predecessors. Whereas the previous two titles offered a serious examination of the emotional, psychological, and spiritual dimensions of parenthood, Javerbaum's parody is lighthearted, comedic, and at times even irreverent. The cover touts the text as "The first-ever guide to pregnancy for the prenatal reader—written by a former embryo!" Along those same lines, the foreword to the book is authored by none other than "The Stork." The chapters that follow offer an equally humorous take on the situation, with titles like "Month 2: Making Mitosis *Your*tosis" and sub-topics such as "Sonograms and Daughterograms" (Javerbaum 51, xiii). In spite of *What to Expect When You're Expected*'s claim to being "A Fetus's Guide to the First Three Trimesters," the book is clearly directed at adults. Indeed, with sub-sections like "It was 'Mom-Dad'; Now it's 'MomYouDad': Guess Who Got Between Them?" and "TITS TITS TITS TITS TITS!," the parody text is adult in more ways than one.[4]

Regardless of the specific tone, content, or audience, works of fetus fiction have increased in both number and importance since the late 1990s. World-Cat, a global catalog of library holdings, created the subject heading "Fetus—Fiction" in 2008 to classify this growing body of literature.[5] This body of narratives written from the perspective of the unborn does more than simply constitute a new narrative category; it also engages with current highly politicized questions about the rights of the unborn and the debate over personhood. Texts like *I Can't Wait to Meet Daddy*, *Angel in the Waters*, and, of course, *MA! There's Nothing to Do Here!* make powerful, if tacit, arguments for life beginning before birth. By personifying the unborn, they make a case for their personhood.

Barbara Park's picture book for adults embodies a particularly rich and interesting example of this phenomenon. *MA!* does more than simply participate in a burgeoning new sub-genre of "fetus fiction"; the text pushes it in a new direction. Park's unborn narrator-protagonist exemplifies the millennium-era shift toward what Lauren Berlant has termed "fetal citizenship." As she explains, the roles, rights, and responsibilities previously associated with adults are now being extended to the young. Whereas grown-ups were formerly regarded as the centerpiece and even the raison d'être of the nation, this position is now being occupied not simply by children but—as *MA!* demonstrates—the unborn.

For centuries, children's literature has commonly been written by adults. In a feature that would be unthinkable in any other genre, very few books intended for young people are actually created by them. Instead, it is adults who write children's books, illustrate them, edit them, publish them, and also routinely select and purchase them. Barbara Park's *MA! There's Nothing to Do Here!* offers a twist on this situation. Whereas children's literature for children is commonly written by adults, her work of children's literature for adults is purportedly "written" by not simply a child, but a fetus in utero. Together with upending a longstanding literary trend, this reversal adds a new element to the social significance and cultural impact of Park's text. While her picture book for adults might be seen as yet another example the encroachment of grown-ups into the world of kids, the point of view that the text privileges points to the opposite phenomenon: it signals the growing power that the unborn have come to possess over adults in the United States. Together with serving as the narrative voice for their literature, children—including those who are still in utero—are also dictating the material, emotional, and psychological expectations for motherhood in the new millennium.

"I Love You, Your Baby": The Debate about Personhood and the Battle over the Rights of the Unborn

Since the *Roe v. Wade* decision in 1973 that legalized abortion in the United States, the pro-life movement has been working to overturn it. The National Right to Life Committee (NRLC) was founded the following year and, in the decades since, it has spearheaded efforts to eliminate or, at least, restrict women's access to abortion. Eric Eckholm has outlined some of the approaches that the NRLC and its affiliates have utilized in the service of such efforts: "sharply restricting the procedures at as early as 20 weeks, requiring women to view ultrasounds of the fetus, curbing insurance coverage and imposing expensive regulations on clinics" (par. 10).

After more than thirty years of lobbying efforts that saw only small, incremental results, the anti-abortion shifted to a different strategy: what came to be known as the "personhood" movement. As Daniel Becker explains, this concept is "the recognition by our culture and our government that each individual human life has an 'unalienable' right to life from its earliest biological origins" (23–24). Under current US law, an individual does not become a person until after they have fully exited the birth canal. More specifically, this moment is defined as

> the complete expulsion or extraction from his or her mother of that member, at any stage of development, who after such expulsion or extraction breathes or has a beating heart, pulsation of the umbilical cord, or definite movement of voluntary muscles, regardless of whether the umbilical cord has been cut, and regardless of whether the expulsion or extraction occurs as a result of natural or induced labor, cesarean section, or induced abortion. (1 USC 8, 2002)

Advocates for personhood seek to change this condition; they argue that life begins at the moment of conception, when the sperm fertilizes the egg (Calhoun, par. 16). In their viewpoint, the distinctions between zygotes, blastulas, embryos and infants are purely semantic. All of them constitute forms of human life and thus all ought to possess the same rights, privileges, and protections afforded to any other developmental stage. Ben DuPré, the director of the organization Personhood Alabama, perhaps best explained this viewpoint when he asked: "What it boils down to is, aren't these little children persons?" (qtd in Calhoun, par. 15).

For this reason, the personhood movement argues that the fight to protect the unborn is akin to other civil rights efforts that seek to aid a vulnerable, voiceless minority. The fact that an embryo or fetus could not survive on its own outside the womb is immaterial. Akin to other demographic groups who require medical assistance—such as the seriously ill, the severely disabled, or the aged—a fetus's state of physical dependency does not negate the fact that it is a human life (Becker 33).

The concept of personhood has altered while it has re-energized anti-abortion efforts in the United States. During the opening decades of the twenty-first century, various other federal regulations, medical research provisions, and criminal statutes have been passed that reflect the growing sense of fetal rights. As Sara Dubow has documented:

> In October 2002, the United States Department of Health and Human Services added human embryos to the list of 'human subjects' whose welfare must be taken into account by the Advisory Committee on Human Research Protections. The next month, in revising the State Child Health Insurance Program (S-CHIP), HHS redefined *child* to begin at the moment of conception, making fetuses eligible for state-sponsored health insurance. In April 2004, Congress signed into law the Unborn Victims of Violence Act, making the death of a pregnant woman and her zygote, embryo or fetus in the execution of a federal crime punishable as two separate criminal violations. (1)

These federal statutes are in addition to the 38 US states that already possess fetal homicide laws (National Conference of State Legislatures, par. 4). In several instances, these laws have been used to prosecute expectant women or new mothers for actions while they were pregnant.

Growing beliefs in the personhood of an unborn fetus are not limited to the pro-life movement; such sentiments can also be traced in American popular culture. According to Sara Dubow, "Stores like 'A Peek in the Pod' are opening, where for $295 expectant parents can buy a 'keepsake package of prenatal memories,' that includes a thirty-minute ultrasound session recorded on DVD, a computer screensaver, and photo frames" (3). Such examples point to the growing presence of what may be called the "fetal child" in the United States. Whereas these two words were formerly mutually exclusive—a fetus was not a child and a child was, by definition, no longer a fetus—this distinction has eroded. Exemplifying this change, Dubow has documented that, during the twenty-first century, an increasing "shift in language from 'unborn' to 'preborn,' a shift that suggests a natural continuum from preborn to born, as opposed to a discrete moment in time in which one changes from being unborn to born" (185).

MA! There's Nothing to Do Here! can be read in dialogue with growing twenty-first century interest in personhood. The narrative not only spotlights an unborn baby, but it endows the fetus with a unique personality, distinct voice, and definite opinions. On the opening pages of *MA! There's Nothing to Do Here!*, for example, the baby-to-be complains about life in utero: "Dear Ma, What's a baby to do in a womb with no view?" More than simply unhappy that he cannot see anything in the outside world, Park's narrator-protagonist is unhappy with the whole process of waiting to be born: it's too cramped inside the womb, it's too Spartan, and it's too lonely. In sum, it's simply dull and boring. On the third page of the book, for example, he grouses that there are "No puppies. No toys" with which he can play. Additionally, there's no one else to keep him company. "No girls . . . zero boys," he grumps. The remainder of Park's narrative is comprised of various complaints along these lines. "I've tried hide-and-seek and I don't even peek," he reports near the middle of the book, "But I'm so intertwined, I'm too easy to find." This disappointment is quickly followed by another lament: "Plus tag is no fun—I've got no place to run." In these and many other passages, Park presents the baby-to-be as a sentient creature who experiences the same depth and breadth of emotion as those outside the womb. Throughout the text, he reveals that he has hopes, dreams, and fears as well as worries, wishes, and even discomforts. This type of psychologizing reinforces arguments that life begins before birth.

Park's word choices and the illustrations by Viviana Garofoli accentuate these elements. In both the book's subtitle and in numerous passages throughout the text, the author calls her central character a "baby-in-waiting" or "baby-to-be" rather than by the less endearing but biologically accurate term "fetus." Moreover, at some points, she drops such qualifiers altogether and makes no distinction between her unborn protagonist and an actual infant. As mentioned before, the opening line of the book reads: "What's a *baby* to do in a womb with no view?" (my emphasis). The cute, colorful drawings reinforce this viewpoint. All of the illustrations greatly downplay the actual conditions inside the uterus. The baby-to-be is shown encased in a bubble of what appears to be clear, blue water; there is no blood, no discernible amniotic fluid, and a greatly reduced presence of the umbilical cord (fig. 6). In fact, in most drawings, the cord is thin, white, and nearly transparent, far different from the thick rope-like and blood-veined organ in reality. Moreover, in the image that accompanies the baby-to-be's comments about looking forward to the day he is born—"Then ready . . . set . . . YAY! I'll be comin' to play!"—the umbilical cord is entirely absent. (fig. 7). Finally, but not incidentally, Garofoli's portrayal of the youngster from the first page of the picture book presents him as far more physically developed than a newborn infant let alone a third trimester fetus. With his eyes fully open and sharply focused, his head nearly perfectly round, and his face tremendously expressive, Park's protagonist more closely resembles an infant who has already aged several months than a fetus who is still developing in utero. These changes make the youngster cuter and, more importantly, they also help readers to forget that he is a still-gestating fetus instead of an autonomous, fully formed infant. Indeed, when viewed collectively, these elements blur the boundary between the born and unborn.

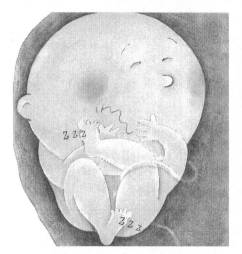 

Figure 6. (*left*) The rendering of the gestating fetus is not a realistic depiction of conditions inside the uterus. Illustration from Barbara Park's *MA! There's Nothing to Do Here! Figure 7.* (*right*) This metaphorical depiction of the baby being born completely omits the umbilical cord. Illustration from Barbara Park's *MA! There's Nothing to Do Here!*

"We, the (Unborn) People": From Fetal Personhood to Nationhood

The boundary between a gestating fetus and a newborn infant is not the only one that fetal personhood challenges. This phenomenon also calls into question the nation's age-based conception of full citizenship. As Lauren Berlant has written, from the founding of the United States, "national democracy was based on principles of abstract personhood (all persons shall be formally equivalent)" (18). However, the initial constitutional construction of a person was extremely limited: it was restricted to white male property owners. Of course, other groups, such as white women and white males who did not own property, were considered "Americans" from the standpoint of their national identity. Accordingly, they were seen as sociopolitical subjects of the United States and were counted in the national census. However, these individuals lacked a key element that defines modern notions of full citizenship: voting rights.

Over the centuries, the legal definition of full citizenship would be revised to include additional groups, such as African Americans with the passage of Fourteenth Amendment in 1868 and women with the ratification of the Nineteenth Amendment in 1920. But whenever the rights and privileges of US citizenship were expanded, it was always to a new demographic of adults. Although the specific constitutional configuration of "We the people" has shifted greatly since 1776, it has always tacitly remained "We the people who are grown men and women."

The rise of the pro-life movement during the closing decades of the twentieth century challenged this understanding. With their insistence that life begins at inception, anti-abortion advocates made a case for the "personhood" of fetuses. While this concept differs from both nationality and citizenship, it forms an important prerequisite to both conditions. As the preamble to the Constitution indicates, you cannot be considered part of "We the people" if you are not first considered a person.

For this reason, making a case that the unborn are persons has been a key strategy in efforts to overturn *Roe v. Wade* because doing so means that they can viewed as part of the nation's citizenry. The pro-life movement has framed fetuses as a group of exceedingly vulnerable Americans whose basic right to life, liberty, and the pursuit of happiness was being violated (Berlant 6, 22). This viewpoint created a zero-sum game between the woman's right to an abortion and what they saw as the fetus's right to life. The pro-life movement asserted that "the fetus, framed as a helpless, choiceless victim, will always lose—at least without the installation of surrogate legal and technological systems" (Berlant 98). The unborn were not simply persons, they were a demographic at risk. For this reason, anti-abortion advocates drew heavily on the language of previous movements for minority rights, arguing "that the fetus is a contingent being, dependent on the capacity of Americans to hear *as citizens* its cries *as a citizen* for dignity of the body, its complaints at national injustice" (Berlant 98; italics in original).

In this way, while babies have long been associated with national futurity, a new conception of what Berlant termed "fetal citizenship" emerged (6, 22). As the pro-life movement asserted, no other demographic of the populace is more blameless for their current imperiled state, more helpless without outside assistance, and thus more deserving of special legal provisions than the unborn. In the words of Berlant: "What constitutes their national supericonicity is an image of an American, perhaps the last living American, not yet bruised by history" (6). A fetus is "not yet caught in the confusing and exciting identity exchanges made possible by mass consumption and ethnic, racial, and sexual mixing; not yet tainted by money or war" (Berlant 6). As a result, an unborn baby is all personal potential and social possibility. It becomes a repository for national hopes, dreams, and aspirations. Because the fetus is not yet able to do anything, there is, ironically, nothing that it cannot do. The fetus may not yet have any personal strengths, but that also means that it has no known weaknesses. Likewise, its particular abilities have not been identified, but that means that neither have any of its limitations. Finally, the fetus may not yet be in possession of any special gifts or exceptional aptitudes, but that also means it is equally devoid of any possible shortcomings. In this way, "the image of fetal personhood [became] the icon of ideal citizenship" (Berlant 22).

Fetal citizenship upended the dynamics of age that had been the basis for civic enfranchisement in the United States for centuries. As Berlant has said, "it changed fundamentally the relative meanings and rules of federal and state citizenship, and it called into crisis the norms and principles of national embodiment" (98). Personhood, from either a Constitutional or an ontological standpoint, had long been predicated on being born. However, now—in an event that was unprecedented in the history of the United States—this status was being extended to a gestating fetus. The movement for fetal personhood had an immediate impact on national civic life. Starting in the closing decades of the twentieth century and accelerating rapidly in the new millennium, "a nation made for adult citizens [was steadily being] replaced by one imagined for fetuses and children" (Berlant 1). The unborn went from simply representing the theoretical future of the nation to being regarded as one of the most important constituencies within the populace. Whereas the primary focus of government life had been on protecting, improving, and ensuring the welfare of the nation's adults, now significant effort, attention, and energy was being expended on the unborn. As Berlant aptly observed about this shift, "the nation's value is figured not on behalf of an actually existing and laboring adult, but of a future American, both incipient and pre-historical" (6).

MA! There's Nothing to Do Here! can be seen as both a byproduct of this phenomenon and a further catalyst for it. Park's "baby-to-be" offers a powerful demonstration of how "The success of the concept of fetal personhood depends on establishing a mode of 'representation' that merges the word's political and aesthetic senses, imputing a voice, a consciousness, and a self-identity to the fetus that can neither speak its name nor vote" (Berlant 98). The picture book bestows thoughts, feelings, and personality traits to its unborn narrator-protagonist in a manner that goes far beyond merely humanizing him; it affirms his personhood. In a detail that exemplifies some of the profound sociopolitical implications of fetal citizenship, the personhood of the baby-to-be in *MA! There's Nothing to Do Here!* comes at the expense of the personhood of his mother. Not only is she entirely silent throughout the text—failing to utter even a solitary word—but her face is also never depicted. On the contrary, she is shown only from the shoulders down.[6] While this decision not to feature the mother's face in any of the illustrations might be explained in purely pragmatic terms as a means to ensure that all expectant mothers can imagine themselves as her, it also has more negative and even nefarious implications. After all, not depicting the mother's head and especially face erases the part of her body that is forms a key facet to her identity, her individuality, and even her humanity. It suggests that she is valuable not as a thinking, feeling, and talking being but as a biological vessel for her gestating baby.

However, the civic inversions precipitated by fetal citizenship do more than simply cause expectant mothers to become secondary to their unborn child. As Berlant has noted, they can also cause the roles between these two individuals to reverse: "the pregnant woman becomes the child to the fetus, which is in turn made more national, more central to securing the privileges of law, paternity, and other less institutionalized family strategies of contemporary American culture" (85). These messages likewise permeate *MA! There's Nothing to Do Here!* The baby-to-be's litany of requested toys, attractions, and amusements suggests that he is dictating the terms not simply of his current gestation, but of his future childhood. Rather than allowing mothers to recognize, identify, and fulfill his needs, he is enumerating them to her, a process that suggests if not her incompetence then certainly his lack of faith in her abilities. Finally, and arguably most importantly, the narrative's storyline also sends a strong message about national priorities during the opening decade of the twenty-first century when the text was published. Park's book makes a case that what is paramount is not the health, safety, or happiness of the expectant mother; but that of her unborn child. Rather than the personal being political in *MA! There's Nothing to Do Here!*, the opposite is true: the political importance of the baby-to-be has a profound personal impact on the expectant mother. Being pregnant causes her to lose her claim to a personal life, personal privacy, and even basic personhood.

When Park's text is viewed in this context, her choice of literary genre assumes a new, and alternative, significance. Although *MA! There's Nothing to Do Here!* is a picture book for adults, the text does not signal the encroachment of grown-ups into the world of kids. On the contrary, the physical format of the book notwithstanding, it demonstrates the opposite phenomenon: the supremacy that the unborn have come to possess over adults in the United States.

"You're Set for Me, Right? You've Got a Night Light?": The Materialism of the New Maternalism

Barbara Park's picture book for adults has implications that encompass more than broad sociopolitical issues like the personhood movement or new linguistic concepts like fetal citizenship. It also engages with the daily lives of individual women. Previous narratives written from the perspective of the unborn had the same basic goal: to ease the minds of expectant parents through humor, information, or appeals to tender emotion. Blease's beautifully illustrated picture book, *I Can't Wait to Meet My Daddy*, for example, addresses the deep love that expectant fathers already feel for their unborn child. Writing in the voice of an unborn male baby, her narrator-protagonist speaks directly to the excited but nervous dad: "We have so many things to see and do. Maybe we can swim in a lake and feed the ducks and smile at each other, then smile at the man . . . in the moon!" By contrast, *What to Expect When You're Expected* opts for a more comedic approach, but the end result is the same. Using satiric humor, the book calms the nerves of mothers- and fathers-to-be by pointing out some of the silly and even absurdist aspects of pregnancy and new parenthood. Organized as a series of "FAQs" from fetuses, chapters provide answers to queries such as the following: "So far Mommy is spending most of her pregnancy in a state of stress, anxiety, and depression. Which one should she focus on?"

MA! There's Nothing to Do Here! both builds on and breaks from this trend. While the narrative does reassure its audience of expected mothers about the powerful love that they will feel for their child, it also catalogs the complaints of their bored, frustrated, and even annoyed baby-to-be. Indeed, far from a sentimental approach, the book has a whiney quality. Park's narrator-protagonist speaks with a nagging tone, relaying long lists of items that he needs, wants, or wishes he had.

By focusing exclusively on an unborn baby's desires, *MA!* adds—however unintentionally or inadvertently—to the tremendous social pressures placed on parents in general and new mothers in particular in the twenty-first century. Pregnant women have long been seen as responsible for ensuring the physical, intellectual, and cognitive development of their baby. To aid in this process, in fact, women are commonly urged to abide by various exhortations, from eating a nutritious diet and getting sufficient rest to taking prenatal vitamins and avoiding drinking and smoking. *MA! There's Nothing to Do Here!* adds another, equal-parts absurdist and alarming, item to this ever-growing list of responsibilities for pregnant mothers: ensuring that their fetus is properly amused or sufficiently entertained.

While mothers have always been expected to be selfless and even self-sacrificing when it comes to their children, these traits assumed a new intensity during the late 1980s and extending through the opening decades of the twenty-first century. After generations of women fought for increased freedom from domestic drudgery through more equitable divisions of household labor and the ability to work outside the home, a shift occurred. In the wake of events such as the ascendency of a more conservative political climate during the Reagan and Bush administrations, the hysteria over various well-publicized (albeit mostly unfounded) cases of child abuse by babysitters and day care centers, and the growing national awareness about the long-term harm that results from being raised in a dysfunctional family,[7] "Working mothers were no longer heroines, symbols of the new and healthy freedoms won by Mother's Lib. They were villains, selfish and 'unnatural'" (Warner 91). Unlike a belief commonly espoused by the previous generation of mothers, this new one did not believe that it was possible "to have it all." A woman who was juggling both a career and family, they concluded from watching many of their own mothers do so while they were young, was stretched too thin and everything suffered: her work, her children, her marriage, and her own well-being. In their minds, if a woman wanted to do a task well—like raising a child—she needed to make it the focus of her attention. Thus, as Judith Warner has written, in both the popular media and in the minds of many women during the late 1980s and early 1990s, "if a woman 'chose' to work, she was doing so at the 'expense' of her child" (117–18).

As a consequence of this shift in cultural attitude, another shift occurred. After decades of women fighting for their right to work outside the home, many of "[Betty] Friedan's daughters—and grand-daughters—[began] opting out of careers in favour of motherhood" (Stonehouse D8). Moreover, this new generation of mothers was not simply returning to domestic life, they were immersing themselves in it. Although calling themselves "post-feminist," they used rhetoric that was more indicative of the pre-feminist era, arguing that mothers "belonged" at home with their kids and that raising children was their "life's work" (Miller, par. 5). By the mid-1990s, such sentiments had become so culturally pervasive that they gave rise to new American social identity: the "soccer mom." A seeming throwback to gender roles from the 1950s, these women "had pretty much renounced all interests or ambition outside the family" (Warner 115). As Republican pollster Kellyanne Fitzpatrick (now

Kellyanne Conway) quipped to the *New York Times*: "If you are a soccer mom, the world according to you [sic] is seen through the needs of your children" (qtd in Warner 115).

In the same way that conceptions of motherhood were shifting during the 1990s, so, too, were ideas about effective and even "appropriate" forms of child-rearing. A generation earlier, women had espoused a philosophy of "good enough" parenting and happily embraced new modern conveniences like frozen dinners, disposable diapers, and bottled formula that made parenting easier, especially for those who worked outside the home. This new generation of mothers, however, rejected anything perceived as labor-saving. To them, parental short cuts shortchanged children. Thus, instead of structuring motherhood in a way that helped them, they constructed it in a manner that they believed most helped their child's development. A slew of parenting books appeared urging women to raise their offspring in what quickly become known as a "child-centric" way. From Penelope Leach's *Children First* (1994), T. Berry Brazelton's *What Every Baby Knows* (1987), and especially William and Martha Sears's *The Baby Book* (1993), these texts outlined a form of childcare that was more labor-intensive but also, they asserted, more beneficial to children. For example, William and Martha Sears stressed immersing children in an environment of safety, comfort, and love. Instead of placing an infant in a lonely crib or prison-like playpen, they advocated for baby-wearing in slings and co-sleeping in a family bed. Likewise, rather than using bottles filled with formula, they made a case for the nutritional as well as psycho-emotional benefits of breastfeeding for at least the first year. Finally, and perhaps most importantly, instead of allowing a fussing infant to "cry it out" as Dr. Richard Ferber had famously advised a previous generation of parents, *The Baby Book* argued that "every baby's whimper is a plea for help and that no infant should ever be left to cry" (Pickert, par. 7). The Sears's called this approach "attachment parenting," and its core principle was "that the more time babies spend in their mothers' arms, the better the chances they will turn out to be well-adjusted children" (Pickert, par. 9). Their tremendously popular *The Baby Book* became "the 'parenting bible of the '90s'" (Douglas and Michaels 318).

Such beliefs only increased in the opening decade of the twenty-first century. As Kate Pickert remarked in a recent article in *Time* magazine, "If you've had a baby in the 21st century, chances are good that . . . consciously or not, you've practiced some derivative of attachment parenting or been influenced by its message" (par. 6). Given that the child-centric principles of this approach being applied not simply to babies and toddlers but to youngsters of all ages, she goes on to assert "the prevalence of this philosophy has shifted mainstream American parenting toward a style that's more about parental devotion and sacrifice than about raising self-sufficient kids" (Pickert, par. 5). Judith Warner characterized this shift as even more deleterious to women: "The icon of the ideal motherhood at the dawn of the twenty-first century was a woman so bound up in her child, so tightly bonded and fused, that she herself—soul, mind, and body—all but disappeared" (68). As one mother described the experience: "We micromanage. We obsess. . . . Gluten free birthday cakes and organic apple juice. Leapfrog toys and bow-tying boards and black-and-white baby toys. No TV; only a half-hour of TV; only educational TV. No sugar. No trans fat. No Disney. No pizza" (Warner 191–92). Unlike previous eras where children were viewed as resilient and resourceful, they were now increasingly regarded as delicate and easily scarred (Schafer 6). One mistake, however seemingly trivial, could cause permanent psycho-social damage, resulting in self-esteem problems, abandonment issues, or attachment troubles that would lead to a lifetime of personal and professional hardship (Warner 48, 102).

While some of this pressure to be a perfect mother in the late 1990s and early 2000s was internally imposed—with women expecting increasingly more of themselves—the external price for failure was both real and high. Louette Harding, profiling author Judith Warner, explains: "one of the main reasons behind our obsessive mothering is economic fear: we have to work harder than our parents just to stand still. We can no longer take a middle-class lifestyle as a birthright" (FB4). Acutely aware that the world into which their children have been born is far more uncertain and competitive, the hope is that, "if we give them just the right combination of winner-producing things—the right swimming lessons and ballet lessons and learning-to-read books and building toys—we can inoculate them against failure" (Warner 162). The onset of the Great Recession in 2008, and the attendant negative consequences that it has had on the job market, funding for public education, and the existence of government assistance and entitlement programs, has only exacerbated the situation. As one mother explained, "We have to [be perfect], because we believe that if *we* aren't perfect, it's our kids who will pay the price for our mistakes" (qtd in Schafer 5; emphasis in original).

The problem inherent in this approach, of course, is that it creates an ever-escalating spiral of expectations. As one woman remarked in sentiments that were shared by countless other mothers: "there remains a nagging doubt. 'I worry I'm not giving my children a competitive advantage,' she admits. 'I'm not instilling a sense of the importance of doing better than other people'" (Harding 4). It becomes impossible to set limits, given the potential costs involved in neglecting to maximize even one small advantage. "So . . . it's off to soccer practice, Kumon Math, piano lessons (which they hate, but playing an instrument is vital), and don't forget to stop at the Montessori school to drop off the pre-registration for the baby (yes, he's only three months old now, but you *know* how long those waiting lists are for good schools)" (Schafer 5; emphasis in original). This increasing cycle of demands quickly spins out of control. As Susan J. Douglas and Meredith Michaels have commented only half-jokingly about the cultural messages with which they struggle, mothers who "really cared" about their children only "got her kids toys that were educational, that advanced gross and fine motor skills, that gave them the special sensibilities and design aptitude of Frank Lloyd Wright, and that taught Johnny how to read James Joyce at age three" (18).

Given the amount of time, energy, and especially money needed to meet these requirements, one might expect that this form of motherhood would be found only among the middle and especially upper-middle classes. However, "this constellation of beliefs is held in common by many American mothers today. These ideas are certainly not followed in practice by every mother, but they are, implicitly or explicitly, understood as the *proper* approach to the raising of a child by the majority of mothers" (Hays 9; italics in original). Indeed, as Douglas and Michaels have commented about this model of motherhood, "Once you identify it, you see [it] everywhere" (8): among women from varying races, regions, ethnicities, and socioeconomic backgrounds. Taken collectively, both the power of this new model of motherhood and its pervasiveness in millennium-era American society has "raised the bar to even more ridiculous levels than during the June Cleaver era" (Douglas and Michaels 9).

Barbara Park's *MA! There's Nothing to Do Here!* participates in and expands upon this new form of twenty-first century motherhood. The book reflects the ever-increasing list of duties placed on women with regard to childcare. Expectant mothers commonly face an array of parental responsibilities long before their baby is actually born. From securing various items like a diapers and clothing to ensuring the baby's proper development by eating well and getting sufficient rest, the work of motherhood far predates the newborn's arrival. *MA! There's Nothing to Do Here!* adds to these extant expectations for pregnant women. Echoing both the current climate of child-centeredness and the anxious nature of parenting in the twenty-first century, it is not the expectant mother in Park's picture book who is making the list of tasks to do and items to purchase, but her unborn child. Moreover, in keeping with twenty-first-century desires to give one's children every possible advantage, the baby-to-be frames these items not as wants but as needs to optimize his intellectual, physical, and psychological development.

While the new motherhood is strongly associated with nonmaterial entities—encouraging children's interests, cultivating their self-esteem, and making sure that they know how much they are loved—it also has a powerful consumer component. As Alyson Schafer has written, the ideal mother in the twenty-first century would not only "never need sleep, always be happy . . . [and] be able to co-exist in three places at once" but she would also "have $100k in disposable cash to spend on the kids" (6). From obtaining the seeming limitless number of educational toys that are available to enrolling them in the obligatory slate of athletic and extracurricular activities, raising children in the twenty-first century requires, as Susan J. Douglas and Meredith Michaels humorously note, "the monetary equivalent of the gross domestic product of Australia" (6). Often, failure to purchase even one of these items is cast as a crass lack of parental concern, both in the public mind and in the minds of many mothers and fathers: "Do you buy the $300 titanium [bicycle] helmet—or do you not quite love your child *that* much?" (Schafer 7; emphasis in original).

MA! There's Nothing to Do Here! reflects the intense consumerism that fuels millennium-era motherhood while pushing it to a new arena: namely, inside the womb. Many of the complaints lodged by the narrator-protagonist identify the cause of his boredom as a lack of specific material items: "Not a sandbox or swing . . . Or those monkey bar things. Not a park or a zoo. MA! There's *nothing* to do!" (italics in originals). Not only is the fetus far too young to actually play with any of these items, but his request for them exacerbates expectations that women devote themselves fully to nurturing, stimulating, and even entertaining their child.

Peter N. Stearns has written about changes in American attitudes regarding childhood boredom. Prior to the Second World War, a youngster who complained about not having anything to do was regarded as being both the source of this problem and the person responsible for solving it. A bored child was one who lacked imagination, initiative, or interests—and needed to deploy these qualities to alleviate the situation (Stearns 170–71). By the closing decades of the twentieth century, however, this belief had shifted so that juvenile ennui was increasingly framed as the fault of the parents. It became the responsibility of mothers and fathers to ensure that their youngster had a sufficient number of amusing toys and an adequate amount of stimulating activities

(Stearns 190–99). "So the child who whined and moaned, whether at home or at school, now became a commentary on parental inadequacy" (Stearns 197). As a consequence, "Car trips, a classic site for boredom, were embellished by the 1980s with specific products to keep kids entertained, including more elaborate games, portable CD players, and video systems" (Stearns 200).

MA! There's Nothing to Do Here! extends this phenomenon into the womb, suggesting that pregnant women are now expected to entertain their unborn baby. "If I just had a truck. Or a small rubber duck. Or a cat or a bug. Or a teddy named Doug," the narrator-protagonist laments (fig. 8). As Park's book progresses, his wish list becomes increasingly age-inappropriate: "I'm so tired of floating. I'd love to go boating. But where's the canoe? MA! There's *nothing* to do!" At the same time though, his tone grows more insistent and demanding: "No, wait! A balloon! But please . . . buy it soon." Advertisers of products aimed at children have long known about the "Nag Factor," or the purchasing power that children possess when they repeatedly pester their parents to buy them a certain item (Linn 32–34). As Elena Morales has reported, "the impact of children's nagging is assessed as up to 46 percent of sales in key business that target children" (35). *MA! There's to Do Here!* creates a new arena for nagging. Now, mothers can experience their child whining for a certain toy or game not simply in a store, but from the womb.

Figure 8. The newborn is presented with physical traits—such as fully opened eyes— that are more indicative of older babies. Illustration from Barbara Park's *MA! There's Nothing to Do Here!*

Not all of the baby-to-be's requests in Park's text involve leisure-time items; in a few passages, his wish list expands to include common baby care products. In a tone that is meant to relay adorable anxiety but instead suggests a lack of confidence in his mother's preparedness and even basic parenting competency, he inquires nervously about some basic necessities: "You're set for me, right? You've got a night light? And diapers? Shampoo?" In these instances, the narrator-protagonist's requests are no longer designed to stave off boredom, but to ensure his proper care. Many expectant mothers worry about their ability to be a good parent, and, in sentiments that exacerbate rather than assuage such fears, so does Park's unborn child.

In a telling indicator of the power dynamic that exists in parent and child relationships during the early twenty-first century, the pregnant woman featured in *MA! There's Nothing to Do Here!* seemingly heeds all of her fetus's requests. In the endpapers to the book, readers see a double-page illustration of the expectant mother sitting in a rocking chair in what appears to be the baby's nursery (fig. 9). She has her feet propped up on a short dresser and is lovingly holding a teddy bear whose baseball cap reads "Doug"—the exact bear that the baby-to-be had requested and was pictured earlier in the book. In *How Picturebooks Work*, Maria Nikolajeva and Carol Scott have written about how paratex-

Figure 9. Echoing the book's omission of the mother's face and thus her identity throughout the book, the mother's head is cropped out in this image. The toy that the baby-to-be requested, however, is featured prominently. Illustration from Barbara Park's *MA! There's Nothing to Do Here!*

tual material in picture books—the cover, front matter, endpapers, title page, copyright page—can serve important storytelling functions. These pages can contain words and especially images that are pertinent to the story (Nikolajeva and Scott 241). The authors go on to assert, "The narrative can indeed start on the cover, and it can go beyond the last page onto the back cover. Endpapers convey essential information" (Nikolajeva and Scott 241). This observation certainly holds true for *MA! There's Nothing to Do Here!* The scene depicted in the double-page illustration that forms the endpapers to the picture book is meant to indicate the woman's already profound love and equally eager excitement for the arrival of her child. However, it also affirms Sharon Hays's observation about the alarmingly high expectations in the late 1900s and early 2000s about a mother with regard to her child: "One must . . . anticipate his every desire" (64).

This closing image serves one final and critically important purpose in Park's text: it clarifies the tone and intent of the narrative. Some readers might be tempted to view *MA! There's Nothing to Do Here!* as an over-the-top and, thus, satiric take both on the increasing amount of consumerism associated with childhood and on the absurd expectations of motherhood. After all, the unborn narrator-protagonist asks for a ridiculous amount of toys, activities, and amusements—many of which he will be too young to enjoy even after he is born. In addition, the clever rhymes and sing-songy cadence of the written text could be regarded as further support for seeing the book as humorous rather than serious. However, the paratextual imagery that bookends the narrative in general and the illustration that appears in the endpapers to *MA! There's Nothing to Do Here!* in particular makes the book's literary aim and cultural objective clear. Both the fact that the mother is contentedly relaxing in the rocking chair and that she is lovingly cuddling Doug on the final double-page spread suggests that the text is intended to be viewed in a sentimental rather than satiric way. After all, a similar illustration also appears on the inside cover of the picture book, prefacing the narrative. It likewise shows the mother in the baby's nursery; she is clutching a teddy bear in her left arm while hanging a colorful mobile above the crib. The closing image to the book returns to this scene, but with a few significant details changed. The same teddy bear reappears, but—as mentioned in a previous paragraph—he is now wearing a baseball cap that reads "Doug," transforming him into the exact bear that the baby-to-be mentioned wanting and was depicted on a prior page. Park's text thus demonstrates that all of the various toys, activities, and amusements that the unborn narrator-protagonist mentioned are not excessive, but accessible. These requests not only could, but—as the baseball cap which now appears atop the stuffed animal's head reveals—even should be accommodated.

The addition of the hat saying "Doug" is not the only noteworthy modification to this scene. So, too, is the proximal relationship that this object has to the mother's body. Whereas the expectant mother was simply clutching the stuffed toy in one arm in the opening image, she is now hugging it against her pregnant belly with both hands in the closing illustration. Far from an insignificant detail, this change in the item's physical placement also suggests a change in its emotional register. The move indicates that she cherishes the toy, rather than derides it. This change sends the message that the content of Park's text is intended to be authentic, not parodic. The book's discussion of fetal needs might be presented in a way that is amusing and even humorous at times, but it is sincere nonetheless. The rhythmic writing makes the subject matter of *MA!* more enticing and enjoyable, not more execrable and egregious.

"Still . . . I Try to Stay Busy. I Slosh Till I'm Dizzy": Fetal Learning and the Prenatally Advantaged Child

Not all of the passages in *MA! There's Nothing to Do Here!* equate baby boredom with a lack of material items. Many of the narrator-protagonist's complaints arise not from his desire for toys or games, but from his longing for sensory stimulation, physical activity, and even intellectual challenges.

Once again, this detail echoes a powerful facet of millennium-era parenthood in general and motherhood in particular. In the late 1980s and early 1990s, during the same time that the expectations for women with regard to childrearing were beginning to change, so too were social and scientific opinions about the intellectual, psychological, and sentient capacity of the unborn. Fueled by advances in medical technology that allowed for greater visual imaging along with more accurate physical monitoring of the unborn, a series of research studies discovered that fetuses could not only detect but respond to various sounds. As Adam Eshleman has written, "hearing is one of the first senses to develop. As early as 16 weeks gestation, a developing fetus begins to perceive the world outside the womb through his or her fluid-filled ears" (par. 4). Although both maternal tissue and amniotic fluid greatly muffle these sounds, there is "a lot of information in that filtered and muted sound stream" (Eshleman, par. 4). Fetal infants acquire valuable knowledge about language as well as the intonation of their mother's voice through the sounds that they hear while in utero. For instance, "There are studies that show a two-day-old infant's preference to the mother's native language, even when spoken by unfamiliar voices" (qtd in Eshleman, par. 5). These observations also proved true for other types of repeated, organized sounds—such as music. Denise Winterman reports: "Numerous studies conclude that playing music to babies in the womb and in the early years helps build the neural bridges along which thoughts and information travel" (par. 3). This phenomenon quickly became known as the "Mozart Effect" after the classical composer whose sonata was used in the 1993 study in which this discovery was made.

Taken collectively, these developments gave rise to a new area of pediatric inquiry known as fetal learning. For centuries, unborn babies were regarded as passive and sequestered—physically cut off from the outside world and thus personally unaffected by it. But, as Curtis A. Sandman has observed, in the wake of scientific discoveries during the late 1980s and early 1990s, the human fetus proved to be "an active participant in its own development and is collecting in formation for life after birth" (qtd in Association, par. 9).

By the closing years of twentieth century, together with the old maxims of eating right, getting enough rest, and taking prenatal vitamins, pregnant women were also encouraged to read, sing, or simply talk to their babies. As one advice column implored: "Anything that you would say to a newborn you can say to your unborn baby. You can read it a story or you can sing it a song. You can express your love and feelings. Talk to your baby very lovingly every day" ("5 Steps").

Babies who have been exposed to music, books, and/or foreign languages in the womb are referred to as "prenatally advantaged children," and a veritable industry of products has sprung up to cater to them. A new cadre of texts—such as Tish Rabe and Dr. Seuss's *Oh Baby, the Places You'll Go!: A Book to be Read in Utero* (1997) and Marissa McTasney's *With Love: A Book to Be Read to Your Child In Utero and Beyond* (2007)—were published to facilitate early language acquisition and parental voice recognition. Meanwhile, a growing number of companies, from well-known ones such as Baby Einstein, Baby Genius, and Baby Mozart to lesser-known entities like BabyPlus and SmarterBabies.info, offer CDs, videos, and informational materials to facilitate fetal learning. Many of them make claims that only the most cavalier and uncaring parent-to-be could ignore. For instance, BabyPlus states in the printable brochure on its website: "By using this revolutionary educational product, parents *can* give their child lifetime mental, social, psychological, and creative advantages" ("BabyPlus"; my emphasis). Later, they go on to make another equally powerful proclamation: "Children *prenatally advantaged* by

BabyPlus *have shown consistent learning gains* in terms of intelligence, social skills, and creative ability, allowing them to develop into high achievers and well-rounded individuals" ("BabyPlus," 2012; my emphasis).

Such observations dovetail with the growing millennium-era pressure for parents to give their children every possible competitive edge—and fear of the lifelong consequences that may arise from not doing so. Psychologist Frances Rauscher, whose research study gave rise to the concept of the Mozart Effect, has observed that the discovery of prenatal learning precipitated a widespread belief in what she calls "infant determinism," or the belief that the positive and especially the negative experiences that a child has early in life have a powerful and even irreversible impact on the course of their development. Although in reality, infants and young children are astoundingly resilient—overcoming challenges and rebounding from setbacks—the past few decades have witnessed a growing belief in both childhood fragility and even predestination. Beginning in the 1990s and accelerating rapidly during the opening decades of the twenty-first century, parents increasingly believed that a child's intellectual capacity was determined exceedingly early in life, sometimes even before birth. Professor Paul Robinson captures this sentiment while discussing the Mozart Effect: "There is compelling scientific evidence that the music we hear at the earliest stages significantly affects the way our neurological pathways are laid down during development" (qtd in Winterman, par. 10). By extension, according to this theory, newborns who have not had the benefit of being exposed to music prenatally have missed out on an opportunity for which there is no possible compensation—or recovery. These youngsters lag behind and are destined to remain there. Given what is at stake, prenatal stimulation has become not merely a parental recommendation but an imperative. As one advice column put it: "parents *must do whatever they can* to maximize growth and development *during all* aspects of embryonic and fetal development" ("How to Maximize," par. 3; my emphasis). Couched in these terms, failing to do so emerges as not simply foolish, but neglectful.

The concept of fetal learning and the accompanying imperative for prenatal stimulation emerged during the same time that the expectations for women with regard to childrearing responsibilities were increasing, and they were quickly folded into them. Although many of these products simply mention the importance of "parents" talking, reading, or playing music to the unborn baby, the person to whom they are most often speaking is a mother. During the period of gestation, women are the physical custodians of the baby-to-be and thus are cast as having the primary responsibility for prenatal education.

Curt A. Sandman echoed this viewpoint when he wrote: "[the fetus is] preparing for life based on messages *the mom is providing*" (qtd in Association, par. 9; my emphasis).

By the opening decade of the twenty-first century, the pressure for parents in general and mothers in particular to give their unborn baby a developmental edge had become so great that it no longer even mattered whether the methods employed were actually effective. For instance, in spite of the emphasis on reading books to unborn babies that were specifically designed to promote early literacy—be it Dr. Seuss's *The Cat in the Hat* or Marissa McTasney's *With Love*—Rick Gilmore reveals "nothing suggests that . . . the kind of material you read matters" (qtd in Eshleman, par. 7). Likewise, after years of parenting magazines touting the nearly magical power of the Mozart Effect, subsequent studies were unable to replicate the findings of the initial research. This lack of reproducibility prompted psychologists to question the validity of the entire premise. Even Frances Rauscher, who had initially created the concept, agreed. As she remarked in an article that appeared in *Scientific American*, "I would simply say that there is no compelling evidence that children who listen to classical music are going to have any improvement in cognitive abilities. . . . It's really a myth, in my humble opinion" (qtd in Swaminathan, par. 9). Nevertheless, parental pressure to prenatally advantage their unborn baby—by talking to them, reading to them, or playing them music in utero—remains high. The website for BabyPlus touts that thousands of families in more than 60 countries have used their system ("BabyPlus").

Barbara Park's *MA! There's Nothing to Do Here!* traffics in both the perceived benefits of prenatal stimulation and the parental fears about the developmental pitfalls of failing to do so. This theme is established in one of the opening lines of the book when the baby-to-be laments the lack of visual stimuli: "There's nothing to see here! Not one scrawny tree here!" Viewed through the lens of fetal learning, this complaint is far from a bratty whine; instead, it can be seen as a cry of anxious concern—and early warning. If Park's narrator-protagonist lacks interesting things to look at, then his neurological pathways are not being stimulated and a myriad of new and potentially life-altering intellectual connections are not being made.

Sensory engagement is not the only activity for which the fetus in *MA! There's Nothing to Do Here!* longs. He also craves additional physical challenge: "I'm all in a heap here. My feet are asleep here. I'm flat out of space. I've got knees in my face. And I'm totally bored with this dumb bungee cord." Once again, this comment echoes one of the most recent tactics for prenatal engagement: physical stimulation. As one website reports to expectant mothers, "Valuable research has shown that stimuli such as stroking the fetus through the belly . . . as well as light and vibrations are pleasurable to the baby" ("Prenatal Stimulation," par. 3). While Park's baby-to-be is complaining more of cramped conditions than a lack of physical contact, the end result is the same. "I'm NOT kidding you . . . there is NOTHING to do," he gripes in an annoyed tone.

Lacking adequate outside stimulation, Park's narrator-protagonist does seek ways to do so for himself. In a passage that is meant to relay his resourcefulness but could also be read as his need to compensate for a maternal deficiency, he explains: "Still . . . I try to stay busy. I slosh till I'm dizzy. I practice my kicking. And hiccup-cup-hicking." Nonetheless, the baby-to-be remains woefully under-challenged. "My choices are slim. There's no room to swim," he reports.

Reflecting growing societal beliefs in "infant determinism," Park's protagonist already seems disadvantaged from his lack of visual, intellectual, and physical stimulation. "I'm working on hair. But my head is still bare," he bemoans. The illustration that accompanies these lines shows the baby-to-be holding the solitary strand that is growing on his head (fig. 10). Indicating the high level of anxiety that his lack of hair is causing him, his eyebrows are raised, his mouth is open wide, and his eyes are firmly fixed on the lone lock. Later, he frets over several other possible shortcomings: "Still a few worries more: Ma, I think that I snore." By the very next page, such feelings of inferiority cause Park's baby-to-be to cast even normal physical limitations of newborns as deficiencies: "Plus my head's kinda wobbly. I'll need support, prob'ly." Perry Nodelman, in *Words about Pictures*, has commented about how the illustrations in picture books provide cues about emotional state of the characters as well as the tone of the printed words (69). This observation is certainly true of *MA! There's Nothing to Do Here!* Throughout the picture book but especially in the pages where Park's fetus is expressing concerns about his developmental state, the illustrations convey his agitation, anxiety, and even alarm. The four small drawings that accompany the passage about his wobbly head, for example, show the fetus's affective state as his head tilts uncontrollably left, right, forward, and back (fig. 11). Based on his facial expressions and body language, he is experiencing not simply emotional distress but physical discomfort.

Alyson Schafer, in *Breaking the Good Mom Myth*, laments the highly competitive, achievement-orientated conception of motherhood that pervades the twenty-first century: "Seems we're now in the *business* of 'people building' and 'unlocking potentials'" (4; emphasis in original). However, as

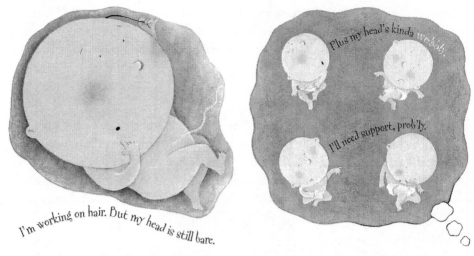

Figure 10. The still-gestating fetus is presented with fully opened eyes. Illustration from Barbara Park's *MA! There's Nothing to Do Here! Figure 11*. The newborn is unable to support his own head, a physical trait that is perfectly normal for his developmental state, but that he regards as an alarming sign of possible deficiency. Illustration from Barbara Park's *MA! There's Nothing to Do Here!*

Judith Warner explains, women who decide to opt out of this results-focused model and make alternative choices for raising their children face an equally hazardous situation: "The flip side of this was, if you *neglected* to nurture and—let's admit it—*create* your child's talents, then you could hold yourself responsible for a lifetime of future academic and professional (not to mention social and psychological) failure" (112).

Both Schafer and Warner were discussing the parenting dilemmas faced by women whose children had already been born. But these observations increasingly apply to those whose offspring are still in the womb. The mounting expectations and even outright imperatives of prenatal parenting raise the bar on motherhood to new and previously unimagined heights. Now, more than ever, a woman can be failing as a mother before her baby is actually even born.

Turning the Tables on Mom (and Dad): From Children's Literature by Adults to Adult Literature by Children

The gestating fetus who is the narrator-protagonist of Barbara Park's picture book can be seen as offering a commentary on another phenomenon: the nature of children's literature. The genre first emerged in Great Britain during the eighteenth century. As M. O. Grenby has discussed, prior to this era, "Children read, certainly, but the books that they probably enjoyed reading (or hearing) most, were not designed especially for them" (par. 2). Instead, these materials were composed either for an audience of adults or for a mixed readership of grown-ups and kids alike (Grenby, par. 2).

This situation changed in the mid-eighteenth century when a small group of publishers in London began releasing books explicitly intended for children (Grenby, par. 3). The subject matter of these texts varied greatly, with books about animals, illustrated histories, and nursery rhymes representing just a few of the many offerings. Whatever the specific focus of these narratives, though, they were united by one common feature: this new crop of books intended for children were overwhelmingly authored by adults. From lesser-known figures, such Thomas Boreman, Dorothy Kilner, and Sarah Trimmer to ones who would become literary giants, including Maria Edgeworth, Sarah Fielding, and, of course, John Newbery, writers for children were adults, not kids. In the words of Grenby, "For the first time it was possible for authors to make a living out of writing solely for children, and to become famous for it. Children's literature, as we know it today, had begun" (par. 5).

In the decades that followed, the genre would change greatly. Nonetheless, this founding feature remained in place. Literature for children overwhelmingly—as well as paradoxically—remained written by adults. Young people only rarely penned books for other young people.[8] This situation remained in place even amidst growing estimation about the intellectual capacity of children and beliefs in the importance of giving them agency. Furthermore, this quality was equally true of picture books as it is of young adult novels. Whether youth readers are in nursery school or high school, the materials that they encounter, even today, are adult-authored. In this way, while children's literature emerged as distinct genre, it also emerged as one that was the literary purview of adults. Adults write children's books, illustrate them, edit them, and publish them. They are not simply involved in, but firmly in control of, every step in the line of production.

Park's *MA!* can be seen as offering a commentary on this situation. Mirroring the oxymoronic fact that books for children are authored by adults, her juvenile-styled narrative for adults purports to be "written" not simply by a child but by a fetus in utero. The text's use of first-person narration, its claim to offer *A Word from Your Baby-in-Waiting*, and its opening salutation of "Dear

Ma" only further suggest that the narrative was "composed" by the unborn infant. Of course, a gestating baby is not actually able to author a book. Nonetheless, Park's text plays with the idea child authorship. After centuries of adults authoring narratives for children, *MA!* turns the tables. By using this narrative approach, it takes the notion of youth authorship as far as it can possibly or—given the subject matter of *MA!* perhaps more accurately—conceivably go. In a detail that can be seen as turning the tables on adults, the text puts adults in the same literary position that children have long occupied: narratives that are intended for them are not written by them.

Viewed from this perspective, *MA! There's Nothing to Do Here!* does far more than simply explore the boundary that exists between a mother and her baby. It probes the longstanding power dynamics between adults and children. Mothers and fathers have long had social, cultural, literary, economic, political, familial, and corporeal authority over boys and girls. For better or worse, *MA! There's Nothing to Do Here!* reverses this situation. The text presents a situation where young people author books for adults, dictate the of terms of parenting, and even redefine the terms of national citizenship. Children's literature for adults can easily be viewed as a genre that allows grown-ups to appropriate, encroach, and even usurp the literary forms historically reserved for kids. As Barbara Park's picture book reveals, however, these narratives also signal how doing so can result in adults ironically becoming subordinated to even the youngest of children. Instead of serving progressive purposes that call into question established modes of thinking, the genre might actually become a platform for reactionary messages and conservative movements.

The chapter that follows continues to explore the political dimensions of children's literature for adults. To that end, it spotlights the rapidly expanding number of adult-audience parodies of classic picture books that appeared as the twenty-first century progressed. In examples ranging from *Goodnight Keith Moon* (2010) and *The Very Hungover Caterpillar* (2014) to Andrew Simonian's *Bi-Curious George* (2012) and Phil Newton and J. Edward's *If You Give a Guy a Beer* (2013), dozens of narratives of this nature were released in these decades. While many of the adult-audience parodies addressed lighthearted topics—alcohol, romance, popular music, etc—a significant subset examined the more serious subject of contemporary US politics. From Erich Origen and Gan Golan's *Goodnight Bush* (2008) and *Don't Let the Republicans Drive the Bus!* (2012) to Dr. Truth's anti-Obama *The Cat and the Mitt* (2012) and Chris Ouellette's libertarian-themed *Dr. Paul* (2011), these books featured both liberal and conservative viewpoints. The chapter that follows explores the use of children's literature for adults as a platform for political commentary and even partisan propaganda. While books like *Goodnight Bush* and *The Cat and the Mitt* may ostensibly be parody texts, I make a case that their true creative and cultural kinship is with a far difference source: the political broadside. Accordingly, the next chapter discusses how the new genre of children's literature for adults can serve as an effective medium for reaching not simply mainstream audiences, but the national electorate.

Learning Left from Right

Goodnight Bush, Don't Let the Republican Drive the Bus!,
and the Broadside Tradition

Linda Hutcheon, in her landmark book, *A Theory of Parody*, traces the pervasive nature of this literary mode across cultures, time periods, and creative mediums. As she discusses, parody is a common form of artistic expression in the West. Works written in this style permeate print, visual, and popular culture from ancient times to the present.

Children's literature is no exception. For centuries, books for young readers have been shaped by the tradition of parody and, in turn, helped to shape it. In examples ranging from Lewis Carroll's *Alice's Adventures in Wonderland* (1865) to Jon Scieszka and Lane Smith's *The Stinky Cheese Man and Other Fairly Stupid Tales* (1992), some of the most critically acclaimed and commercially successful narratives for children contain parodic characters, themes, and plot points. Moreover, books for young people have also been the subject of parodies. As Linda M. Shires, Kimberley Reynolds, and John MacKay Shaw have all discussed, *Alice's Adventure in Wonderland*, along with its sequel, *Through the Looking-Glass, and What Alice Found There* (1871), have so frequently been the subject of imitation that they have given rise to their own parodic tradition.

Over the years, parodies of children's books have also been directed at an adult readership. John Kendrick Bangs's *Alice in Blunderland* (1907) constitutes an excellent early example. The narrative features the same characters from Lewis Carroll's *Alice's Adventures in Wonderland*, but the plot offers a pointed critique of the foibles and failures of municipal government. With chapters bearing titles such as "The Immovable Trolley" (19) and "The Aromatic Gas Plant" (37), Bangs tackles subjects such as civic bureaucracy, administrative incompetence, and corporate corruption.

Lewis Carroll's *Alice*, however, was not the only children's book to be rewritten for adult audiences. As David Blamires has documented, Heinrich Hoffmann's *Struwwelpeter* (1845) has also served as a vehicle for socio-political satire.

In 1899, for example, Harold Begbie released *The Political Struwwelpeter*. The text lampooned political life in Great Britain, reimagining Struwwelpeter as a lion who had long, unkept claws. Meanwhile, each story examined a different aspect of governmental affairs.

During the opening decades of the twenty-first century, narratives of this nature experienced a boom in the United States. While adult-audience parodies of well-known children's books had existed for centuries, a variety of commercial, material, and especially technological conditions at the start of the new millennium helped them to become especially pervasive. These elements included the rise of the personal computer, the ease and affordability of desktop publishing, and the marketing, sales, and distribution opportunities made possible by the internet. Taken collectively, these developments allowed such books to be created, printed, and sold in faster and simpler ways than ever before. As a result, while authors had been penning parodies of well-known children's books to provide a satiric look at various socio-cultural issues for adults for generations, the opening decade of the twenty-first century saw an increase in their number, their variety, and their popularity.

Kate Merrow Nelligan's *Pat the Husband* (2008)—a retelling of Dorothy Kunhardt's classic interactive text *Pat the Bunny* (1940)—can be seen as a starting point for this trend. For generations, Kunhardt's narrative has been helping young children practice their fine motor skills and explore their sense of touch. Through the assistance of central characters Paul and Judy, young readers get a chance to rub a patch of soft plush fur on a bunny, slide their finger over a strip of sandpaper that simulates daddy's scratchy beard, and lift a swatch of fabric to play peek-a-boo. Featuring Paul and Judy as newlyweds, Nelligan's *Pat the Husband* allows its presumably adult married female reader the chance to lampoon some stereotypical male peccadilloes. For instance, one page invites them to pull the tab in order to get Paul to ask for directions when he gets lost while driving; meanwhile, another allows them to remove a tiny milk jug so that Paul can find the ketchup in the refrigerator and see that its absence "is not a conspiracy."

Not surprisingly, *Pat the Husband* soon inspired a companion text, *Pat the Bride* (2009). Written with an adult female audience in mind once again, Nelligan's follow-up invites its readers to use a swatch of cloth to polish Judy's engagement ring, cinch her into her wedding gown using a real zipper, and place various Velcro-attached hairstyles to help Judy experiment with up-dos. The following year, Nelligan released the final book in her *Pat the Bunny* parody trilogy for adults: *Pat the Daddy* (2010). The text follows the same formula, but this time it takes on the subject of parenthood. One page permits readers to put the lens cap on the video camera that Paul brings into the birthing room, while another allows them to Velcro a piece of duct tape over Paul's mouth whenever he comments on Judy's struggle to lose the last few pounds of baby weight.

Nelligan was not the only writer to see the potential for adult-audience humor in Kunhardt's classic. In 2011, two more parodies of *Pat the Bunny* appeared: *Pat the Zombie* and *Pat the Foodie*. The former text was written by Aaron Ximm and illustrated by Kaveh Soofi. As its title implied, *Pat the Zombie* offered a gothic twist on the childhood classic. Instead of feeling Daddy's scratchy beard, readers touch his decaying face, complete with exposed jawbone. Likewise, instead of putting their finger through Mommy's wedding ring, they can insert it into her empty eye socket. Lest either the gruesome content or intended older audience of the text is unclear, the subtitle calls the narrative *A Cruel (Adult) Spoof*. *Pat the Foodie*, which is subtitled *A Culinary Pull and Poke Parody*, is far less macabre. The text offers a comedic look at some of the joys—but mainly the hassles—associated with trying to "live green" and eat healthy. An opening page, for instance, queries readers: "Judy loves petting her free-range chickens. Do YOU want to pet her chickens?" By contrast, a subsequent scenario offers the sarcastic assertion: "Paul likes standing in line at the gourmet Korean food truck. Do YOU want to stand in line too?" A fold-out flap on the facing page reveals the numerous individuals who have queued up in front of Paul.

In the next few years, a bevy of parodies based on a variety of classic picture books followed. Eric Carle's *The Very Hungry Caterpillar* (1969) was reimagined first by Michael Teitelbaum as *The Very Hungry Zombie* (2012) and then by Josie Lloyd and Emlyn Rees as *The Very Hungover Caterpillar* (2014). This same writing duo also released *We're Going on a Bar Hunt* (2013), which was modeled after Michael Rosen's well-known *We're Going on a Bear Hunt* (1989). Reese Ling, in *Are You My Wine? A Children's Book Parody for Adults Exploring the World of Wine* (2017), reinterpreted P. D. Eastman's classic *Are You My Mother?* (1960) for oenophiles.

Laura Numeroff's classic *If You Give a Mouse a Cookie* (1985) received similar treatment in *If You Give Mommy a Glass of Wine* (2016) by Renee Charytan and *If You Give a Guy a Beer* (2013) by Phil Newton and J. Edward. Meanwhile, Dr. Seuss's *Oh, the Places You'll Go!* (1990) was revamped first as *Oh, the Sh*t You Don't Know!: College Graduate Edition* (2016) by Antonio Carter and then as *Oh, the Meetings You'll Go To!: A Parody* (2017) by "Dr. Suits." During those same years, writer Katie Blackburn and illustrator Sholto Walker released two parodies of Maurice Sendak's *Where the Wild Things Are* (1963): *Where the Wild Moms Are* (2015) and *Where the Wild Dads Went* (2016). Likewise, Dan Zevin updated the well-known Mr. Men series for the cell phone era, with *Mr. Selfie: A Parody* (2015). Shel Silverstein's classic *The Giving Tree* (1964) was spoofed as *The Taking Tree: A Selfish Parody* (2010). Written by an individual using the equally parodic pseudonym "Shrill Travesty," the book begins: "Once there was a kid who spent every day under a tree / The tree was his best friend. / Which shows what a loser the kid was."

Some millennium-era parodies of popular children's picture books have employed naughtier themes. *Bi-Curious George: An Unauthorized Parody* (2012), by Andrew Simonian, embodies a vivid example. A sticker affixed to the cover cautions readers "For Mature Audiences Only," and the narrative does not disappoint: "One day George saw a man. / He had on a sassy purple beret. / And George got excited, despite himself," a representative passage reads.

By contrast, both C. B. Bryza's *Are You My Boyfriend?* (2014) and Ross Mac-Donald and James Victore's *In and Out with Dick and Jane: A Loving Parody* (2011), are far tamer. The former text reimagines the P. D. Eastman's classic *Are You My Mother?* (1960) for single heterosexual women trying to find a husband. Meanwhile, the latter book, *In and Out with Dick and Jane*, encompasses a variety of themes and topics. Contrary to the text's moniker, none of the vignettes are actually sexually explicit. Instead, most mock the idealized view of American family life that is presented in this popular series of picture books.

A few adult-audience parodies lampoon more than merely an individual picture book; they engage with a well-known series of texts. For example, Simon Max Hill and Shannon Wheeler's *Grandpa Won't Wake Up* (2011) offers a satiric variation on Little Golden Books. The text physically resembles the size, appearance, and format of these narratives, but with a far different plot and passages: "We lit a candle in his butt, / but Grandpa won't wake up. / Grandma punched him in the nuts, / but Grandpa won't wake up." Meanwhile, Arthur C. Gackley's *Bad Little Children's Books* (2016) satirizes the Little Golden Books along with an array of other well-known titles. Examples include *Little Dysfunctional House on the Prairie, James and the Giant Preach,* and *The Very Hung Caterpillar* (6, 74, 100).

Finally, Margaret Wise Brown's beloved bedtime story, *Goodnight Moon* (1947), has provided frequent fodder for adult-audience parodies in the early twenty-first century. In 2010, Bruce Worden and Clare Cross released

Goodnight Keith Moon. Mimicking the narrative style as well as aesthetic look of Brown's text, the book begins: "In the great green room / There was a telephone / And a dead Keith Moon / And a picture of / Townshend jumping over the moon. / And there were four little gents pissing on cement." Matt Cole's *Fuck You Sun* (2011) echoes some of this content: the book takes Brown's relaxing bedtime story and rewrites it as a tale about a bunny who is waking up with a terrible hangover. The cover image shows the pajama-clad rabbit burying his face in the pillow to shield it from the bright sunlight streaming in through the window. Also in 2011, Ann Droyd—a punny pseudonym, the jacket flap informs us, for an established children's author who wishes to keep her identity secret—released *Goodnight iPad: A Parody for the Next Generation* (2011). Directed at "the child in us all" and shelved in the adult humor section, the publisher provided the following comment about the book's intent: "Modern life is abuzz. There are huge LCD WiFi HD TVs and Facebook requests and thumbs tapping texts and new viral clips of cats doing flips. Wouldn't it be nice to say goodnight to all that?"

Goodnight Husband, Goodnight Wife (2012), by Eric Stangel and Justin Stangel, is another parodic variant on Brown's text. The jacket flap provides the following synopsis: "In this humorous parody of a children's literature classic, familiar to generations of married couples, the gentle sarcasm and clever illustrations combine to make a perfect book for the end of every frustrating, exhausting, utterly priceless day." *Goodnight Nanny-Cam: A Parody for Modern Parents* (2014), written by Jen Nessel and Lizzy Ratner and illustrated by Sara Pinto, can be seen as a close corollary to this subject. *Goodnight Mr. Darcy*, released that same year, takes an entirely different tack. Written by Kate Coombs and illustrated by Alli Arnold, the narrative offers a Jane Austen spin on the classic story. A representative passage reads: "And Jane with a blush and / Mr. Bingley turned to mush / and a gossiping mother / and a father saying 'hush.'" Finally, *Goodnight Brew: A Parody for Beer People* (2014) and *Good Morning Brew: A Parody for Coffee People* (2015), both written by Karla Oceanak and illustrated by Allie Ogg, form the most recent offerings along these lines.[1]

A sizable cadre of these adult parodies of classic picture books possessed political themes.[2] In 2004, Julie Marcus and Susan Carp inaugurated this trend with the release of their bipartisan narrative, *Pat the Politician*. Yet another retelling of Dorothy Kunhardt's classic interactive text *Pat the Bunny* (1940), the book not only presented characters Paul and Judy as voting-age adults, but it also, as the subtitle indicated, permitted its audience to "pull and poke" their favorite politicians.[3] On one page, for instance, readers can lift a flap to look inside George W. Bush's head, only to see a large black empty space. Meanwhile, in another scenario, they are invited to feel Bill Clinton's briefs—and not just his legal ones. Two years later, in 2006, Ellis Weiner and Barbara Davilman continued this tradition with the release of *Yiddish with George and Laura*. Modeled after the popular Dick and Jane series, the book offered lessons in the Yiddish language through its poignant critique the 43rd president of the United States. The opening page provides a representative example. Beneath an illustration of the smiling-and-waving Commander-in-Chief, the text reads: "See George. / He is our president. / He lives in a fancy white house / and is a big *shmegegge*" (Weiner and Davilman 3).

George W. Bush was not the only US President to be the subject of politically charged parodies. The two men who have succeeded him in the Oval Office thus far have likewise been lampooned in this way. In 2016, as the second term of the 44th president was coming to an end, bestselling conservative author Jerome Corsi released *Goodnight Obama*. The parody text was not a loving farewell to the nation's first black commander in chief. Instead, the book bids adieu to all of Obama's policies and practices that will (allegedly) not be missed, including "forcing government run health care upon the greatest nation" and "web sites [that] crash upon implementation."[4] The presidency of Donald J. Trump has likewise been the subject of a variety of parody books, including *If You Give a Pig the White House* (2019) by Faye Kanouse and *Goodnight Trump* (2019) by Erich Origen and Gan Golan.[5] As these titles imply, neither book offers a flattering portrayal of him or a supportive view of his administration. Kanouse's text, for example, presents Trump as a porcine president whose demands are never-ending as well as ever-escalating: "If you give a pig the White House," the opening pages relay, "he'll ask to watch TV. When you let him watch TV, he'll want to tweet."

Given the sheer number and wide variety of adult audience parodies of classic picture books, narratives of this nature constitute their own distinct sub-genre or, at least, specialized category of children's literature for adults. More than simply forming a compelling cluster, they embody a key component to this phenomenon. Texts like *A Very Hungover Caterpillar*, *Pat the Husband*, and *Goodnight Brew* occupy the cultural forefront of children's literature for adults. Their clever content, parodic recognition, and humorous appeal cause them to be a highly visible examples of this new genre.

This chapter places adult-audience parodies of classic picture books in the spotlight. More specifically, it investigates a specific subset of them: ones with political content. In the pages that follow, I examine four of the most commercially successful and critically discussed adult-audience political parodies of popular picture books that have been released in the opening decades of the twenty-first century. Two of these texts emanate from the political left: *Goodnight Bush* (2008) and *Don't Let the Republican Drive the Bus!* (2012), both by Erich Origen and Gan Golan. Conversely, two are affiliated with the political right: *The Cat and the Mitt* (2012), by Dr. Truth, and *Dr. Paul* (2011), by Chris Ouellette. These books represent a broad spectrum of political viewpoints, not simply Democrat and Republican, but liberal, conservative, independent, and libertarian. Consequently, although these books might be somewhat dated from a pop culture perspective, they offer a more timeless portrait of the full political possibilities of children's literature for adults. More contemporaneous examples of adult-audience parodies of other historical moments and presidential administrations—such as *If You Give a Pig the White House* (2019) and *Goodnight Trump* (2019)—reflect only one political perspective. Meanwhile, critiques that represent alternative partisan viewpoints, such as *Goodnight Obama* (2016), have not been nearly as popular as their predecessors. In this respect, these four titles blazed the trail or established the formula for narratives of this nature. I would even assert that books like *If You Give a Pig the White House* and *Goodnight Obama* would not exist without the popularity of titles like *Goodnight Bush*. Had these four narratives not been written and released, the others might not have followed.

Goodnight Bush, Don't Let the Republican Drive the Bus!, The Cat and the Mitt, and Dr. Paul parody some of the most popular and beloved picture books of all time: Margaret Wise Brown's *Goodnight Moon* (1947), Mo Willems's *Don't Let the Pigeon Drive the Bus!* (2003), Dr. Seuss's *The Cat in the Hat* (1957), and Dr. Seuss's *Green Eggs and Ham* (1960), respectively. Much of the discussion about these books has focused on how well they mimic the originals. Articles in newspapers, on blogs, and in customer reviews online comment on how perfectly *Don't Let the Republican Drive the Bus!* captures the essence of Mo Willems's feathered character, how well *The Cat and the Mitt* matches the cadence of Dr. Seuss's rhyme, and how accurately *Goodnight Bush* replicates Margaret Wise Brown's famed bedtime story. The success of these books has been attributed to their success as parodies.

In the pages that follow, I make a case that the true literary, ideological, and cultural kinship of *Goodnight Bush*, *The Cat and the Mitt*, and *Don't Let the Republican Drive the Bus!* is not with the classic children's picture book on which they are ostensibly based. Instead, it is with is with a far different genre: the broadside. Emerging in England in the fifteenth century and experiencing their heyday in the United States during the Federalist period, broadsides were among the most ubiquitous and efficacious forms of print communication. Posted in public places or sold cheaply by street hawkers and merchants, these single-sheet missives served a wide array of purposes, ranging from disseminating information about new laws, taxes, or military campaigns to publishing advertisements about local events, the lyrics to the latest popular verse ballad, or the last speech of a condemned criminal. In both Great Britain and the United States, one common and important function that broadsides performed was providing a populist forum for the discussion of pressing sociopolitical topics. As Angela McShane has written, these broadsides offered announcements, news, and controversies that were conveyed as "panegyrics, satires, libels, and prose polemics" (342). Employed in the service of progressive and conservative causes, the main goal of broadsides was to influence public thought (McShane 342).

I argue that *Goodnight Bush, Dr. Paul, Don't Let the Republican Drive the Bus!,* and *The Cat and the Mitt* revive this once vibrant but now largely defunct print tradition for a new audience in a new era. Possessing an array of characteristics associated with this facet of Anglo-American print culture that served as an important site for political debate and public protest through the nineteenth century, these parodies ought not to be viewed as dyadic texts that possess a relationship only with the picture book that they are parodying. Rather, they contain rhetorical, commercial, and material connections that reveal them as both polyphonic and transhistorical.

An awareness of the broadside tradition that permeates *Goodnight Bush, Dr. Paul, Don't Let the Republican Drive the Bus!,* and *The Cat and the Mitt* does more than simply complicate the mimesis that is operating within these texts; it also reveals compelling new insights about the state of political discourse in the United States during the twenty-first century. Released into a media-saturated environment where it is challenging for any message to get noticed, these adult-audience parodies form an effective means to catch the public's attention, spotlight pressing sociopolitical issues, and spark cultural debate. They embody a new venue by which to engage the citizenry. Political parodies of popular picture books call attention to the long, storied, and important role that print culture has historically played—and continues to exert—in American politics. At the same time, they add to ongoing discussions about politics and children's literature. Rather than engaging with the long-standing question of what relationship books for young readers should have with political topics, these books highlight the relationship that politics may choose to have with children's literature.

Since their widespread appearance in American popular culture during the opening years of the twenty-first century, political parodies like *Goodnight Bush* and *Dr. Paul* have largely been viewed as works of comedy. Regarded by critics and readers as mere entertaining narratives intended for amusement, they are commonly shelved in the humor section of bookstores. However, given both the populist purposes that they serve in American culture during the early twenty-first century and their link to important past forms of print protest, I demonstrate in the pages that follow that these narratives are no laughing matter. Books like *Don't Let the Republican Drive the Bus!* and *The Cat and the Mitt* seek to do nothing less than influence public opinion and, by extension, the actions of voters. Adult-audience parodies of children's classic picture book constitute powerful modes for political communication, public protest, and partisan solidarity. More than merely amusing the electorate, these books energize it.

"To Instruct, Exhort, Entertain, and, Perhaps Above All, to Persuade an Audience": The Anglo-American Broadside as Print Mainstay—and Public Mouthpiece

In their most elemental sense, broadsides are individual pieces of paper that have printing on just one side. The most typical dimensions for a broadside are ten inches by fifteen inches, but this size is far from standardized. Georgia B. Bumgardner has documented how some broadsides are quite small, measuring a scant five inches; meanwhile, others are poster-sized, measuring two feet by three feet.

The content of broadsides has been as varied as their dimensions. As the Library of Congress discusses, "Historically, broadsides have been used to inform the public about current events, publicize official proclamations and government decisions, and announce and record public meetings and entertainment events . . . advertise products and services, and celebrate popular literary and musical efforts" (par. 3). Whatever their specific subject matter, broadsides share three core qualities: they are cheaply produced, they are disseminated widely, and they are put to various socio-political uses. These items embody one of the earliest forms of mass communication. Inexpensive to produce, fast to print, and exceedingly easy to circulate, broadsides offered a highly effective means to disseminate information. As Angela McShane has discussed, these documents made their way into the hands—or, at least, sightlines—of individuals in a variety of ways. While some were distributed through the postal system, most were available for sale in shops or from peddlers hawking them on the street. Interestingly, a significant portion of broadsides were not sold, but disseminated for free: they were handed out to the public, posted on walls, fences, and doors, and even shouted from street corners or proclaimed from town squares. In this way, broadsides are often regarded as important precursors to newspapers, magazines, and tabloid "extras." Akin to these journalistic counterparts, "The principal functions of most broadside literature were to instruct, exhort, entertain, and, perhaps above all, to persuade an audience, even if only to part with a penny" (McShane 341). Available for sale in almost any shop, seen lying on tables in gathering places like saloons and boarding houses, and often affixed to buildings around city centers, they were an ever-present facet of daily life. For this reason, although broadsides have often been dismissed as mere ephemera, "they had an important impact on people's lives" (McShane 362).

Broadsides originated as a means of official government communication, and these items always maintained a strong connection with this purpose. The first extant example of the genre was a letter of indulgence written by Pope Nicholas V in 1454 (Bumgardner). For centuries afterward, according to the *Continuum Encyclopedia of Popular Music of the World*, broadsides continued to be "used for the dissemination of royal proclamations, edicts of the church and other official announcements." They were utilized as a means to effectively and efficiently distribute information to the public "so that none [may] pretend ignorance thereby" (McShane 348).

Almost from the moment that broadsides were employed to exert hegemonic political power, however, they were used for popular protests against that power: "[F]rom the beginning of the seventeenth century the press was used for ever more audacious and satirical attacks on political enemies, religious opponents, or those who had fallen short of social expectations" (McShane 354–55). To be sure, within a century after the broadside made its debut in Great Britain, it had become such a common and effective means of socio-political protest that the government sought to regulate them: according to the *Continuum Encyclopedia of Popular Music of the World*, "The authorities' increasing concern over the power of the new medium of broadsides to influence public opinion, and to spread dissent, was apparent in the passage of the Act for the Advancement of True Religion and the Abolishment of the Contrary (1543), which referred to the seditious effects of recent 'printed ballads, rhymes, etc' in 'untruly' instructing the king's subjects, and specifically the 'youth of his realm.'"

Politically charged broadsides have been just as materially prevalent and culturally powerful in the United States. The first one that appeared in

British America, in fact, was political in nature. Titled "The Oath of a Free-man" and making its initial appearance in 1639, the document was an affirmation of loyalty to the Crown.[6] The period of the American Revolutionary War gave rise to what is perhaps the most numerous and diverse array of broadsides in the nation's history. The American Antiquarian Society, for example, houses a bevy of examples from this era containing everything from pronouncements of patriotism and calls for enlistment in the military to ballad versions of "Yankee Doodle Dandy" and information about battles, troop positions, and casualties (see *American Broadsides*). Given the variety and popularity of these items, Michael Warner included broadsides among what he calls the "counterpublic print discourse" of the colonial and Federalist era (24). As he explains, "In their routine dispersion, and in the conventions of discourse that allowed them to be political in a special way, these artifacts represented the material reality of an abstract public: a *res publica* of letters" (Warner 61).

Broadsides remained a significant political tool in the United States long after the cessation of revolutionary hostilities. Noble E. Cunningham has discussed how, "[i]n the 1790s, as major political parties developed and election campaigns became more strongly contested and increasingly heated, the political broadside became an important campaign device in some sections of the United States" (70). For example, many candidates kicked off their campaigns for office by posting handbills or circulating printed fliers. Finally, and perhaps most notably, these documents were used "to influence the voters in favor of a particular candidate or party" (Cunningham 71). In this regard, broadsides served much the same function as modern-day political commercials or direct mailings.

Broadsides were likewise utilized by private American citizens for socio-political purposes. They embodied a staple of communication in advocacy both for and against numerous causes, including women's rights, temperance, labor, and abolition. For instance, the Massachusetts Historical Society archives various broadsides originally published in the Southern states announcing slave auctions and then, after the passage of the Fugitive Slave Law in 1850, advertisements of rewards for the capture of escapees. Meanwhile, others in their collection denounce these exact practices.

In spite of the important cultural, literary, and political position that broadsides held for generations, the genre experience a marked decline beginning in the late nineteenth century. Facing competition, first from the proliferation of daily newspapers and then from new inventions like radio, these single-sided, single-sheet documents were overshadowed by other forms of media. While broadsides might be regarded as still existing in a modified form today—via posters, fliers, and even postcards that are sold, pasted, or handed out in public places—their presence is more one of literary influence than literal reincarnation. The word "broadside" remains, if not an entirely antiquated term, one that is not in common use. In a telling index of this phenomenon, the most recent textual example for "broadside" in the *Oxford English Dictionary* dates from the 1860s. Their legacy, however, extends firmly into the present day. These items, according to the *Continuum Encyclopedia of Popular Music of the World*, "were the first, or at least the prototype, mode of mass communication, and one that spanned the entire period from medieval minstrelsy to the emergence of modern mass media."

"So I Will Check Off His Box. / And I Won't be Swayed by CNN or FOX": Parodying Popular Picture Books to Educate, Engage, and Energize the Electorate

Political parodies of popular picture books recapture the material, cultural, and literary function of broadsides. While *Goodnight Bush, Dr. Paul, Don't Let the Republican Drive the Bus!,* and *The Cat and the Mitt* use a well-known past or present children's narrative as the basis for their physical appearance, their content embodies an array of characteristics that are highly evocative of this once culturally ubiquitous and politically powerful genre. From their partisan nature and hyperbolic rhetorical style to their methods of persuasion and even their participation in parody, these texts revive the longstanding tradition of the political broadside in the United States.

Of course, this assertion ought not to imply that literature for children is devoid of either sociopolitical content or even calls for political action. On the contrary, as Julia L. Mickenberg's *Learning from the Left: Children's Literature, the Cold War, and Radical Politics* (2005) and my own *Raising Your Kids Right: Children's Literature and American Political Conservatism* (2010) demonstrate, narratives for young readers have a long history not only of containing messages that emanate from both sides of the political aisle but also of trying to influence the opinions of their readers.[7] Dr. Seuss, for example, engaged with a number of sociopolitical issues in books throughout his career: from the importance of civil rights in *Horton Hears a Who!* (1954) and the dangers of dictatorships in *Yertle the Turtle* (1958) to the hazards of environmental pollution in *The Lorax* (1971) and the perils of nuclear proliferation in *The Butter Battle Book* (1984). To varying degrees, each book makes a case for young people not simply to become more informed about these issues, but to take action. The closing lines to *The Lorax*, for example, offer the now-famous exhortation about the ongoing destruction of the environment and the urgent need for individual conservation efforts: "UNLESS someone like you / cares a whole lot / nothing is going to get better. / It's not."

Politically engaged picture books remain a fixture of children's literature in the twenty-first century. As Julia L. Mickenberg and Philip Nel have documented in their article, "Radical Children's Literature Now!," titles like Vera Williams's *Amber Was Brave, Essie Was Smart* (2001), Davide Cali and Serge Bloch's *The Enemy* (2007), and Janet S. Wong and David Roberts's *The Dumpster Diver* (2007) encourage young people to get involved with the serious sociopolitical issues of poverty, peace, and environmentalism, respectively (445–58).

By the same token, the opening decades of the new millennium were not the first historical era when political-themed parodies of children's books were being written and released for adult audiences. On the contrary, this phenomenon also has a long history. Steven Heller has written about the "venerable tradition of satire dating back to the nineteenth century, when kings, queens, prelates and presidents were transposed onto characters from children's literature for the sole purpose of ridicule" (par. 2). Titles such as Harold Begbie's *The Political Struwwelpeter* (1899) and John Kendrick Bangs's *Alice in Blunderland* (1907), mentioned at the start of this chapter, spotlighted political events occurring in Great Britain.[8] But books of this nature were also released in the United States. The social, economic, and political upheavals precipitated by the Great Depression, for example, inspired Paul Johnson's *A Political Mother Goose* (1932). A few generations later, the Watergate scandal provided fodder for another parody—Joseph Wortis's *Tricky Dick and His Pals: Comical Stories, All in the Manner of Dr. Heinrich Hoffmann's Der Struwwelpeter* (1975).

The current cadre of titles such as *The Cat and the Mitt* and *Don't Let the Republican Drive the Bus!* do more than simply carry on this tradition; they expand it. The opening decades of the twenty-first century gave rise to what can be regarded as a heyday or golden era of political-themed adult-audience parodies of children's books. Whereas books of this nature had been written and released before, they were generally limited to an isolated title that had appeared during a particularly tumultuous time: the Great Depression, the Watergate scandal, etc. The new millennium, however, witnessed multiple texts released in the span of just a few years that seemed to be occasioned by the election cycle. *Goodnight Bush, Don't Let the Republican Drive the Bus!, The*

Cat and the Mitt, and *Dr. Paul* all draw on a wide array of classic children's books, and they also feature an equally broad spectrum of political viewpoints. They move political-themed adult-audience parodies from being occasional occurrences within American print, material, and popular culture to being a fixture within them.

Titles like *The Cat and the Mitt* and *Don't Let the Republican Drive the Bus!* differ from their literary predecessors in another significant and overlooked way. The attraction, appeal, and effectiveness that these texts have experienced can be attributed in many ways to the powerful kinship that they possess with the American tradition of the broadside. Targeting voting-aged adults whose opinions can have an immediate impact on the outcome of elections and the enactment of public policy, *Dr. Paul* and *Goodnight Bush* contain many suggestive echoes of a print format that has long been used to educate, engage, and energize the American electorate.

The connection between broadsides and political parodies of popular picture books commences even before readers open the cover to titles like *Goodnight Bush* or *The Cat and the Mitt*. This kinship begins with their cultural status, marketing strategies, and means of public consumption. Unlike highbrow products of print culture like bound books, broadsides were seen as ephemera—and treated in kind. As Bumgardner has discussed, "They were read once or twice, perhaps handed around to friends, and then were usually discarded." Those that were not thrown away were often repurposed: used to decorate boxes, adorn walls, or line drawers (McShane 355). Thus, from the standpoint of their original print purpose and their subsequent circulation in society, broadsides "were the most demotic of print products" (McShane 341).

Political parodies of popular picture books are commonly viewed in the same way. Akin to broadsides, they are seen as ephemera that are read once or twice, and then set aside or given away. While these texts may not be physically discarded—in light of the powerful cultural aversion to destroying books—they are often forgotten. Especially after the election season that inspired them, titles like *Dr. Paul* or *Goodnight Bush* are often donated, put away in a box, or simply thrown away. On the eve of the inauguration of Barack Obama, for example, Jennifer Schuessler wrote an opinion piece for the *New York Times* that urged: "let us pause to remember the books that once ruled the best-seller list in the most powerful country on earth only to be dumped into the remainder bin of history" (par. 1). *Goodnight Bush* was not only included on the list, but it was categorized as one of the "novelties" within this category (Schuessler, par. 9). Schuessler's assessment was far from inaccurate;

Goodnight Bush is no longer available as a physical text, only as an e-book for download. Loren Spivack's spoof of *The Cat in the Hat* experienced an even more rapid plummet from public view. Within months after Mitt Romney's loss in the 2012 presidential election, the author transformed *The Cat and the Mitt: A Parody for Conservatives* into *The New Democrat: The Parody for the Tea Party Movement*. These changes first appeared in a video offering a sample reading of the book on Spivack's website and will presumably be codified in a forthcoming print version of the text ("Hear a Sample"). While the critique of President Obama remains the same in *The New Democrat*, the scolding goldfish has been changed from a caricature of Mitt Romney to one of Glenn Beck ("Hear a Sample"). Even before this occurrence, *The Cat and the Mitt* had already been relegated to the fringes of official print culture. In spite of its impressive sales figures, the text is not listed in WorldCat, a global catalog of print, visual, and audio materials.

Meanwhile, in another link to broadsides, these political parodies are inexpensively priced. In spring 2013, a hardback version of Erich Origen and Gan Golan's *Don't Let the Republican Drive the Bus!* sold for $10.19 on Amazon.com; by comparison, a paperback version of Mo Willems's *Don't Let the Pigeon Drive the Bus!* was priced at $13.59. Meanwhile, echoing the longstanding tradition of broadsides being performed or posted in public for free, Christopher Ouellette's *Dr. Paul* is available at no cost. His narrative does not take the form of a physical printed book; rather, it exists as a video on YouTube. Using a software program like Photoshop, Ouellette replaced the original words from a scanned-in copy of *Green Eggs and Ham* with ones about Ron Paul. Anyone wishing to examine *Dr. Paul* can simply play the video on YouTube, which displays images from the book page-by-page as Ouellette reads the text aloud.

The Cat and the Mitt reached its audience via a method that is equally suggestive of broadsides. In a detail that recalls how many of these documents were hawked by street vendors, Hope Hodge reported from the Republican National Convention: "Outside the convention hall Monday, braving tropical storm wind and rain and pushing throngs of convention-goers, [Loren] Spivack, of Springfield, Mass., hawked copies of 'The Cat and the Mitt'" (par. 2). Forming yet another link between these genres, Gan Golan, the illustrator of *Goodnight Bush* and *Don't Let the Republican Drive the Bus!*, recalls the long tradition of politically minded broadsides being publicly proclaimed on the street. When Golan is not doing graphic design work, he is involved in public performance art, much of it offering the same political messages as his parody books.

The connections between broadsides and political parodies only increase once readers begin examining the content of these texts. Broadsides routinely trafficked in what is perhaps the most basic feature of books like *Goodnight Bush* and *The Cat and the Mitt*: the use of parody. Some of the earliest politically charged broadsides were parodies of those issued by the government. Imposters, claiming to be civic leaders, circulated false proclamations, counterfeit edicts, and satiric announcements throughout early modern England (McShane 348). Similar acts occurred in the United States. Alison Gilbert Olson has commented about the methods employed by political satirists during the Federalist period: "They did this by parodying the officials' [*sic*] self-serving political speeches and pompous proclamation, by embellishing political gossip through fables, silly poems, mock ads, fake news items, and ridiculous stories about governors whose characters were easy to spot" (365). Through such tactics, individuals could challenge and even undercut government authority and hegemonic power.

Of course, the parody present in political broadsides was not merely reserved for proclamations that had been issued by the official government; these single-sheet missives also offered satirical accounts of other topics and texts. For instance, because of their massive popularity, well-known songs and poems were commonly parodied on broadsides for comedic and political purposes. Eric Nebeker has discussed the parody-fueled verse war that erupted between Thomas Camel and Thomas Churchyard in the mid-sixteenth century. The exchanges moved "through a number of rhetorical registers, from serious discussion of appropriate public speech to almost childish insult and mockery" (Nebeker 1). They also eventually expanded to include contributions from outsiders.

Titles like *Goodnight Bush* and *Dr. Paul* function in an analogous way. These narratives take their participation in parody as seriously as their concern with sociopolitical issues. In fact, akin to the political broadsides that mocked official proclamations, these two elements are inextricably linked: much of the political commentary offered in these books arises from their parodic features. Christopher Ouellette's *Dr. Paul* forms a poignant example. The book mimics the story of *Green Eggs and Ham* but reconfigures it as a means to persuade readers to support Ron Paul for president. Thus, Dr. Seuss's original refrain, "I do not like green eggs and ham," is reimagined as "I do not like that Dr. Paul."

Likewise, rather than holding up a tray containing green eggs and ham, he is holding up one that has copies of some of Paul's most well-known books: *End the Fed* (2009), *Liberty Defined* (2012), and *The Revolution* (2008).

Goodnight Bush (2008) makes similar use of parody, though it offers a far different political message. Mirroring the cadence of Margaret Wise Brown's classic bedtime story, the text begins: "In the situation room / There was a toy world / And a flight costume." The illustration that accompanies these lines greatly adds to their political poignancy (fig. 12). Every single item depicted has a powerfully satiric meaning. George W. Bush takes the place of the bunny sitting up in bed. He is wearing not striped pajamas as in the original picture book, but the aforementioned flight suit that is suggestive both of his much-questioned service in the Texas Air National Guard and of his disastrous "Mission Accomplished" public relations stunt aboard the *USS Abraham Lincoln* in 2003. Likewise, the comb and brush on the side table have been replaced with a tray of cocaine, a nod to the president's infamous penchant for party-

Figure 12. Illustration from Erich Origen and Gan Golan's *Goodnight Bush*, a political parody of the classic bedtime story *Goodnight Moon*. The book was released on the eve of the 2008 presidential election.

ing when he was a young man. Meanwhile, the basket of wood that sits by the fireplace in the original now holds two ballot boxes marked "FLORIDA 2000," a nod to the hanging chad debacle that played a decisive role in George W. Bush winning the 2000 presidential election. Finally, but far from inconsequentially, the small mouse running along the floor has been replaced with a diminutive Osama bin Laden. In a seeming commentary on Bush's failure to capture the al-Qaeda leader, bin Laden is clearly visible but also completely unnoticed by the president.

Once again, the presence of such politically charged imagery provides a further link to broadsides. As the Library of Congress has said about the genre, it is "[r]ich in detail and variety, and sometimes with striking illustrations" ("Introduction," par. 3). Whereas some of the images that appeared on broadside ballads were stock and did not directly relate to the text on the page (Library of Congress, par. 6), those that were showcased on political broadsides were usually highly relevant. Akin to the illustrations in parody books like *Goodnight Bush*, these images greatly heightened the political poignancy of the text's message. One of the best-known political broadsides in the United States forms an excellent example: the infamous "Coffin Handbill." The document was created anonymously and circulated nationally during the 1828 presidential election cycle (fig. 13). The broadside relays several unflattering episodes in the life of candidate Andrew Jackson, including "a vivid account . . . of Jackson stabbing a man in the back with [a] sword-cane, and a poem about Jackson's cruel treatment of six unwitting army deserters" (Howell 294). While the broadside is predominantly comprised of text, it also contains several key images. The section discussing the incident with the sword-cane features an engraving that depicts Jackson performing the gruesome act ("Coffin Handbill"). To further illustrate Jackson's vicious character, the broadside includes an even more poignant series of illustrations: eighteen coffins are printed at various locations around the page, "representing white men killed by Jackson in his capacities as general, duelist, and aggrieved private citizen" (Howell 294). Though *Goodnight Bush* and *The Cat and the Mitt* are certainly modeled aesthetically after the original picture books that they parody, the way in which they ideologically and formally function draws on many key facets of the broadside genre.

Almost as prevalent as the strategic use of illustration, another common feature associated with political broadsides was their highly partisan nature. Whether authored by an individual person or issued on behalf of a group, these documents contained a viewpoint that was unmistakable. One broadside

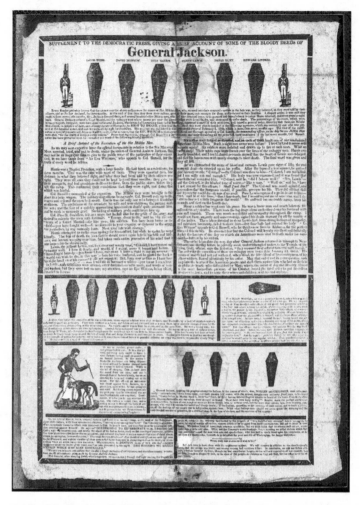

Figure 13. The "Coffin Handbill" (1828), which was created anonymously and circulated during the 1828 presidential election. Wikimedia Commons.

housed in the collection of the American Antiquarian Society, for example, offers a clear message concerning the question of female suffrage: "Show Your Faith in the Women of Massachusetts, Vote Yes on the Amendment Enabling Women to Vote." Likewise, another broadside, titled "The Career of a Know-Nothing!", functions in a similar way. The document informs its audience in no uncertain terms about the dubious political history of a current candidate: "Samuel J. Randall, The Candidate of the Sympathizers with Secession, Was Originally A Whig, When That Party Was Powerful, But Deserted

It on Its Own Decline to Become a Leading Know-Nothing!" ("Career"). As Paula McDowell has noted, given the exceedingly biased perspective of most political broadsides, historians, librarians, and museum curators found these materials too partisan to justify archiving them. Noted British antiquarian Joseph Ritson went even further. More than simply believing that the biased perspective contained in these documents rendered them unfit for archival collection, he felt that it also made them untrustworthy as a means of sociopolitical information. "In a remark that sounds somewhat disingenuous coming from one of the eighteenth century's most vituperative of critics, [Ritson] state[d], 'all of them are too strong tinctured with the venom of party, to retain the least appearance of merit'" (qtd in McDowell 172).

Political parodies of popular picture books are just as unapologetically partisan. These narratives do not offer a satirical view of the American political landscape writ large; rather, they lampoon a particular faction of it from a particular partisan perspective. *The Cat and the Mitt*, for example, offers a less-than-flattering assessment of the current state of the US economy near the end of Barack Obama's first term. During the course of the narrative, it presents the forty-fourth president of the United States as Dr. Seuss's cavalier cat and the Republican presidential candidate Mitt Romney as the sensible goldfish who is alarmed by his reckless behavior. When the caricature of President Obama first appears in the text, for example, he announces: "I know you are poor / And the outlook's not sunny, / But we can have fun / With other people's money!" (7). On the following page, Cat Obama explains his plan: "We can bail out the banks. / I'll find the money with ease. / We can borrow it all / From my friends the Chinese!" (8). In a detail that furthers Obama's allegiance with China while simultaneously reflecting conservative accusations that he is secretly a socialist or even a communist, the hat that his avatar in the book is wearing is a Russian ushanka, or winter hat (fig. 14). It is adorned with two prominent symbols of the communist party: the red star and the hammer and sickle.

As *The Cat and the Mitt* progresses, its partisan portrayal of Cat Obama becomes not simply acerbic, but absurd. The "DemoCat" offers the following summary of his environmental policy: "We'll stop global warming / By killing the jobs / Of working class people. / (Besides, they're all greedy slobs!)" (45). When Cat Obama's sidekicks Dem One and Dem Two—who bear a strong resemblance to Democratic congressional leaders Nancy Pelosi and Harry Reid—arrive, they behave in ways that are even more preposterous. One of the first acts by these politically charged variations on Dr. Seuss's Thing One and Thing Two is to deface the Constitution: "Those Dems got to work; / And they

Figure 14. The figure on the left is Barack Obama. He is holding a teleprompter in one hand and—in a detail that echoes conservative beliefs that he is secretly a socialist or even a communist—a Russian ushanka in the other hand. Illustration from Dr. Truth's *The Cat and the Mitt*.

got to work quick. / Tore up the Constitution / And then gave it a kick!" (42). In lines that epitomize *The Cat and the Mitt*'s viewpoint about the Democratic Party as a whole, the narrator reports about the duo: "They undermined the freedom / On which our republic depends. / And took tax payer's [sic] money / To spend on their friends" (42).

Don't Let the Republican Drive the Bus! is written from the opposite side of the political aisle but offers an equally partisan perspective. In a detail that provides a telling index of the book's overall portrayal of the GOP, the pigeon protagonist from Mo Willems's original picture book is reimagined by Erich Origen and Gan Golan as a Republican vulture. The bird's desire to drive the bus—which, for Willems's pigeon, is a literal wish—is a thinly disguised metaphor in the parody book for his desire to be at the helm of government and steer the nation's social, economic, and political policies. Throughout *Don't Let the Republican Drive the Bus!*, the avian avatar is presented not simply as obnoxious and entitled, but racist, classist, ageist, and homophobic. In one of the opening passages of the book, for example, the vulture matter-of-factly says about himself: "True, I only like a few kinds of people. But that's all we need in this great country of ours—*right!?*" Lest the racially charged meaning of this remark remains unclear, the vulture explains on the following page: "I mean, they call it the White House for a reason."

In a multi-panel series that appears near the middle of the text, the Republican vulture articulates his philosophy about driving/governing: "Run over the little guy! And unions! And gay unions! Teachers! Firefighters! Veterans! Women. . . ." On the following page, he continues in an equally crass, crude, and uncaring manner: "Oops! Old man under the wheel! No more social security for you! Probably had a victim mentality. Take responsibility for me running you over!" A few pages afterward, realizing that he is not going to receive permission to drive the bus, Origen and Golan's protagonist asks for a compromise position: "Okay, can I at least change the bus route?" In side-by-side pages, readers can compare and contrast the bus's previous route with the one that the Republican vulture declares is "Much better." The modifications draw heavily on liberal stereotypes that political conservatives are wealthy, white gun-lovers who dislike minorities almost as much as they dislike art, the poor, and government entitlement programs (fig. 15). The vulture has changed the bus's former stop at the "Public Park" to one at a "Private Club." Likewise, he has eliminated the previous pick-up point at the "Local Bank" to an "Offshore Bank." Meanwhile, the destination of the "Art Gallery" has been exchanged for a "Shooting Gallery," the "Retirement Home" has been replaced with the "Debtor's Prison," and the "Wishing Well" has been abandoned in favor of a stop at the "Bigot Spigot."

One rhetorical feature that greatly enhanced the partisan nature of political broadsides was their tendency toward hyperbolic language presented in equally dramatic ways. Exclamation points, large fonts, heavy typeface, and use of all capitals were commonplace. One broadside dating from the period of the American Revolution, for example, screamed, "WAR! WAR! WAR!" (qtd. Cunningham 73). Another emphatically warned the American people: "Look before you leap!" Others sought to catch the attention of its readers by imploring: "Electors of New York!," "Fellow Citizens!," "Friends of the People!" (qtd. in Cunningham 73).

In the same way that political broadsides used dramatic fonts, typefaces, and marks of punctuation, they presented their viewpoints in the most

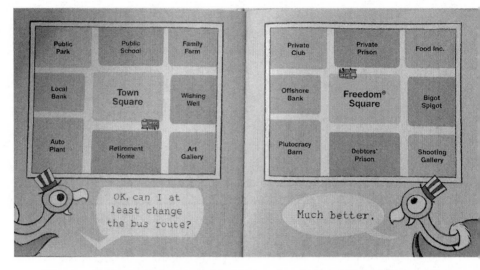

Figure 15. A before and after view of the changes that the Republican bird has made to the stops along the bus route, as shown on the recto and verso sides of the double-page spread. Illustration from Erich Origen and Gan Golan's *Don't Let the Republican Drive the Bus!*

animated, absolutist, and even apocalyptic ways. A broadside distributed in New York in 1799, for example, reminded its readers "how much you have to fear from an insidious federal representation" (qtd. in Cunningham 73). As a result, it advised them "be firm—be vigilant—be enterprising:—Maintain the ground you have hitherto acquired" (qtd. in Cunningham 73). The consequences of failing to do so were dire. As the broadside flatly stated: "The existence of our Constitution and our Liberties are at stake—By our fortitude and unanimity at this crisis, the Rights and Freedom of our Country may be secured forever" (Cunningham 73; caps in original). In this and countless other examples, "broadsides allowed for ample expression of emotion or opinion" (Bumgardner).

These features are equally endemic to political parodies of picture books. This observation holds true despite the fact that several of the original narratives on which these books are based contain strong emotions. The title character in Mo Willems's *Don't Let the Pigeon Drive the Bus!* throws what amounts to a massive temper tantrum by the end of the book. "LET ME DRIVE THE BUS!!," he screams while flailing around on the page. The unnamed character in Dr. Seuss's *Green Eggs and Ham* grows emphatic about his refusal to taste the titular dish, shaking his fist at one point and asserting:

"I would not, could not, in a tree. / Not in a car! You let me be!" (30–31). Both the mischievous Cat and the rule-abiding goldfish in *The Cat in the Hat* become agitated and emotional. In fact, the alarmed goldfish raises his voice at the Cat's plan for mayhem at one point: "Do I like this? / Oh, no! I do not. / This is not a good game,' / Said our fish as he lit. / 'No I do not like it, / Not one little bit!'" (22). The illustration that accompanies these lines conveys his distress. The drawing shows the alarmed fish nearly being thrown out of a teapot when it comes crashing down onto the table. His facial expression is equal parts worry and alarm.

Even with such elements in the originals, the type of emotion, degree to which it is expressed, and severity of language used to convey those feelings are all greatly enhanced in the political parodies. In *The Cat and the Mitt*, for example, the fish's rebukes are far more strident. While his counterpart in the original text may get alarmed by the Cat's antics, he never gets openly angry with him. By contrast, this emotion is not only felt but openly named in the political-themed parody. In a passage that forms the counterpart to the goldfish's admonishment of the Cat quoted above, the narrator notes: "And boy, Mitt was angry! / His collar was hot! / He said, 'Do I like this? / Oh, no! I do not!'" (27). The addition of the two opening lines—stating the fish's anger and then underscoring it further with the idiom that he was hot under the collar—amplifies the severity of emotion.

This same observation applies to *Dr. Paul*. The retelling replaces several of the interrogatory and declarative passages from the original with ones that are now imperatives.[9] For example, in the picture book by Dr. Seuss, Sam-I-am inquires about green eggs and ham: "Would you like them / in a house? / Would you like them / with a mouse?" (19). Meanwhile, in the parody by Christopher Ouellette, the second question has been transformed into an exclamatory statement: "Would you like him / In the White House? / He'd move in / With his original spouse!" Likewise, a few pages later, "I will not eat them here or there. / I will not eat them anywhere. / I do not like green eggs and ham. / I do not like them, Sam-I-am" (34). In Ouellette's political parody, these lines have been reimagined as an even more adamant refusal: "We need our army here and there. / We need to show the world we care. / Vote for Ron? / I do not dare!"[10]

Finally, and perhaps most persuasively, such replacements appear throughout *Don't Let the Republican Drive the Bus!* While Mo Willems's original text contains several passages in which the titular pigeon pleads, implores, and pesters the reader about being permitted on the bus, his Republican counterpart in Origen and Golan's parody goes much further. This process begins even before the text officially commences, with their rendering of the dedication page. In Mo Willems's original, the pigeon peeks his head onto the edge of the page, but says nothing. By contrast, in the parody, the Republican bird has not only intruded much further into the text—his shoulders are clearly visible—but he is also uttering an epithet. In a speech bubble that appears above his head, the Republican dismissively calls Uncle Sam, who appears on the facing page, "Socialist." This modification is indicative of many others that appear throughout the text. In Mo Willems's original picture book, the first page presents the pigeon saying about the bus driver: "I never thought he'd leave." Meanwhile, in the politically charged parody, the Republican vulture offers the far more blunt statement: "I hate public transit. Then again, I hate anything with the word 'public' in it." Even the scene where the vulture erupts in a temper tantrum after his repeated requests to drive the bus have been denied are more dramatic and hyperbolic. Whereas the pigeon flaps his wings, rolls on the floor, and jumps up and down in Willems's original picture book, the vulture foams at the mouth, throws money, and goes on a shooting spree with an assault rifle in Origen and Golan's retelling (fig. 16).

The kinship between broadsides and parodies extends to extratextual issues, such as the question of legal permission and copyright. Linda Hutcheon, in *A Theory of Parody*, discusses how these works are commonly seen as

Figure 16. The central character is furious that he has not been permitted to drive the bus. Illustration from Erich Origen and Gan Golan's *Don't Let the Republican Drive the Bus!*

threatening cultural understandings of creative ownership and even legal defi-
nitions of intellectual property (xiv). By offering an imitation or variation on
a copyrighted narrative, parodic texts raise an array of complicated questions
regarding the meaning as well as limits of "fair use." As Hutcheon explains, an
array of protracted legal battles have erupted in which arguments about fair
use have failed to spare parodists from rulings that they violated copyright
protections (xv). The outcome of such cases has made parodies a risky enter-
prise: for authors, for publishers, and even for booksellers.

   The political parodies of popular picture books are acutely mindful of this
phenomenon. The front cover to Erich Origen and Gan Golan's *Goodnight
Bush* includes the disclaimer: "an unauthorized parody." The back cover to
their *Don't Let the Republican Drive the Bus!* contains an even stronger quali-
fier: "This book is a parody and has not been prepared, approved, or authorized by the creators of *Don't Let the Pigeon Drive the Bus!* or their heirs or
representatives." *The Cat and the Mitt* offers a similar statement on its copyright page: "This book is a work of parody that humorously represents numerous public figures past and present. It is not authorized by, endorsed by or
affiliated with Mitt Romney or Romney for President, Inc. It is not authorized
by, endorsed by or affiliated with Theodor Geisel, his heirs or Dr. Seuss En-
terprises." Finally, Christopher Ouellette likewise seeks to curb any potential
legal liability. The title page to *Dr. Paul* displays the clear proviso "with Apol-
ogies to Dr. Seuss." Meanwhile, the closing credits reiterate this remark, asserting, "There is no association between this work and any work by Dr. Seuss.
This is presented for entertainment purposes only, and under fair parody laws
[*sic*]." Oulette also disavows any official connection to Ron Paul; the very next
statement to appear in the closing credits to *Dr. Paul* says, "This is not associated with any campaign."

   Similar legal concerns have been historically associated with broadsides. In
1557, in the United Kingdom, the Company of Stationers was established by
royal charter. The agency had one simple goal, according to the *Continuum
Encyclopedia of Popular Music of the World*: "to restrict all printing and publishing to its members. The titles of all books, plays and broadsides published by
members of the Company had to be registered with it, and the Company's
agents were authorized to search for, and if necessary destroy, illegal printing
presses." Even in the face of such threats, merely a small fraction of these items
were ever actually recorded. Instead, this law—along with many subsequent
ones regarding printer's licensure and authorial copyright that were passed
during the sixteenth, seventeenth, and eighteenth centuries—"were often, and

increasingly, evaded. In 1660, for example, of 160 ballad titles on the subject of the Restoration none appeared in the Stationers' Register" (McShane 346). The stakes for omission were even higher when the content of the broadside was politically charged criticism of the government. Akin to the consequences experienced by modern-day parodists, these individuals faced lawsuits, the confiscation of their property, and even jail time.

Once again, this trait is reflected in political parodies of popular picture books. While some, such as *Dr. Paul* and *Goodnight Bush*, feature the actual names of their authors, others are released under a pseudonym. *The Cat and the Mitt*, for example, is listed on the cover as the work of the suggestively named "Dr. Truth"; the title page announces that the narrative has been merely "Related by Loren Spivack."

Whether they were attributed to an actual person or merely a fictitious pseudonym, political broadsides served an important social role and exerted demonstrable cultural influence. "By bringing people together into public spaces to share information or entertainment," McShane documents, "broadside literature provoked public debate and at the same time created a truly public record that could be stored and revisited" (341). These documents embodied platforms for the maintenance of socio-political hegemony and for efforts to overthrow it. For this reason, Noble E. Cunningham has remarked about their presence in the United States, "How many votes were won or lost by the appeals or the attacks of campaign handbills no one would venture to decide; but their widespread use suggests that they were considered by contemporary contestants as effective weapons in political campaigns" (73).

The same remarks could be made about political parodies. These books do not merely seek to provide a passing moment of amusement; rather, they encourage sociopolitical change. All of them present their readers with a particular ideological point of view and then urge these individuals to act on such beliefs at the voting booth. Throughout *The Cat and the Mitt*, for example, Mitt Romney's aquatic avatar is presented as the sensible voice of reason who is rightly alarmed by Cat Obama's unwise and even irresponsible ideas. After the "DemoCat" suggests borrowing money from the Chinese, for instance, the piscine presidential candidate scolds:

> Then Mitt said, "No! No!
> Make that fool go away!
> Tell that Democrat Cat

That your grandkids will pay
For his profligate spending,
His lust for power and pelf.
He's not helping you.
He only cares for himself!" (11)

Of course, the endpoint for these comments is not simply ideological persuasion, but political action. Echoing the open-ended finale to Dr. Seuss's *The Cat in the Hat*, the parody version concludes on the eve of Election Day:

So America waited
On that cold, cold, wet day
To see what the voters
Would do with their say.

Would they learn to love socialism?
Keep the cat and his crew?
Or would they strike back for freedom?
What would you do? (55)

The closing question, "What would you do?," is not a theoretical exercise. It is in an invitation—and even exhortation—for the reader to become personally involved. After having encountered the information presented by the text, they now need to translate these viewpoints into action.

Christopher Ouellette's *Dr. Paul* is even more explicit in its desire to convince readers of the wisdom of its political message and then inspire them to take personal action in response. The book seeks to persuade its audience that Ron Paul as the paramount choice for president. Akin to the unnamed central character who initially dislikes or, at least, is disinterested in "That Dr. Paul," Ouellette believes that even his most resistant reader will embrace Paul's candidacy after learning about his positions. In language that is clearly meant to mirror the reaction of his audience, his unnamed new convert asserts after reading Ron Paul's *Liberty Defined*, *End the Fed*, and *The Revolution*: "Say! / I like the ideas of Dr. Paul. / I do! I like them, I like them all!" (59). This experience has not only inspired him to be a supporter of Ron Paul; it has also ignited his desire to participate in the American political process: "And it would be good to have less [fiscal] bloat! / And it would be good to cast our vote . . ." (59). Ouellette's newly convinced supporter of Ron Paul goes on to utter remarks that read more like a voter pledge than the finale to a story book:

So I will check off his box.

And I won't be swayed by CNN or FOX.

And he WILL go to the White House.

And He [sic] will go there with his spouse.

And sow the seed of liberty . . .

Here and there.

Say!

Liberty will grow everyWHERE! (61; caps in original)

Of all the political parodies, *Don't Let the Republican Drive the Bus!* is by far the most direct in its call for political engagement. In the closing pages, Uncle Sam, the bus driver, returns. Taking charge of the now badly damaged vehicle that is clearly labeled "USA," he tells readers: "C'mon people—you deserve better than this. But you have to demand it." Lest readers are uncertain how to enact such change, Uncle Sam adds in a speech bubble that appears directly below these comments: "And remember to vote!" In a final reiteration of the efficacy of political engagement and personal action, the Republican vulture appears on the facing page, looking forlorn and commenting "The more people who vote, the less likely I'll win." *Don't Let the Republican Drive the Bus!* includes an afterword by Origen and Golan that contains additional information about the history of the Republican party, along with the GOP's current stance on various social, political, and economic issues. The discussion concludes with the following emphatic exhortation: "Ideologies get passed down from one vulture to the next via regurgitation. We hope this book helps inoculate you against this strain of bird flu. In the meantime, if you don't want to get thrown under it, then please . . . DON'T LET THE REPUBLICAN DRIVE THE BUS!"

Historian William Huntting Howell, in an essay that appeared in 2010, proposed two maxims about the American political landscape in the new millennium: "First: All politics is literary. . . . Second: All literature is politics" (293). Government leaders routinely employ various narrative devices—metaphor, symbolism, irony, etc.—when they articulate their positions. Likewise, language is inherently political: what is said, as well as how it is phrased, is informed by ideology and generates it.

Political parodies of picture books give a new significance or, at least, added dimension to this phenomenon. These narratives make visible the inherently political nature of all forms of literature, along with the highly literary nature of political discourse in the United States. Titles such as *Goodnight Bush* and

The Cat and the Mitt present high-profile government leaders like George W. Bush, Dick Cheney, Mitt Romney, and Barack Obama as characters in a literal sense. Whether cast as protagonists or antagonists, these men are key participants in a plot. Given that the parodic personifications of these civic figures are modeled on some of the best-known figures from children's literature, the texts invite readers to revisit the original children's books for possible evidence of political latency. Either consciously or unconsciously, narratives like *Goodnight Bush* and *The Cat and the Mitt* shape popular perceptions about these beloved childhood stories, giving them a new form of political significance. They raise the question of whether, after encountering the parodic version of Cat Obama, readers are able to view Dr. Seuss's original character in the same way again, free from partisan associations. They present the possibility that, while reading Margaret Wise Brown's story featuring the "old lady whispering hush" to their children, parents may be reminded of Dick Cheney sitting in a rocking chair with his xylophone of the terror index. If so, then titles like *Goodnight Bush* and *The Cat and the Mitt* become not simply parodies of their source material, but—in keeping with the nature of parody—palimpsests of them.

Even if adult readers are able to keep the parodic texts separate, they signal another significant socio-literary event. None of the original picture books on which these narratives are based engage with political issues. Nevertheless, the adult-audience parodies demonstrate how they may still be used for political purposes. These texts present a compelling variation on the now-hoary debate concerning the relationship of children's literature and politics. Rather than contemplating the role that sociopolitical issues ought to play in narratives for young readers, works like *Don't Let the Republican Drive the Bus!* and *Dr. Paul* demonstrate the relationship that politics may choose to have with children's literature, be it with or, as in the case of these unauthorized parodies, without its consent. Even when books for young readers avoid commenting on political issues, these texts can be conscripted by these concerns and then re-scripted as a means to discuss them with adult audiences.

The connection between politics and children's literature has long been framed as unidirectional, with books for young readers cast as moving into the realm of sociopolitical issues. Parodies like *The Cat and the Mitt* and *Goodnight Bush* reveal that this relationship is actually reciprocal. For decades now, various genres of children's literature have given voice to political subjects; these adult-audience parodies reveal that political subjects, in turn, may embrace children's literature as an effective rhetorical device for their viewpoints.

Goodnight Bush (But Hello Voters): A New Literary Medium becomes a New Cultural Megaphone

Since the publication of Alvin Toffler's *Future Shock* in 1970, it has become commonplace for cultural critics to discuss the problem of "information over-load" in the United States. Every day, individuals are bombarded with an onslaught of information via newspapers, television, magazines, and the internet. A significant portion of this information concerns national politics. As Luis Villa has commented, "we've probably never been so deluged by political information as we are now" (par. 2). From newspapers, magazines, and cable shows to radio programs, blogs, and twitter feeds, individuals in the United States encounter "political commentary from everyone you know (and everyone you don't)" (Villa, par. 3).

With their novelty appeal, humorous tone, and familiar format, texts like *Goodnight Bush* and *The Cat and the Mitt* are able to break through the information overload that typifies the millennium-era American political landscape and get their messages heard. To be sure, these narratives have enjoyed brisk sales, sparked public debate, and energized voter bases—on both sides of the political aisle. *Goodnight Bush*, for instance, was a phenomenal success, appearing on the *New York Times* Best Sellers list a total of ten times during the summer and fall of 2008.[11] Articles and opinion pieces about the book appeared in venues ranging from *Newsweek*, the *Huffington Post*, and the *Village Voice* to *NPR*, *Daily Kos*, and *Politico*. Origen and Golan's follow-up book, *Don't Let the Republican Drive the Bus!*, likewise received a bevy of print, internet, and radio coverage. The two parody books that emanate from the opposite sides of the political aisle have enjoyed an equally impressive cultural impact. Spivack peddled *The Cat and the Mitt* at the Republican National Convention in 2016, earning positive publicity and lucrative sales (de Valle, par. 17).[12] Meanwhile, Christopher Ouellette's *Dr. Paul* may not boast as large a readership. The YouTube-based e-book has received a formidable, but not massive, number of viewings, tallying just over 32,000 to date. But its impact can be measured in other ways. The video has received positive reviews on popular right-leaning political blogs such as *The Daily Paul*. In addition, it has been a featured link on web pages like *YouTube Idol* and *Live Burst*. On the latter site alone, which touts itself as reposting "Funny, Interesting, Addictive Videos," *Dr. Paul* has been viewed an additional 10,000 times.

The public popularity of these political parodies make a compelling case for the important role that print culture can play in participatory democracy during the twenty-first century. Over the past decade, social media has been credited with ushering in a new era of grassroots political protest. In *Why It's Kicking Off Everywhere: The New Global Revolutions*, journalist Paul Mason discusses how, beginning with the uprisings in Greece in 2008, continuing through the events that collectively became known as the Arab Spring, and reaching its apogee in many ways with the Occupy Wall Street movement, nations around the globe witnessed "a revolution planned on Facebook, organized on Twitter and broadcast to the world via YouTube" (14). However, *Goodnight Bush, Dr. Paul, Don't Let the Republican Drive the Bus!*, and *The Cat and the Mitt* demonstrate that adult-audience political parodies of classic children's books—be it in the format of a physical book or an electronic narrative—continues to embody a central feature of the public's access to, information about, and engagement with the sociopolitical process in the United States, just as it did during the heyday of the political broadside. As Amy Reynolds and Gary R. Hicks remind us, "A participatory conception understands democracy as a system in which ordinary people have meaningful ways to participate in the formulation of public policy, not just in the selection of elites to rule them" (4). These parodies provide a means by which individuals may do so. With their nonthreatening picture book formats and already-familiar characters and color schemes, these texts seek to make engagement in current political debates as easy and accessible as "child's play."

Parody books like *Goodnight Bush* and *The Cat and the Mitt* attest to the ongoing efficacy of print culture during an era when the future of books is being called into question. As Robert Coover remarked in a 1992 article tellingly titled "The End of Books": "in the world of video transmission, cellular phones, fax machines, computer networks, and in particular out in the humming digitalized precincts of avant-garde computer hackers, cyberpunks and hyperspace freaks, you will often hear it said that the print medium is a doomed and outdated technology" (par. 1). Political parodies of picture books push back against this phenomenon. While several of these titles are available as electronic texts, their existence in either print or digital form affirms the ongoing cultural relevance of literary narratives in the twenty-first century along with the tremendous potential that they embody for political communication, public outreach, and grassroots organizing. Parodies like *Don't Let the Republican Drive the Bus* and *Dr. Paul* serve as a mouthpiece for public protest as well as a means for energizing the electorate. While none of these highly partisan narratives will likely change the minds of readers who do not already agree with their specific political viewpoint, they do invigorate them.

In so doing, this form of children's literature for adults emerges as an effective means to engage with political issues. Adult-audience parodies of classic children's books are able to capture the attention of the public in ways that other forms of politically themed communication are not during the opening decades of the twenty-first century. Erich Origen and Gan Golan's book may bid *Goodnight Bush* but it and the parodies like it are really saying "Hello voters."

The next chapter can be seen as a continuation of this one in many ways. Several of the focal texts for my discussion—including *Go the F**k to Sleep* (2011), *If You Give a Kid a Cookie, Will He Shut the F**k Up?* (2011), and *The Littlest Bitch* (2010)—are parodies of well-known books for young readers. But while these texts mimic popular bedtime stories, picture books, and illustrated narratives, the focus of their satire is very different. The adult-audience parodies profiled in this chapter lampoon aspects from the world of grown-ups: from dating and drinking to politics and hipster culture. By contrast, as their titles imply, books like *Go the F**k to Sleep*, *The Littlest Bitch*, and *If You Give a Kid a Cookie, Will He Shut the F**k Up?* take aim at children. The tone and subject matter of these texts suggest a new variation on this genre: children's literature for adults that is anti-children.

CHAPTER 6

Not Kidding Around

Go the F**k to Sleep and the New Adult Honesty about Parenthood

By the second decade of the twenty-first century, children's literature for adults was firmly established. The texts profiled in the previous chapters were accompanied by a bevy of additional titles, many of which had been released to positive critical reviews and strong commercial sales. Kathryn Petras and Ross Petras's *B is for Botox: An Alphabet Book for the Middle-Aged* (2009) and their follow-up text, *1, 2, Can't Reach My Shoe: A Counting Book for the Middle-Aged* (2010), delighted adult audiences with their humorous re-introduction to the rudimentary subjects of spelling and counting, respectively. Joel Rickett's *H is for Hummus: A Modern Parent's ABC* (2013) did the same for family life: in this book, A is for "Au Pair," B is for "Babyccino," C is for "Controlled Crying." Meanwhile, pop-up books for adults appeared with increasing frequency, becoming reader favorites. Most famous among these was Gary Greenberg and Matthew Reinhart's *The Pop-Up Book of Phobias* (1999), which made a variety of bestseller lists around the nation and inspired a sequel, *The Pop-Up Book of Nightmares* (2001). In 2015, the coloring book craze for adults arrived the United States. Titles such as Johanna Basford's *The Secret Garden: An Inky Treasure Hunt and Colouring Book* (2013), Lacy Mucklow's *Color Me Calm: 100 Coloring Templates for Meditation and Relaxation* (2014), and Marjorie Sarnat's *Cats Coloring Book* (2015) sold thousands of copies. Finally, the 2016 presidential election cycle and the subsequent inauguration of Donald J. Trump inspired G. Thomas Mandel's *T is for Trump: A Candidate's ABC Book* (2016) and Ann Telnaes's *Trump's ABC* (2018). Lest the intended readership for these alphabet texts was in question, the former contained entries such as "F" is for "the finger" and "V" is for "vulgar," while the latter text featured rhyming couplets such as the following: "G is for grabbing pussies with ease / H is for helping elect such a sleeze." As even this brief overview suggests, children's literature for adults had emerged as a full-fledged literary phenomenon. From picture books, counting texts, and pop-ups to ABC books, bedtime stories, and coloring books, the genre encompassed seemingly every conceivable type of narrative traditionally intended for young readers.

In spite of the wide range of schools, styles, and subjects represented by these texts, one element united them: a largely positive perception of childhood. Mabel Maney's Nancy Clue and Cherry Aimless narratives are popular with LGBTQ readers not only because of their campy nature, but also because they traffic in nostalgic memories that adults have about reading the original versions when they were young. Meanwhile, one of the primary reasons why the baby-to-be in Barbara Park's *MA! There's Nothing to Do Here!* is so eager to be born is that there are so many wonderful things to enjoy outside of his mother's womb. He is looking forward to his childhood with gleeful anticipation. Along those same lines, a large part of the parodic humor inherent in titles like *Goodnight Bush* and *Don't Let the Republican Drive the Bus!* arises from the discussion of serious political issues in the seemingly incongruous format of a picture book. In these and other examples, juvenile-styled books for adults traffic either explicitly or implicitly in views of childhood as a carefree and enjoyable time.

While adult memories of childhood might be happy and nostalgic, the experience of parenting actual children is often far different. Mothers and fathers feel profound love for their sons and daughters, but they also routinely feel frustrated, exhausted, and overwhelmed with them. For generations, expressing such sentiments publicly was taboo. By the second decade of the twenty-first century, however, this trend was beginning to change. Parents were being more open, honest, and candid about the experience of rearing children, including the aspects that were unpleasant.

A new subset of children's literature for adults provided a poignant cultural platform for these viewpoints. Appearing first in Kelly and David Sopp's board book *Safe Baby Handling Tips* (2005), expanding in Marcy Roznick's picture book parody *If You Give a Kid a Cookie, Will He Shut the F**k Up?* (2011), and then reaching full fruition in Adam Mansbach's bedtime story *Go the F**k to Sleep* (2011), they offered a new honesty about an aspect of adulthood that had previously gone unspoken—or even been silenced. The frustrations associated with parenting that are presented in these narratives make visible the simultaneously celebrated and criticized place that young people occupy in twenty-first-century American society as well as the powerfully mixed feelings that many adults have about children, especially their own. Parenthood has long been regarded as one of the major signposts of being an adult. The blunt honesty of *If you Give a Kid a Cookie* and *Go the F**k to Sleep* reveals how caring for children is so physically, emotionally, and logistically demanding that it engulfs and even eclipses their lives. Having children marks adulthood—and paradoxically just as quickly erases it.

Go the F**k and *If You Give a Kid a Cookie* demonstrate how having and caring for children swallowed up adulthood. However, in a detail that reflects the twisty, bendy, and even circular nature of the human lifespan by the opening decades of the twenty-first century, the inverse was also true. Another work of children's literature for adults that was released during this same period examined how childhood had been swallowed up by adulthood. The narrative was tellingly titled *The Littlest Bitch* (2010). Written by David Quinn and Michael Davis and illustrated by Devon Devereaux, it made a case that children were not simply growing up too fast—they were skipping childhood entirely.

Reading *The Littlest Bitch* in tandem with *Go the F**k to Sleep*, *If You Give a Kid a Cookie*, and *Safe Baby Handling Tips* makes visible the complex relationship between childhood and adulthood that emerged by the second decade of the twenty-first century. Much attention had been given to how adulthood had been radically altered by its growing embrace of aspects of childhood. The latter three titles reveal the equally powerful impact that raising children has on adult lives and identity. Meanwhile, as *The Littlest Bitch* demonstrates, childhood had been just as significantly transformed by its association with previously off-limits facets of adulthood. In many respects, it had been thoroughly—and, in many regards, distressingly—subsumed into it.

Even Moms and Dads Get the Blues: Challenging the Romanticization of Parenting

While being a parent can be a source of profound joy, it can also be one of equally profound misery. As any mother or father can attest, raising children is exhausting, stressful, and expensive. Many parents simply discover that being a mother or father isn't what they expected: they realize that they aren't very good with children or they don't actually like being around them all the time. Whatever the specific reason, Sonja Lyubomirsky notes that many mothers and fathers consider parenthood "a heavy burden" (83). While this situation is disheartening on its own, it is exacerbated by the fact that discussing it is taboo. In the words of Lyubomirsky, "to top off these unwelcome feelings, you feel like an aberration and misfit in a culture of fierce family nuclearity, afraid to voice your true feelings about parenting and risk being rebuffed by others" (84). As a result, many mothers and fathers do not admit their unhappiness about parenthood, sometimes even to themselves (Lyubomirsky 84).

In the opening years of the twenty-first century, a new crop of children's books for adults tackled this issue. These texts sought to give voice and visibility to the frustration, exasperation, and dissatisfaction that mothers and fathers often feel about parenthood, but have been unable to publicly discuss and maybe even to personally acknowledge. Kelly and David Sopp's board book, *Safe Baby Handling Tips*, can arguably be seen as inaugurating this trend. Released in 2005, the text offers an array of comedic childrearing do's and don'ts for new parents. As one panel informs novice moms and dads, the effective method for amusing baby is by playing peek-a-boo; the ineffective approach is by challenging the infant to a game of chess.[1] Likewise, another illustration informs first-time parents that the proper way to check if the baby's diaper needs changing is by peeking inside; the improper approach is by stuffing your hand down the back of it.

Such humorous examples of clueless parenting practices are coupled with others that seem to emanate not from ignorance, but from frustration. For example, one early page presents the correct way to feed a baby—by giving the infant a nice, fresh bottle—and the incorrect method: by shoving an oversized turkey leg in their mouth. Similarly, another page presents the do's and don'ts for corralling baby: yes, for placing the tot in a playpen, and no for locking him or her in a gerbil cage. Meanwhile, a subsequent illustration spotlights how to dry a baby. The proper method, readers learn, is by swaddling the infant in a soft towel, while the improper method is by tossing the baby in the clothes dryer. Many other pages contain similar suggestions that are meant to be seen as comedic because they are obviously inappropriate but also wholly understandable. The panel dedicated to washing baby indicates that a good method is by gently wiping with wet cloth and a bad method is by squirting with a garden hose. Likewise, the illustration explaining where to let the baby sleep informs new parents that the correct place is in a crib, and the incorrect one is stuffed inside a dresser drawer.

The widespread popularity and strong sales of *Safe Baby Handling Tips* inspired a sequel, *Safe Baby Pregnancy Tips* (2006). The basic premise of the book is the same, only it spotlights the time when the mother is still carrying the baby rather than after she has given birth. One pregnancy tip, for instance, endorses simple swimming as an acceptable means of getting exercise; meanwhile, it frowns upon acrobatic high diving for this purpose.[2] Another page offers appropriate and inappropriate methods for choosing your baby's name: do browse through the book *1000 Baby Names* for ideas; don't decide on an appellation after reading a list of "1000 War Criminals."

Most recently, Kelly and David Sopp have released *The New Parents' Fun Book* (2008). The text is designed as a "baby book" for parents to document all of the landmark moments of being new moms and dads. Many of the pages contain evidence of the exasperation that comes from being an exhausted and overwhelmed first-time parent. A "Fun Fill-in-the-Blank" exercise for Mom, for example, begins with the lines: "Last night I woke up _____ times! I totally deserve a _____!" (20). Meanwhile, the one for Dad commences with the exasperated sentence: "Man! If I have to _____ one more time I'll _____" (41). Other activities include a "Curse Word Puzzle" (12) and a chart to document all of the hobbies that Mom enjoyed when she "had a life of [her] own" before baby came along (4).[3]

Lisa Brown's board book *Baby, Make Me Breakfast* (2005) offers a different take on similar sentiments. Rather than lamenting all of the activities that parents have given up in the wake of having children, her adult-audience narrative humorously suggests that infants should help with a variety of daily tasks, such as the titular act of making breakfast for mom and dad. While the humor of the book arises from the sheer absurdity of this premise—an infant cooking eggs—its appeal can also be connected to parental annoyance with the large amounts of time, care, and attention that young children require. Viviana A. Zelizer, in *Pricing the Priceless Child: The Changing Social Value of Children*, discusses the shift during the second half of the nineteenth century from a national culture that held children in esteem on the basis of the paid as well as unpaid labor that they could perform to one that prized them for the joy that they brought to the household. As Zelizer notes, "The emergence of this economically 'worthless' but emotionally 'priceless' child has created an essential condition of contemporary childhood" (3). Much of the comedic effect of Brown's *Baby, Make Me Breakfast* arises from its suggestion that parents shift back to an earlier time when children were seen as valuable because they were domestically and economically useful, not because they were emotionally rewarding. The humor of Brown's book is rooted in the belief that such views are not simply antiquated but absurd: adults do not have a child so that the youngster can perform tasks like making breakfast for them. On the contrary, mothers and fathers have a baby knowing that they will be performing a vast array of tasks—cooking, cleaning, etc.—for their son or daughter.

The popularity of *Baby, Make Me Breakfast* prompted Brown to release an entire series of books along these lines: *Baby, Mix Me a Drink* (2005),[4] *Baby Do My Banking* (2006), *Baby Fix My Car* (2006), *Baby Get Me Some Lovin'* (2009), and *Baby Plan My Wedding* (2009). These texts used the same premise as the original title, but apply it to different settings, scenes, and situations. As the publisher's summary says about *Baby, Mix Me a Drink*: "Are you a parent? Are you thirsty? Too many of us allow our infant sons and daughters to lay about idly: napping, drinking milk, and sometimes 'turning over.' Why not put them to work?" ("Baby, Mix Me," par. 1). As before, such remarks are intended as satiric humor, but they encapsulate sentiments that have been experienced by countless tired, grumpy, and exhausted parents.

Marcy Roznick's *If You Give a Kid a Cookie, Will He Shut the F**k Up?* (2011) is even more candid about the frustrations that often accompany raising kids. Whereas previous narratives that discussed the difficulties of being a parent focused on newborns, babies, and toddlers, Roznick's text spotlights a boy who is elementary-school aged. The youngster featured in the picture book might be older, but he is behaving in ways that are typical for his developmental stage: namely, testing adult boundaries. The book is subtitled *A Parody for Adults*, and it lives up to this claim. Roznick's narrative reimagines Laura Numeroff's classic *If You Give a Mouse a Cookie* (1985) for exasperated parents. The opening two pages repeat the main title—"If you give a kid a cookie, / will he shut the fuck up?"—and they depict a haggard father sitting in a recliner and forlornly offering a cookie to his rambunctious son. The boy is playing a trumpet while wearing a snare drum around his waist and waving a lightsaber. Meanwhile, his younger sister sits off to one side, crying. She is surrounded by building blocks scattered across the floor, an overturned toy car, a raggedy-looking teddy bear, and a broken robot. On the side table next to the father is an open can of beer and neglected TV dinner. The man's exhaustion is visually apparent: his eyes are half-closed, his face has noticeable stubble, and one of his socks has drooped down to his ankle.

The father's attempt to quiet his son by giving him a cookie, however, backfires. On the following page, the narrator reveals: "Well, the sugar rush will make him crazy." The illustration that accompanies this statement shows the young boy running wildly around the room: his trumpet is flying off to one side, toys are strewn hither and thither in his wake, and his young sister is covering her head for protection.

From there, in keeping with the premise of the original story, the situation escalates. The father puts "on a TV show to calm him, but a purple dinosaur will tell him scissors are dangerous . . . / So he'll reach for a pair, and knock over your beer." In the illustration, the young boy stands on a living room side table to reach a pair of scissors on a high shelf. The table teeters precariously, upending not simply the father's beverage but also his TV dinner and the telephone. The ordeal doesn't end with this event, however. As the narrator relays: "The smell [of beer] will remind him of Uncle Billy, so he'll want to call. / Of course, the old drunk won't answer. / And your kid'll throw a tantrum until you drive over to roust your useless brother-in-law."

At this point, the father's predicament, which was already perilous, spirals wholly out of control. While driving to your brother-in-law's house, the text relays, "you'll pass a cockfight. / He'll want to stop and watch the birdies . . . / Then he'll rat you out for a lollipop, / When a police raid sends you into hiding." Arrested and thrown in jail, "You'll be bailed out by your wife, who will hand you divorce papers." On the way back home, the father crashes the car after taking his eyes off the road because—as the narrative says about the son—"he'll whine until you play a game." Once safely back home, the boy starts a fire by tying his sister's doll to a toilet plunger and lighting it with a match. The father manages to put out the fire. The combination of his heroism and the smoke "will remind you and your wife of the rock concert where he was conceived." Unfortunately, the child finds the ensuing amorous overtures between his parents upsetting. "He'll cry hysterically . . . / And chances are if you want him to shut the fuck up, / You'll have to give him a cookie"— causing the cycle to begin all over again.

In 2017, one more title joined this growing cadre: *Baby Don't Sh!t Your Pants*. Written by White Cedar and illustrated by Vivian Mineker, the text spotlights an important but often acutely frustrating aspect of parenting: toilet training. Mirroring the wishes of countless mothers and fathers, the publisher describes the plot of the book as "a poetic invocation for sanitary defecation where a toddler is implored by his parents to poo-poo in the porcelain." As those who have been through this experience know all too well, however, the toddler refuses, defecating seemingly everywhere and anywhere else but the desired place. *Baby Don't Sh!t Your Pants* documents this process, showing poop so ubiquitous that it rains from the sky and acquires magical qualities, assuming its own identity and personality. Far from mere fictional fantasy, the author includes the following anecdote about his inspiration for the book: "His muses include his two little mud-covered boys, who defecate in their pants, on the kitchen floor, on the carpet, in the bathtub, in the sink, in their sandbox, and in their father's hands, Amen." In so doing, Cedar's picture book depicts just how crappy (pun intended) the process of toilet training children can be. Echoing the theme of frustration that permeates previous books of this nature, the back cover asserts: "As parents, you love your children. It's a biological fact and you would do anything for them. But when it comes to some things,

eventually, enough is enough." Lest Cedar's picture book be seen as a potential comedic read for young children as well, the opening line of the blurb
from the publisher states flatly: "*Baby Don't Sh!t Your Pants* is a children's
book, but it's not for children. It's for their parents."

In these and other examples, this new type of juvenile-styled book for adult
readers challenges the longstanding romanticization and even idealization of
parenting. As titles such as *Safe Baby Handling Tips* and *Baby Don't Sh!t Your
Pants* demonstrate, far from being a fulfilling and even pleasurable role, raising a child is often exasperating. Mothers and fathers are expected to glean
personal satisfaction and even delight from raising their child. However, the
emotions that parents frequently experience could more truthfully be described as despair and even misery. Much of the frustration in *If You Give a
Kid a Cookie* arises from the fact that caring for children is more than merely
time-consuming, it is all-consuming. Instead of parents having children, it often feels like the children have them. The time, work, and responsibility associated with parenting are massive and, thus, exhausting. From feeding,
dressing, and bathing to disciplining, education, and socializing, the physical,
emotional, and logistical tasks involved with parenting seemingly never end.
As a result, for many mothers as well as fathers, having children does not simply transform adulthood, it devours it. The childhoods of their sons and
daughters engulf and even erase the adulthoods of mothers and fathers.

From Romance to Realism: Advocating for Honesty in *Go the F**k to Sleep*

Whereas the source of parental frustration in *Safe Baby Handling Tips* and *If
You Give a Kid a Cookie* arises from a series of circumstance-specific events,
the plight of the beleaguered parents in Adam Mansbach's *Go the F**k to Sleep*
(2011) is far more common: youngsters delaying bedtime. The book, which is
written and illustrated in the style of Nancy Tillman's *It's Time to Sleep, My
Love* (2008), is told from the perspective of a parent who is exasperated by repeated unsuccessful attempts to get a young child to go to sleep. In telling
this story, the text shatters lingering nineteenth-century conceptions of the
always-pleasant, cherubic child and more modern twenty-first century beliefs
in the endlessly patient, never frazzled, child-centered parent. The opening
lines of Mansbach's narrative read: "The cats nestle close to their kittens, / The
lambs have laid down with the sheep. / You're cozy and warm in your bed, my
dear. / Please go the fuck to sleep."[5] As the narrative progresses—and the child
continues to stall sleep—the adult voice grows increasingly annoyed: "All the

kids from day care are in dreamland. / The froggie has made his last leap. / Hell no, you can't go to the bathroom. / You know where you can go? The fuck to sleep." In time, the parent's frustration becomes directed not simply at the recalcitrant child, but at all of the material accoutrements of childhood. Mansbach writes: "The tiger reclines in the simmering jungle. / The sparrow has silenced her cheep. / Fuck your stuffed bear, I'm not getting you shit. / Close your eyes. Cut the crap. Sleep."

Even before *Go the F**k to Sleep* was published, the text sparked controversy for its frank portrayal of parental annoyance and even anger. Karen Spears Zacharias, in an article that appeared on CNN, called the text "Crass in concept and execution" (par. 1). Similar sentiments were echoed on blog posts, parenting websites, and discussion boards. One commentator on Amazon called *Go the F**k to Sleep* "The battle cry of a generation of young parents in their war against their kids" ("Customer Discussions"). Meanwhile, another poster was even more frank in their condemnation, writing the pithy prediction: "Child-hating parents cry out for Mansbach's sequel: 'Change Your Own F—ing Diapers, You Stinking Little S—t'" ("Customer Discussions").

Given the tragic frequency of child abuse, neglect, and mistreatment, such concerns are understandable. As Zacharias notes, Mansbach may have intended to be humorous, "But sadly, his book accurately portrays the hostile environment in which too many children grow up" (par. 17). She continues: "For far too many kids, the obscenities found in Mansbach's book are a common, everyday household language. Swearing is how parents across the social, educational, and economic strata express their disappointments or anxieties, their frustrations and outright anger at their children" (Zacharias, par. 18). For this reason, Zacharias goes on to assert: "The violent language of 'Go the F**k to Sleep' is not the least bit funny, when one considers how many neglected children fall asleep each night praying for a parent who'd care enough to hold them, nurture them and read to them" (par. 20).

Not all readers of *Go the F**k to Sleep*, however, view the book in such a disparaging light. Defenders of Mansbach's text offer an alternative explanation for its creation and appeal. Rather than condemning *Go the F**k to Sleep* as yet another disturbing example of the ill treatment of children in modern American culture, they make a case for the role that it plays in neutralizing and even nullifying such sentiments. Phrased in a different way, Mansbach's book is not designed for child-hating adults; rather, it is aimed at loving but exhausted parents as a cathartic way for them to vent some of the perfectly normal frustrations that come with child rearing. As the publisher of *Go the*

F**k to Sleep says about the text in its official publicity materials: "Profane, affectionate, and radically honest, it captures the familiar—and unspoken—tribulations of putting your little angel down for the night." At a time when child-centered parenting makes it even more taboo for mothers or fathers to express irritation towards their children, *Go the F**k to Sleep* reveals that such feelings are perfectly normal—even inevitable.

The full-color illustrations that permeate Mansbach's book, which were created by Ricardo Cortés, reflect this state. The images, which mimic the style of those created by Eric Metaxas in Nancy Tillman's *It's Time to Sleep, My Love*, do not follow the exploits of just one parent and just one child. Instead, each double-page spread spotlights a different child and thus the experiences of a different but equally exasperated parent. *Go the F**k to Sleep* demonstrates that while the specific way by which a child delays bedtime—asking for another drink of water, pleading for just one more story, etc.—may be different, this parenting experience is the same. Indeed, it is universal. Showing households big and small, black and white, affluent and modest, urban and rural, Mansbach and Cortés assert that mothers and fathers all over the world have dealt with this same problem—and felt these exact emotions. In this way, *Go the F**k to Sleep* gives voice and visibility to sentiments that parents privately think during these moments but do not publicly share.

The tremendous commercial success of *Go the F**k to Sleep* avers this claim. The initial idea for the text itself began as comedic comment that Mansbach posted on Facebook during one of his toddler-daughter's sleepless spells: "Look out for my forthcoming children's book, 'Go the — to Sleep'" (Harmanci, "Whim" par. 1). But, after receiving an array of positive comments and encouraging feedback from other exhausted parents, Mansbach decided to turn this fantasy project into reality. In early May 2011, more than a month before the book was scheduled for release, a pirated copy of the full, 32-page narrative began circulating around the internet. This seeming publishing blunder was actually a marketing boon. As Reyhan Harmanci commented, "While it's impossible to calculate the number of emailed documents shared, media outlets such as the *New Yorker* [began] to speculate that one of the biggest engines of its success has been booksellers and other industry folk circulating the 32-page PDF to the wider world" ("Go" par. 5). Within weeks of the pirated edition of *Go the F**k to Sleep* circulating the internet, Mansbach's book catapulted to "the #1 spot on Amazon's bestseller list" (Harmanci, "Go" par. 4). Then, once the book appeared in print, it shot to the top of the *New York Times* bestseller list. Clearly, the profanity-laced inner monologue of an exhausted, exasperated parent was one that held a tremendous attraction and appeal for many other adults.[6]

Giving further credence to this observation, the success of Mansbach's book inspired a popular audio version, narrated by critically acclaimed actor Samuel L. Jackson. Once again, recordings of the book quickly vent viral, boosting its popularity even more. *Go the F**k to Sleep* has also spawned two sequel texts thus far: *You Have to F**king Eat* (2014) and *F**k, Now There Are Two of You* (2019). Both books use the same format, premise, and narrative style, only they feature a difference source of parental frustration. As the title of the first book implies, *You Have to F**king Eat* spotlights the tendency of young people to be exceedingly fickle about food. One representative quatrain reads: "Your cute little tummy is rumbling / And pancakes are your favorite treat. / I'm kind of surprised you suddenly hate them. / That's bullshit. Stop lying and eat." Meanwhile, Mansbach's most recent text offers a candid take on what it's like to have a second child. "I have wonderful news for you, darling," the book begins. It continues with the author's trademark candor: "A little brother or sister is coming—what fun! / As for me, my life's pretty much fucked now. / Because two's a million more kids than one."

*Go the F**k to Sleep* may be the most vocal and visible example of parental frustration, but it is far from the only text to articulate such sentiments. The 2011 picture book participates in a long tradition of narratives that articulate the antipathy and feature the fantasies that mothers and fathers occasional have about their sons or daughters. As I discussed in my book *Bloody Murder: The Homicide Tradition in Children's Literature* (2013), some of the most famous and beloved fairy tales are filled with antagonism towards children. Tales such as "Cinderella," "Hansel and Gretel," and "Snow White" form poignant examples.

More than three decades ago, Adrienne Rich broke a longstanding silence surrounding such feelings in her landmark book *Of Woman Born: Motherhood as Experience and Institution* (1976). She quotes the following passage from a journal that she kept in 1960 when she was a young mother: "My children cause me the most exquisite suffering of which I have any experience. It is the suffering of ambivalence: the murderous alternation between bitter resentment and raw-edged nerves, and blissful gratification and tenderness" (21–22)

Mansbach's picture book echoes these sentiments. Even though the narrator is repeatedly telling a small child to "Go the fuck to sleep," such sentiments do not mean that he is not also a devoted and loving parent. Many of the passages begin with tender terms of endearment for the youngster. For instance, the fourth quatrain commences: "The wind whispers soft through the grass, hon." Meanwhile, even many of the lines that contain profanity-laced mandates are softened by loving asides, such as "Lie the fuck down, my darling, and sleep" and, a few pages later, "A hot crimson rage fills my heart, love." Finally, the book itself is lovingly dedicated to Vivien, the daughter whose bedtime-stalling antics inspired the text.

The numerous blog posts, book reviews, and online comments made by adults who have purchased or at least read *Go the F**k to Sleep* echo such assertions. One anonymous parent on Amazon encapsulated such viewpoints in a post bearing the apt title "Raw Honesty": "For those who have called this 'abusive' and 'disgusting' you are actually missing the whole point not to mention you are either not parents . . . or [are] liars. The point of this book, if you would have taken the time to read some of the statements made by the author, is to remind parents that we all go through the frustrations of parenting and the strain of getting our kids to cooperate" (par. 1).

The National Children's Book and Literacy Alliance (NCBLA), a non-profit organization that advocates on behalf youth literacy, libraries, and literature programs around the United States, has a section of their website devoted to the question "Why Do Kids Need Books?" The lengthy page provides more than a dozen reasons why literature is not simply important but essential to the intellectual, emotional, and psychological development of young people. Among the points the NCBLA makes include that "Books comfort us," "Books entertain and offer a great escape," Books are great companions," "Books provide the opportunity to share cultural experiences," and "Books help us to understand ourselves."

An analogous observation applies to titles like *Go the F**k to Sleep*. In the same way that kids need books to share cultural experiences, help them understand themselves, and allow them to learn about other lives and ways of being, grown-ups enjoy books like *Safe Baby Handling Tips* and *If You Give a Kid a Cookie, Will He Shut the F**k Up?* A well-known adage reminds us that simply denying the existence of evil does not mean that it goes away. Likewise, denying upsetting thoughts and emotions—whether about one's own children or other issues—and pretending that they do not exist does not make them disappear. On the contrary, such suppression can cause them to fester and grow, perhaps erupting to the surface when the individual least expects it. However, if these feelings can be given a safe outlet, they can be defused. The frequent frustration as well as occasional resentment that adults experience towards children is an unpleasant and unflattering but nonetheless real facet of life. As a result, for the way in which they give voice and visibility to this shared experience, books like *Go the F**k to Sleep* and *Safe Baby Handling Tips* embody the most iconoclastic form of children's literature for adults but one that is also, ultimately, the most important. Parents are able to see that they are not alone. Even though they may experience moments of annoyance towards their children, such feelings do not mean that they are bad parents or even bad people. On the contrary, it just means that they are human.

In an article about *Go the F**k to Sleep* that appeared on the website for CNN, journalist Karen Spears Zacharias asserted: "Nobody is suggesting that there's a connection between Adam Mansbach's book and child abuse or child neglect" (par. 6). In many ways, in fact, the opposite might be true. Texts like *Go the F**k to Sleep* and *Safe Baby Handling Tips* do not encourage the mistreatment of children. On the contrary, the cathartic emotional release that these books provide beleaguered, on-the-edge caretakers may help to prevent it. There has been a great deal of discussion in recent years about the importance of adults being more open and honest with children. Books like *Go the F**k to Sleep* and *If You Give a Kid a Cookie* reveal the presence of a parallel phenomenon: the need for parents to be more open and honest with themselves and with each other about the difficulties, disappointments, and frustrations of raising children.

Children Taking Over Adulthood, Adulthood Overtaking Childhood: *The Littlest Bitch* and the Return of the Little Adult

While *Go the F**k to Sleep* and *If You Give a Kid a Cookie* offered a candid portrayal of the way that the childhoods being experienced by sons and daughters engulfs the adulthoods of many parents, this scenario was not the end of the story. A book tellingly titled *The Littlest Bitch* revealed how the reverse was also true: young children were also preociously moving into the realm of adulthood. The illustrated narrative featured a protagonist who is physically a young child, although few would describe her psychologically in this way. The preadolescent main character looks, acts, and thinks more like a jaded middle-aged woman. *The Littlest Bitch* reveals how, at the same time, adulthood was overtaking childhood.

Young people have commonly yearned to be more grown up. After all, the older you are, the more freedoms you generally enjoy. Unlike children, adults can stay up as late as they want, eat whatever they wish, and do whatever they feel like for as long as they desire.

While young people have routinely longed to grow up faster so that they could be free from the restrictions placed on children, this phenomenon assumed a new form in the closing decades of the twentieth century. Kids were not merely imaginatively wishing that they were older, they were literally growing up faster than in previous generations. The duration of youth was rapidly shrinking. In areas such as their taste in music, their interest in activities, and especially their choice in clothing, elementary-aged boys and especially girls were adopting the actions, attitudes, and accouterments commonly associated with adolescence—and even adulthood. For example, as Jan Hoffman reported, the Nancy Drew mystery novels were "Originally intended for girls ages 13 to 16" but "the books are now read by elementary school-age girls" (par. 27). Likewise, when Barbie dolls first appeared on the market in 1959, girls as old as twelve routinely played with them (Goldman). As Abigail Goldman has discussed, however, "as 12-year-olds grew more sophisticated, the dolls quickly moved down the age range, settling to today's target Barbie audience of 3- to 5-year-olds" (par. 8). This trend is not limited to these two isolated items. It applies to a myriad of children's material goods. In the field of advertising, this phenomenon has become such an essential consideration that it received its own acronym: "what marketers refer to as KGOY—Kids Getting Older Younger" (Orenstein, par. 3). Commonly seen as providing an "explanation for why 3-year-olds now play with toys that were initially intended for middle-schoolers" (Orenstein, par. 3), it also encompasses instances when they become consumers of products that are designed for individuals who are far older. Susan Linn, for example, noted that one of the fastest-growing demographics of customers for thong-style underwear are pre-adolescent girls (211). Changes of this nature prompted Neil Postman to argue that the late twentieth century and opening decade of the new millennium marked the "disappearance of childhood."

The Littlest Bitch offers a poignant portrayal of this phenomenon. The text is visually modeled after the popular children's picture book *Pinkalicious* (2006) by Victoria Kann and Elizabeth Kann. The cover contains the same pink color palette. In addition, the eponymous character is wearing a frilly dress and—akin to Pinkalicious—a bejeweled crown. The similarities between the two books, though, end there. As the title of *The Littlest Bitch* indicates, the protagonist to Quinn and Davis's narrative is not a sweet little girl like Pinkalicious. She is an abhorrent and even detestable individual. The source of much of her odiousness arises from the fact that she possesses the actions, attitudes, and accoutrements of adulthood.

The summary of *The Littlest Bitch* provided by the publisher describes the protagonist in the following way: "Little Isabel is not quite what she seems—

think of a ruthless CEO trapped in a five-year-old's body." This description is far from hyperbole. On one of the opening pages, the title character's mother asserts: "Yes, Isabel is a very, very grown-up girl." Although this figure is only five years old, she seems more like fifty. Both the gifts that she receives at her birthday party and her reaction to them offer a telling snapshot. "Black crocodile briefcase. Check. Cell phone. Check. Mummy, I'm not seeing my Black-Berry," she details. While many children desire electronic gadgets intended for individuals who are older, the remark that she makes next reveals a far different mindset: "And who sent me this doll? Come, on people! If I want a baby, I can buy one wholesale in California or some other third world country!"

In these and other similar comments throughout *The Littlest Bitch*, Isabel exemplifies what Anne Higonnet termed the "knowing child" (12). For generations, young people were seen as blissfully unaware of humanity's unsavory aspects, including greed, violence, and corruption. Beginning during the era of the Vietnam War and accelerating rapidly in the decades that followed, American attitudes about both the accuracy and the perceived benefit of childhood innocence began to change. Instead of young people being regarded as rightly and happily unaware of life's difficulties, they were regarded as already being in the know. In the Hollywood film *Paper Moon* (1973), for example, the nine-year-old female protagonist not only smokes regularly, but skillfully swindles, lies, and manipulates the adults who surround her. Far from being seen as lamentable, this behavior is presented as commendable. The bulk of the adults that she encounters are con artists who are more interested in financially cheating her than lovingly caring for her. Similarly, in Alice Childress's young adult novel *A Hero Ain't Nothin' But a Sandwich* (1973), thirteen-year-old Benjie sees the hypocrisy, inequity, cruelty, and injustice that permeate the adult world—and rebels against it, often self-destructively. In these works, young people were presented as being acutely aware of how the world operates. The stakes for not knowing were simply too high.

Isabel does not want a briefcase, cell phone, and BlackBerry simply for the purposes of imaginative play. Furthering her portrayal as nothing more than a diminutive adult, she puts these items to practical use. Over the next few pages, the protagonist subjects her family to a corporate-style "Performance Review." Predictably, neither her parents nor any of her siblings fare very well. Isabel's assessment of her mother leaves her wondering how they could "share the same genetic balance sheet." Meanwhile, the review of her siblings concludes with her deeming them "drooling cretins." Her father, however, receives the most scathing assessment. In a drawing that shows Isabel visiting his office on what a poster in the background reveals as "Bring Your Child to Work Day," she delivers the news. Precociously calling her father by his first name, Isabel tells him flatly: "Larry, it's time to man up and admit it—you feel like a loser because you are a loser."

In a telling commentary on the state of the corporate world, such attitudes help land Isabel a position as CEO of a large corporation in New York City. Her first act, of course, is to heartlessly fire as many employees as possible. When one newly terminated employee bursts into tears and laments "How am I supposed to feed my two young babieeeees," Isabel is completely devoid of sympathy. "Please. I can't strategize with you whimpering like a constipated Chihuahua," she says. The kindergarten-aged executive is equally cold when it comes to her family. Placing a call from her mother on hold, she shouts to her administrative assistant in one illustration: "Who gave this parasite my direct line?"

The Littlest Bitch depicts how adulthood has thoroughly swallowed up the childhood of its elementary-aged protagonist. Accordingly, it seems only fitting that the picture book ends with an adult literally swallowing up Isabel after she gives yet another ruthless, cold-hearted presentation during a breakfast meeting. A faceless man wearing a business suit picks her up with his fork and puts her in his mouth. The drawing at the bottom of the page makes this turn of events unmistakable. The illustration is focalized from inside of his mouth, placing the viewer roughly on his tongue. Peering over his teeth which frame the top and bottom of the image, readers can see Isabel sitting atop his fork, heading directly towards them. Her eyes are open wide in surprise and even fear, and the speech balloon beside her head contains one word: "Mummy!"

The following page, which is the final one in the book, features a close-up of the man's fork. It holds only the string of pearls that Isabel has been wearing throughout the narrative. Presumably, she has been consumed and this inedible accessory is all that remains. In spite of such seeming certainty, the book ends with a question rather than a statement. "The End?," it asks in large white lettering above the drawing. This query does more than simply cast doubt on Isabel's fate. It also suggests that this saga may not be over. Even if Isabel has been eliminated, there could be others like her.

One of the most profound transformations to take place in Western civilization was the advent of childhood during the mid-eighteenth century. The assertion that young people were not merely diminutive adults, but individuals inhabiting a distinct, unique, and important stage of human development, altered more than merely understandings of the human life cycle. It transformed the whole structure of society. This phase of life that had previously not existed quickly came to be seen as the most important one. During the ensuing decades, childhood began to drive and even dictate social, political, familial, educational, and cultural arenas.

The Littlest Bitch makes a case that, by the start of the twenty-first century, this revolutionary development may be over. Instead of experiencing a separate and distinct period of childhood, boys and girls have returned to being nothing more than "little adults." As the portrayal of Isabel affirms, this phenomenon is not commendably radical and revolutionary—it is utterly repellent and repulsive. In a banner that appears in multiple places inside and outside of the book, Quinn and Davis dub *The Littlest Bitch* a "Not for Children Children's Book." Ironically, though, their text reveals how many children are no longer children. Childhood has disappeared; an odious version of little adulthood is all that remains.

Comedian Jerry Seinfeld, in his HBO special *I'm Telling You for the Last Time* (1998), reflected on the relationship between parents and children and, by extension, adulthood and childhood. "When you're little, your life is up," he observed, "the future is up, everything you want is up: Wait up. Hold up. Shut up. Mom, I'll clean up. Let me stay UP." The period of youth is commonly spent yearning for maturity. Rather than cherishing and savoring their childhoods, kids often wish it away.

Ironically, while young people long to be adults, adults often look back fondly on the period of youth. The romanticization of childhood is a wholly adult construct. It is grown-ups who idealize this period of life, not kids. So, as Jerry Seinfeld noted, while children are always wanting to go up, "Parents, of course, are just the opposite. Everything is down. Just calm down. Slow down. Come down here. Sit down. Put that down." In many regards, they would also like to age themselves down: to be younger and, for many, even to be kids again.

Go the F**k to Sleep, *If You Give a Kid a Cookie*, and *The Littlest Bitch* embody compelling examples of the ways in which adults and children are no longer imaginatively switching places, but have socially, psychically, and materially done so. For the exhausted parents in *Go the F**k to Sleep* and *If You Give a Kid a Cookie*, children have thoroughly eclipsed and even usurped their adult lives. Caring for their son or daughter consumes every waking moment, squeezing out any adult activities, interests, or even identities. By contrast, in *The Littlest Bitch*, the reverse is true: the "Not for Children Children's Book" shows how childhood in the early twenty-first century has been thoroughly consumed by adulthood. The five-year-old protagonist doesn't merely wish she were older. She exhibits all the traits of adulthood, including and even especially the worst ones.

Given its basis in blurring age-based divisions, children's literature for adults offer a rich and productive platform to explore both of these phenomena. The name of the genre suggests the movement of a cornerstone feature of childhood into adulthood. But it also compels us to confront the possibility that neither children nor adults occupied the socio-cultural places where we had previously positioned them. Instead of creating these chronological slips, developmental reversals, and cultural elisions, children's literature for adults serves as a platform by which to document them more vividly.

Both Radical and Reinforcing

The Complicated Cultural Significance of Children's
Literature for Adults

Each of the works of children's literature for adults profiled in the previous chapters teases out a particular aspect of how the line between childhood and adulthood has blurred. In examples ranging from the way that the elderly are infantilized in Dr. Seuss's *You're Only Old Once!* and the process by which adult-audience retellings of children's books can shed new light on stories intended for young people in Mabel Maney's *The Case of the Not-So-Nice Nurse* to the portrayal of how times of national crisis cause adults to occupy positions of vulnerability more commonly experienced by young children in Art Spiegelman's *In the Shadow of No Towers* and the growing power that children—including those who have not even been born—have come to possess over adults in Barbara Park's *MA! There's Nothing to Do Here!*, these narratives map the twisty, bendy, and even circular nature of the human lifespan by the opening decades of the twenty-first century.

When the titles profiled in the previous chapters are viewed not merely as compelling individual narratives but as a collective cross-section of a new genre, they provide a telling portrait of the rich, diverse, and complex transformations that have taken place with regard to age and audience since the closing decades of the twentieth century. These books demonstrate that it is not merely our theoretical understandings of the human lifespan that are shifting, but our daily lived experiences. Formerly linear concepts of growing up and growing older are looping, leaping, and lurching back upon themselves in ways not previously acknowledged, discussed, or perhaps even realized. Moreover, these events are not abstract pie-in-the-sky potentialities, but actual current realities. Children's literature for adults provides a platform to represent such phenomena, while it also continues to push those boundaries, exploring new possibilities and investigating new developments.

These features raise a number of questions. What does the blurring of divisions regarding age and audience that appear in children's literature for adults mean for this generation of readers and, even more importantly, for the next?

What are the literary and cultural ramifications when audiences no longer regard children's literature as the exclusive domain of children? Even more significantly, what happens when the phases of life cease to be independent and instead are regarded as intertwined, interdependent, and interlocking? Childhood and adulthood have long been theoretically defined, historically constructed, and socially understood in oppositional ways: being a child means not being an adult, and vice versa. Children's literature for adults opens up the murky and messy but simultaneously rich and compelling arena where these phases of life include rather than exclude each other.

Much has been written in recent decades about the fluidity of gender. After generations of masculinity and femininity being framed as fixed, firm, and oppositional, these two modes of expression are increasingly regarded as existing along a spectrum. As theorists such as Judith Butler, Riki Wilchins, and Susan Stryker pointed out, no man is uniformly masculine and no woman is exclusively feminine in their activities, interests, and appearance. A woman might love wearing dresses, heels, and makeup, but she may also be an avid football fan. Conversely, a man may work in traditional male professional like construction, but he may also enjoy activities that are more commonly coded as feminine, such as gardening, cooking, or singing. These scenarios reveal how gender is not only a social construct—it is also a continuum.

In the same way that the field of LGBTQ studies has made a case for recognizing the nonbinary nature of gender, children's literature for adults invites us to consider the nonbinary nature of age. No individual fully and exclusively embodies adulthood or childhood—nor should they. A grown man or woman may be married, have a fulltime job, and own a home—all traditional markers of adulthood—but they also may belong to a kickball league, enjoy board game nights with their friends, or color in the evenings as a way to relax. Likewise, a tween boy or girl may still be in elementary school and not yet experienced the onset of puberty, but they may also have a sophisticated understanding about seemingly adult subjects like consumer capitalism and media technology. These phenomena demonstrate that, if we truly seek to understand the complexities of life, we must view human existence as a totality. This process includes those aspects that are challenging, confusing, and contradictory. Rather than ignoring, overlooking, or minimizing the ways that childhood and adulthood mix and merge, we must recognize, explore, and contend with them. Approached from this vantage point, the category of children's literature for adults becomes not simply more understandable, but appropriate and even necessary.

Daniel Donahoo, in his book *Idolising Children*, examines the longstanding tendency in Western cultures to idealize childhood. As he argues, this seemingly positive phenomenon has many unintended negative consequences, both for young people and also, albeit less expectedly, for adults. Not only does this tendency cast children in an unrealistic light—setting a standard of perfection that is impossible for any actual child to embody—but the privileging of childhood also, by definition, disparages adulthood. As Donahoo explains, "our idolising of childhood and youth and all that comes with it means we have created a negative image of ageing [sic] and growing old" (22). The primacy placed on youth via the idolization of childhood has contributed to the creation of binaries such as "Youth is beautiful; ageing [sic] is ugly" (Donahoo 226). Of course, such attitudes harm adults, causing them to associate their own stage of development with unflattering traits and qualities. But, as Donahoo points out in a more surprising consequence, the devaluing of adulthood also does "a disservice to us and our children. Our children need people of all ages to help raise and guide them towards adulthood" (Donahoo 22).

For this reason, Donahoo advocates something much more radical than simply abandoning the longstanding Western practice of placing children on a pedestal. Instead, he makes a case for eliminating all age demarcations, be they generational or developmental. "We shouldn't divide ourselves into ages and stages. We don't need the tags like baby-boomers or Generation X or Y; instead we should be working to create a society for all ages, where birth and death are triumphant bookends to an entire life and where there isn't innocence in childhood or inflexibility in older age" (16–17). As Donahoo asserts: "We don't need a philosophy of children first, we need one of a society for all ages: inclusive, supportive and diverse" (23).

Forming what can perhaps be viewed as its final paradox, children's literature for adults both heeds and ignores this advice. On one hand, this iconoclastic genre breaks down seemingly sacrosanct barriers separating youth from so-called maturity. It invites us to imagine an environment where the formerly rigid distinctions between children and adults have been blurred. The appearance of picture books, alphabet texts, and bedtime tales for grownups marks the moment when these literary schools, narrative styles, and material formats are no longer confined to a specific period in the human life cycle. In embracing this diversity, children's literature for adults does not indicate the end of this genre; rather, it signals the expansion.

At the same time, of course, these books are intended for an exclusively adult audience. As a result, while titles like *Goodnight Bush, MA! There's*

Nothing to Do Here! and *Go the F**k to Sleep* break down the barriers of age and audience in some regards, they paradoxically reinforce them in other ways. As the name "children's literature *for* adults" suggests, the genre still affirms the existence of two separate and distinct literary modes—as well as phases of the human life cycle. Although these narratives may use literary schools and styles traditionally associated with kids, they remain books that are written for and directed to grown-ups. Indeed, with passages such as "And if the right wing fanatics/Push some radical scheme/Like balancing the budget/We'll just call it 'extreme!'", it is difficult to imagine an elementary-aged child finding *The Cat and the Mitt* interesting let alone satirically amusing. Likewise, as numerous customer comments about *MA! There's Nothing to Do Here!* attest, it is expectant mothers, not young children, who most enjoy Park's picture book. Finally, along those same lines, it is challenging to envision any parent actually reading *Go the F**k to Sleep* to their son or daughter at bedtime. The book is intended to amuse adults, not their offspring. Affirming this observation, in 2012, Adam Mansbach released a child-friendly version of his narrative. Called *Seriously, Just Go to Sleep*, the book removed all of the profanity that appeared in the original as well as the strong expressions of parental frustration and anger. The story still focused on a young child stalling bedtime, but it discussed the issue in a way that Susan Carpenter aptly called "G-rated" (par. 3). In the original version, for example, the narrator says: "I know you're not thirsty, that's bullshit. Stop lying. Lie the fuck down, my darling, and sleep." Meanwhile, in Mansbach's new edition, this passage was rewritten to read: "I know you're not thirsty. You just had a drink. Stop goofing around now, and sleep."

As even these few examples suggest, while children's literature for adults breaks down the divide separating adults from children in some respects, it reinforces the distinction in other ways. The name of this new genre is paradoxical, and, perhaps appropriately, its social, cultural, and literary impact is paradoxical as well. Far from signaling the wholesale elimination of age and audience, therefore, it can more accurately or, at least, consistently be said to reconfigure it.

For centuries, the category "children's literature" has been regarded as an endpoint. The name of the genre refers to the individuals who are intended to receive, read, and consume these narratives. In this way, the moniker denotes the final destination of, or even societal terminus for, these texts. By contrast, children's literature for adults frames the same school, style, and format of texts in a far different way. Instead of seeing picture books, bedtime stories, or ABC books as an ending point, it positions them as a starting point. Of course, the name "children's literature *for adults*" still signals the individuals who are ultimately intended to receive and read these books. But, children's literature serves as the beginning, not the ending. Children's literature for adults casts books of this nature as being creatively generative, rather than demographically conclusive. This change embodies if not a radical shift then at least a significant alteration in how children's literature has historically been regarded in the United States.

From the growing popularity of children's literature for adults in the closing years of the twentieth century with the success of *You're Only Old Once!* to its widespread prevalence by the second decade of the new millennium amidst the national coloring book craze, this phenomenon has emerged as a powerful commercial, literary, and cultural force. While the canon for the genre is still taking shape, one characteristic has become clear: these books invite us to reconsider the boundaries of age and audience on a scale that has arguably not occurred since children's literature itself was founded nearly three centuries ago. Whatever place these books ultimately occupy in American literary history, it seems apparent that neither narratives for young people nor those intended for grown-ups will ever be the same again. Even more radically, this same observation holds true for childhood and adulthood.

Introduction · A Is For Adult

Epigraph. Quoted in Christopher Noxon's *Rejuvenile: Kickball, Cartoons, Cupcakes, and the Reinvention of the American Grown-up* (New York: Two Rivers, 2006): 101.

1. Georgina Howlett, in an article that appeared in the *Guardian* in February 2015, reported: "One of the most important things to note about the teen and YA market in particular, though, is that the majority of its readers (55%, according to a 2012 study) are actually adults. Yes, you read that right: adults" (par. 2). For more on this issue, see my discussion of the growing millennial trend of adults reading young adult literature that appears later in this introduction.

2. The phrase "children's literature for adults" has appeared in scholarly discussions about literature. However, the phrase has not been used to signal juvenile-styled narratives written for adult readers. For example, in 1981, Martha L. Brunson authored an article in the *ADE Bulletin*—the journal of the Association of the Departments of English—with this title. Even so, the phrase "children's literature for adults" referred to the first peer-reviewed academic journal that was devoted to the scholarly study of children's literature, which was the focus of her discussion. Nearly two decades later, Leona M. English and Susan C. Unher both released essays that bore the title "Children's Literature for Adults," but these articles also used this phrase in a far different way. The essays by English and Unher addressed the benefits of using children's books in the context of adult literacy programs. They did not examine narratives that have been released in a material format or participated in a literary style that has been commonly associated with young people, but were written for adults.

3. In this post, Conway claims to coin the phrase "Children's Literature for Adults," but my work on this topic predates his comments. In January 2017, for example—more than nine months before Conway's blog post—I gave a conference paper on this topic at the Modern Language Association Convention. My talk was titled "Adultescents, Kidaults, and Rejuveniles: Children's Literature for Adults and Remapping the Boundaries of Age and Audience." So, again, my work on this topic—not merely the private individual research and writing, but also the public sharing and discussing of it at major academic conferences—predates Conway. Throughout my January 2017 conference talk, in fact, I used the exact same phrasing—"what I call 'children's literature for adults'"—as Conway does in the opening sentence to his blog post from later that year.

4. I discuss retellings of children's books for adults that contain implicit or explicit sexual content, along with Tribunella's work on this topic, in greater depth and detail in chapter two.

5. In the opening pages of his essay, Tribunella does assert that "adult retellings of children's books clearly constitute a vital literary and cultural phenomenon" (136). However, his scope remains limited, since it is restricted to adult-audience retellings of already-published children's works rather than new and original narratives of children's literature for adults.

6. I say "in the United States" here—and I reiterate this detail frequently throughout my discussion in the subsequent chapters—because my analysis is limited to this country and its popular culture. The works of children's literature for adults that I spotlight, along with my analysis of issues like the construction of adulthood, is focused on the United States. But books of this nature have appeared in other countries around the world, as I discuss later in this introduction.

7. Of course, the phenomenon that I am examining may also be happening in other parts of the world. Indeed, as I have already discussed, the adult coloring book craze started in the United Kingdom. My focus, though, is on the United States. Looking at this issue from a global or transnational perspective is outside the scope of this project, and it is also outside my own area of expertise. It is my hope, however, that this study will inspire additional research

into the ways that conceptions of adulthood have evolved, changed, and shifted in other countries and cultures. Furthermore, given the neocolonial influence that American popular culture has around the globe, similar events may be happening in other nations in light of occurrences that are taking place in the United States.

8. This project was funded from 2000 to 2008. The survey from the MacArthur Research Network on Transitions to Adulthood that I cite is from 2002. Meanwhile, the information about generational attitudes from Stephanie K. Taylor appeared in 2006. Finally, the findings from Richard Stetterson and Barbara Ray were published in Spring 2010. I chose these dates deliberately and I have not included data from any more recent years intentionally, since these dates form the rough backdrop to the texts that I profile in chapters three through five along with the conclusion. In so doing, they encapsulate attitudes from the chronological period that constitutes the bulk of this volume.

9. As Nodelman explains, "This in itself makes the term highly unusual as a category of literature. *Victorian literature* or *women's literature*, for instance, are terms that refer to the writers of the texts more than to their audiences" (3). Even so, "while Victorian literature was all written by Victorians, and most women's literature is written by women, few children write the literature published professionally as 'children's literature'" (3).

10. Examples of this nature can also be found in Great Britain. Lynne Rosenthal, for example, has written about Florence Montgomery's 1869 novel *Misunderstood*, which she describes as "A Victorian Children's Book for Adults" (94). Meanwhile, Felicity A. Hughes, Marilynn S. Olson, and Claudia Nelson have explored instances of what Nelson calls "literary age inversion" in nineteenth-century British print culture. While none of the materials profiled by Hughes, Olson, and Nelson are juvenile-styled narratives intended for a readership of men and women rather than boys and girls, they can be placed on a continuum with children's literature for adults. As Nelson explains, "the terms 'child-woman,' 'child-man,' and 'old-fashioned child' appear often enough in Victorian writings to prompt critical questions about the motivations and meanings of such generational border crossings" (1–11).

11. Of course, fairy tales also have a long tradition of being retold and reimagined for adults. Angela Carter's *The Bloody Chamber* (1979) embodies one of the most famous print examples along these lines. Still, as scholars like Maria Tatar and Jack Zipes have repeatedly pointed out, fairy tales began as narratives intended for adults, not children. As I have written elsewhere, "Although critics hotly debate whether fairy tales have their root in an oral or written tradition, few contest that they began as stories that were initially created by and for adults" (39). Maria Tatar has noted how "traditionally folktales were related at adult gatherings after the children had been put to bed for the night" (23). Given this child-free atmosphere, Tatar wrote, "peasant *racounteurs* could take certain liberties" (23), although as the nineteenth century progressed, fairy tales gradually began "being appropriated by parents as bedtime reading for children" (xiii). Perhaps as a result of this literary lineage, fairy tales have always retained a connection—however tenuous and even vestigial—to their original audience of men and women. In examples ranging from the repeated appearance of expensive collector's editions of stories by Charles Perrault or the Grimm Brothers to the powerful appeal that Disney fairy-tale movies have for many women, they can be seen as enjoying a dual audience or, in some cases, of being cross-written. Given that fairy tales have routinely moved back and forth between the realm of stories for children and those for adults, I have omitted them from this project. As the title suggests, I am interested in literary forms and narratives styles that have formerly if not exclusively been associated with young people moving into the realm of adults. Fairy tales not only have the opposite history—starting out as narratives for men and women—but they have also frequently crisscrossed audiences.

12. To be clear, Beckett's primary focus is on children's texts that—as the title to two of her books demonstrates—have crossed over from juvenile audiences to adult ones, or on texts

that were written with a dual audience of children and adults in mind. As I have repeatedly asserted, these two phenomena differ from that of children's literature for adults. Books that enjoy crossover status or are written for both children and adults simultaneously are not the same as juvenile-styled narratives that are originally and exclusively intended for an audience of adults. So, while Beckett's work demonstrates the fluid, permeable, and expanding boundaries of children's literature, it charts different literary developments than that of children's literature for adults and, by extension, what I am doing in this project.

13. I wish to thank an anonymous outside reader of my manuscript for alerting me to these titles.

14. A variety of lesser-known texts could also be added to this list. Examples include Andrew Vachss's inspirational title *Another Chance to Get it Right: A Children's Book for Adults* (1995) as well as Anthony L. Hall's self-help picture book *The Fear Equation: A Children's Book for Adults* (2006). Along those same lines, Mark Yablonovich and Juliet Kaska's *The ABC's [sic] of Happiness: NOT for Children* (2008), Ken Tanaka's *Everybody Dies: A Children's Book for Grown-Ups* (2014), and Norman Twisted's *The Elf On Our Shelf Must Die: A Picture Book for Adult Children* (2015) also belong to this category. Finally, two parody texts—Gregory P. Dorr's picture book *Santa's Lil' [sic] Gimp: A Book NOT for Children* (2003) and P. A. Hayden's *My Little Book of Big Bugbears: Nursery Rhymes for Grumpy Grown-ups* (2012)—are both juvenile-styled books that are intended for a readership of men and women rather than boys and girls.

15. It is tempting to include David Carter's artistically innovative and materially intricate pop-up books in this category as well. However, as the subtitles for texts like *One Red Dot* (2005), *600 Black Spots* (2007), and *Yellow Square* (2008) directly state, they are pop-up books "for children of all ages." This study is interested in juvenile-styled narratives that have been written intentionally and exclusively for adults, not merely those that participate in the longstanding (and often discussed) phenomenon of having a dual audience of grown-ups and young people. For more on the tradition of cross-writing in children's literature, see Beverly Lyon Clark's *Kiddie Lit: The Cultural Construction of Children's Literature in America* (2003) and Sandra L. Beckett's *Crossover Picturebooks: A Genre for All Ages* (2013).

16. I discuss this issue—including more examples along these lines—in more detail in chapter five.

Chapter 1 · "A Book for Obsolete Children"

1. *You're Only Old Once!* is not paginated.

2. Of course, this image of Whelden the orderly pushing the main character in the wheelchair is showcased on the cover to *Old Once!* As Maria Nikolajeva and Carole Scott have written, illustrations from the interior pages of a picture book that are reproduced on the cover assume added symbolic significance and narrative importance: "A cover picture that is repeated, even with a slight variation, inside the book anticipates the plot and . . . provides some information about the book's story, genre, and addressee" (245).

3. Once again, indicating the centrality of this scene, the line of doctors on "Stethoscope Row," peeking out from their dark rooms, eager to "scope" the protagonist, forms the top half of the cover image to *Old Once!*

4. Between 1981 and 1987, whites comprised 59.9% of all AIDS cases, while blacks constituted 25.5%. Given that blacks represented about 11% of the total U.S. population in the 1980s, their rate of infection was much higher than whites. For more on this issue, see "HIV and AIDS—United States, 1981–2000," *Morbidity and Mortality Weekly Report*, Centers for Disease Control and prevention, vol. 50, issue 21 (June 1, 2001): pp. 40–44. Available online at https://www.cdc.gov/mmwr/preview/mmwrhtml/mm5021a2.htm.

5. This drawing of Seuss's narrator-protagonist clad only in his boxer shorts and lying in the Wuff-Whiffer is reproduced in the front matter and in the endpapers of the picture book. This repetition, of course, suggests its importance to the story.

Chapter 2 · Off to Camp

1. This color has a long history of being associated with lesbianism in the United States, especially during twentieth century. Most notably, perhaps, was in the early 1970s, when a group who called themselves the "Lavendar Menace" protested the exclusion of queer women and their issues in the second-wave feminist movement. For more on this issue, see Lillian Faderman's *Odd Girls and Twilight Lovers: A History of Lesbian Life in Twentieth Century America* (New York: Columbia UP, 1991).

2. Tison Pugh, in his book *Innocence, Heterosexuality, and the Queerness of Children's Literature* (London: Routledge, 2011), takes this paradoxical condition one step further: he argues that it is so iconoclastic and even unusual that it can, ironically, be deemed queer. As Pugh explains, "queerness provides an apt metaphor" for the "confused interplay" of how children are viewed as sexually innocent, how their association in homosocial peer groups is not simply condoned but encouraged, and how they are also expected to grow up to be heterosexual (6). But Pugh makes clear that he is using "queerness not as a synonym for *homosexuality* but as a descriptor of disruptions to prevailing cultural codes of sexual and gender normativity" (6; italics in original). Thus, the phenomenon that he is discussing differs from what Mabel Maney is doing in her lesbian-themed parody texts. Whereas Pugh is discussing figurative queerness, Maney's books are showcasing literal forms of homoeroticism.

3. As Bill Phillips has documented, this feature would remain a hallmark of the genre until the early twenty-first century. In an article published in 2014, Phillips discusses the longstanding absence of religious belief in detective fiction, and then declares: "This has, however, recently changed. The detective, once the acme of rational thought and deductive flair—incarnated in the figure of Sherlock Holmes, for example—has now been replaced, on occasions, by investigators with overt religious beliefs" (139).

4. The other black characters in the book are presented in an equally stereotypical manner. When Nancy and her companions first arrived at the estate of Bess's relatives, "an elderly colored couple, wearing a maid's and a butler's uniforms, came from the house. They were introduced as Mammy Matilda and Pappy Cole. The two smiled pleasantly. Then, as Pappy Cole started to unload the car, Mammy Matilda said to the visitors: 'I sure hopes you all have a fine time durin' your visit here'" (41).

5. Lamentably, blacks are not the only racial or ethnic group who are presented in stereotypical ways in *The Haunted Showboat*. When Nancy and her companions contemplate costumes for Mardi Gras, they deride another minority: "Instantly [George] bent double and began to do a dance that resembled that of an Indian ceremonial. Then Bess began to chant a song in the manner of a three-year-old reciting a nursery rhyme. All but Donna Mae burst into laughter" (59).

6. The success of Hoff's books notwithstanding, *The Tao of Pooh* and *The Te of Piglet* were also the subject of a variety of criticism. Hoff's use of popular children's texts that were written by a white Westerner to introduce religious practices about non-Western beliefs and tradition were seen by many not as insightful retellings, but as problematic cultural appropriation. In the words of Eric Reinders, "Hoff makes Taoism and Chinese culture as a whole into an enchanted fantasy, a child's world." Reinders goes on to assert that throughout both *The Tao of Pooh* and *The Te of Piglet*, "Taoism is reduced to only a happy attitude. Certainly this description has little to do with the Taoism (tao-chiao) of most Chinese."

7. As mentioned in the introduction, fairy tales were originally composed for adult audiences and later became adapted for and associated with young readers. For this reason, I have excluded them from my examination of children's literature for adults. Nonetheless, fairy tales are commonly associated with children, so my discussion of Angela Carter's decidedly adult take on many of these stories in *The Bloody Chamber* seems appropriate.

Chapter 3 · Material Matters

1. *In the Shadow of No Towers* is a difficult text to cite. Its unpaginated opening essay— "The Sky Is Falling! The Sky Is Falling!"—is followed by Spiegelman's ten original comics; although each one occupies a double-page spread, they are all given a single sequential Arabic number, from one to ten. The second half of the book opens with another unpaginated essay by Spiegelman, "The Comic Supplement." Finally, the volume closes with seven reprinted plates of comics from the early twentieth century. Although some plates occupy a single page whilst others encompass a full double-page spread, each reprinted comic is given its own solitary Roman numeral, starting at one. Given the unconventional mode of organization used in *No Towers*, I have done my best to preserve Spiegelman's original pagination and to ensure that readers can locate the material that I am referencing.

2. This phrasing, of course, recalls the infamous headline about President Gerald Ford that appeared in the *New York Post* on October 30, 1975: "Ford to City: Drop Dead" (Van Riper). The headline referred to Ford's refusal to give the city federal assistance that would keep it from declaring bankruptcy. Since this allusion would not be readily recognized by young people, it further suggests that Spiegelman's *No Towers* is directed at an audience of adults. I am indebted to an anonymous reader of my manuscript for this insight.

Chapter 4 · Baby Talk

1. Once again, this phenomenon is not limited to the United States. As Åse Marie Ommundsen has discussed, several picture books released in Scandinavia in recent years have been written from the perspective of a fetus. More specifically, Ommundsen cites *De skæve smil* (*The Crooked Smile*, 2008) from Denmark and *Krigen* (*The War*, 2013) from Norway. But these texts offer a vastly different view on the experiences of the unborn than any of the titles that I discuss in this chapter. In the words of Ommundsen, "*De skæve smil* is a challenging picture-book about aborted foetuses [sic], 'those who were never born'" (71). Meanwhile, *Krigen* examines different understandings of the concept of war, including the battles that erupt between expectant parents who are divorcing (Ommundsen 71). Given the atypical narrative voice as well as the equally unusual subject matter of these texts, Ommundsen explores the questions that they raise about literary aim, cultural intent, and even readerly audience. For more on this issue, see her chapter "Who Are These Picturebooks For? Controversial Picture-books and The Question of Audience," in *Challenging and Controversial Picturebooks: Creative and Critical Responses*, edited by Janet Evans (New York: Routledge, 2015), pages 71–94.

2. I have not included *Oh Baby, the Places You'll Go!: A Book to be Read in Utero* (1997), adapted by Tish Rabe from the works of Dr. Seuss, to this list. While the narrative does have some areas of overlap with the phenomenon of "fetus fiction" that I am discussing, it is not a work of children's literature for adults. Instead, as *Oh, Baby!* is both marketed by its publisher and widely used by the general public, it is a book "for doting parents-to-be to read aloud to their adorable baby-to-be" (inside jacket flap). For this reason, while *Oh, Baby!* does embody another example of the growing power and importance of the unborn in American culture, it is a book that is still intended for young readers—the youngest among them, in fact. Indeed, the premise that *Oh Baby, the Places You'll Go!* will actually be read to a fetus in utero is not comedic; it is serious. As I discuss later in this chapter, *Oh, Baby!* was composed and released during the height of American societal beliefs in fetal learning and prenatally advantaged babies. While *Oh, Baby!* certainly appeals to expectant parents who believe that reading, singing, talking and/or playing music to their child in the womb will stimulate their brain activity, the book's audience remains—at least in part—young people. So, once again, it cannot be classified as a work of children's literature for adults.

3. *Angel in the Waters* is not paginated.

4. It should be noted that, in addition to the picture books, bedtime stories, and parodies of nonfiction texts about pregnancy mentioned above, a number of novels for adults have been released in recent years that are narrated by a fetus. Micah Perk's *What Becomes Us* (2016), Ian McEwan's *Nutshell* (2017), and Eric Goodman's *Womb* (2017) are all told from the perspective of a gestating baby in utero. Meanwhile, Sarah Cohen-Scali's novel *Max* (2017) begins with the title character still in his mother's womb, eagerly awaiting to be born. The novel is told in first person, and the narrator's tone does not change over the course of the text. Max's voice remains the same observant, mature, and knowing one from the time that he is in the womb. As a result, even as a fetus, Max possesses what can be regarded as a very adult personality.

5. I am basing this date on when the authority record for this heading was created. It should be noted, however, as cataloguer Susan A. Vandale explained to me via email, "the date that record was created doesn't necessarily mean that 2008 is the first time the combination of the 'Fetus' subject heading with the form subdivision 'Fiction' was used. It's more like 2008 is the time at which that subject heading had been used often enough that creating a proper authority record for it made it easier for our library catalogs and OCLC (etc.) to work. It's probably impossible to determine when exactly the subject heading was first used, unfortunately." Nonetheless, 2008 marks the moment when a "critical mass" of these tags appeared, sparking the creation of the authority record.

6. There are two slight exceptions to this trend. First, on the double page spread in which Park's baby-to-be discusses how "nights might get bumpy. I'll wake, full of grumpy," the mother's head is shown, but from a distance and only in silhouette. Then, a few pages later, when the narrator-protagonist zooms down the slide and into his mother's waiting arms, a portion of her head is shown from the back. However, her face is still occluded, in part by her long hair and in part by the angle or perspective of the image.

7. For more information about each of these phenomena along with their interplay, see chapter three, "Threats from Without: Satanism, Abduction and Other Media Panics," in Susan J. Douglas and Meredith Michaels's *The Mommy Myth*.

8. For a discussion of these instances, see David Sadler's article "Innocent Hearts: The Child Authors of the 1920s" (*Children's Literature Association Quarterly*, 17.4, Winter 1992: 24–30); Jill Medersha McClay's essay "World Enough and Time: The Handmade Literacies of Young Adolescent Writers" (*The Lion and the Unicorn*, 29.1, January 2009: 87–101); and Laurie Langbauer's book *The Juvenile Tradition: Young Writers and Prolepsis, 1750–1835* (Oxford 2016).

Chapter 5 · Learning Left from Right

1. Together with parodies of classic picture books that have been published as full-length narratives, there are even more covers that have been satirically reimagined through photoshop. Sites like Pinterest contain collections of them. Examples include *Richard Scarry's Public Erections*, *Why is Mommy Moaning?*, a supposed Berenstain Bears book, and *Chicken Nuggets Come From Little Shits Who Don't Listen*, based on *The Little Red Hen*.

2. My overview here is neither exhaustive nor all-inclusive. There are additional adult-audience political parodies of well-known children's picture books that appeared in the new millennium. The controversial 2000 presidential election, for example, gave rise to Bill Maher's "How the Grinch Stole the Election" monologue (2000), Ward Sutton's "The Cat in the Chad" comic (2000), and—mirroring the title by Maher—Salman Rushdie's poem, "How the Grinch Stole America" (2001). These narratives did not appear in book format. Instead, they were released via television, magazine, and newspaper, respectively. Thus, while their content certainly places them in dialogue with the phenomenon that I am tracing, their format or medium sets them apart.

3. The novelty appeal of *Pat the Politician* sparked a sequel, *Pat the Politician #2*, which was released for the 2008 presidential election season. In this edition, readers join Paul and

Judy while they engage in activities such as scratching "John McCain's rough and tumble war rhetoric" and fluffing "John Edward[s]'s high-priced hair."

4. It should be noted that the text in *Goodnight Obama* appears in all caps. For both ease of reading and accessibility, I have chosen to reproduce it in mixed-case lettering.

5. It is tempting to add Michael Ian Black's *A Child's First Book of Trump* (2016) to this list. After all, the *New York Times*–bestselling title does imitate a popular series for young readers. However, the text is marketed as being for both adults and children. Indeed, *A Child's First Book of Trump* was released by Simon and Schuster's Books for Young Readers division.

6. The opening statement to "The Oath of a Freeman," for instance, asked that its reader, who was presumably white and male, "to bee the fubject of the govern-ment thereof; and therefore doe here fweare, by the great & dreadfull name of the Everyliving-God, that I will be true & faithfull to the fame, & will accordingly yield affiftance & fupport thereunto. . . ."

7. For even earlier examples of children's narratives that have clear political content, see *Tales for Little Rebels: A Collection of Radical Children's Literature*, edited by Julia Mickenberg and Philip Nel. The anthology reprints works such as M. Boland's "A B C for Martin" (1935). As the title implies, this text relays the letters of the alphabet through a decidedly Marxist lens: "A stands for Armaments—war-mongers' pride," "B is for Bolshie, the thorn in their side" (20). While the presence of such overt ideological content might call into question the audience of such texts, all of the authors whose work appears in *Tales for Little Rebels* assert that their narratives are intended for young people.

8. Of course, there many additional examples. The outbreak of the Second World War, for example, served as the impetus for the British parody *Struwwelhitler*. Written and illustrated by Robert Spence and Philip Spence, the text mimicked *Struwwelpeter*, "the German fable about a nasty and unkempt little boy whose misbhevaior has disastrous consequences" (Heller, par. 3). As Steven Heller has said about the book, "Hitler and his henchmen are thwarted at every turn, or punished for carrying out their evil deeds. And when not being thwarted or punished, they are ridiculed" (par. 3). The following excerpt provides a representative example of the tone and the content of *Struwwelhitler*: "Just look at him! There he stands / With his nasty hair and hands. / See! The horrid blood drops drip / From each dirty fingertip: / And the sloven, I declare, / Never once has combed his hair; / Piecrust never could be brittle / Than the word of Adolf Hitler." A copy of *Struwwelhitler* is held in the National Archives.

9. To be fair, there are a few instances where the reverse occurs in *Dr. Paul*: passages that were exclamatory in Dr. Seuss's original picture book appear as declarative or even interrogatory in Ouellette's parody. One of the opening pages, for example, changes "That Sam-I-am! / That Sam-I-am! / I do not like / That Sam-I-am!" to "That Dr. Paul. / That Dr. Paul. / I do not like / That Dr. Paul." However, changes along these lines are relatively minimal, occurring only occasionally during the course of the parody text. Moreover, in many cases, the author's vocal performance of these passages seemingly eradicates the modifications in tone. Ouellette reads these lines on the YouTube video of his book with such force and emphasis that they seem to embody impassioned, exclamatory statements regardless of their actual marks of punctuation.

10. These examples are not the only instances where declarative or interrogatory passages from the original *Green Eggs and Ham* are reconfigured as exclamatory remarks in the parody. Several others exist. For example, while Dr. Seuss's two characters are riding the train car through the darkened tunneled, Sam-I-am inquires about green eggs and ham: "Say! / In the dark? / Here in the dark? / Would you, could you, in the dark?" to which his nameless counterpart replies: "I would not, could not, / in the dark." In Ouellette's *Dr. Paul*, this query concerns the possible collusion by mainstream media to ignore Ron Paul's campaign, and his counterpart's reply becomes the far more adamant: "I do not think / There's a [media] black out.'"

11. *Goodnight Bush* made its debut on the list in the category of "Advice, How to and Miscellaneous" on July 6, 2008; it then appeared from July 27, 2008 through September 14, 2008, giving it a total of ten appearances.

12. In the years since *The Cat and the Mitt*, Spivack has released two more political-themed parodies: *The Gorax*, a parody of Dr. Seuss's *The Lorax* that features Al Gore as the titular character; and *The Wizard of Iz*, which uses the basic premise of L. Frank Baum's famous story to offer, as its subtitle indicates, *A Parody of Hillary's America*. Both books are available for sale only through Spivack's Facebook page, "Free Market Warrior Loren Spivack."

Chapter 6 · Not Kidding Around

1. *Safe Baby Handling Tips* is not paginated.

2. *Safe Baby Pregnancy Tips* is not paginated.

3. Along those same lines, J. D. Simone's *Mommy's First Picture Book: What Nobody Told You about Parenting!* (2013) has a similar focus, theme, and message. As the publisher's summary explains, the text "is for moms who don't buy into the popular myth that motherhood is blissfully free of poop, terror and adrenaline-inducing embarrassment."

4. *Baby, Make Me Breakfast* and *Baby, Mix Me a Drink* are the only two titles that have a comma after the word "Baby." The other three books in the series present this statement as a continuous phrase.

5. *Go the F**k to Sleep* is not paginated.

6. Giving further credence to this observation, the success of Mansbach's book inspired a popular audio version—narrated by Samuel L. Jackson—and then a sequel text: *You Have to F**king Eat*. Released in 2014, the follow-up book used the exact same format, premise, and narrative style, only this time it spotlighted the tendency of young people to be fickle about food.

Introduction · *A Is for Adult*

Abate, Michelle Ann. *Bloody Murder: The Homicide Tradition in Children's Literature.* Baltimore, MD: Johns Hopkins UP, 2013.

Abraham, Tamara. "Peter Pan Syndrome: Does the Rise of Women Mean Men Will Never Grow Up?" *Daily Mail Online.* 22 February 2011. http://www.dailymail.co.uk/femail/article-1359186 /Peter-Pan-syndrome-Does-rise-women-mean-men-grow-up.html. Accessed 3 March 2012.

"Adult, *Adj.* and *N.*" *Oxford English Dictionary.* Third edition, October 2011; online version December 2011. http://o-www.oed.com.fintel.roanoke.edu/view/Entry/2821. Accessed 04 March 2012. An entry for this word was first included in *New English Dictionary*, 1884. Accessed 3 March 2012.

"Adultescent, *N.*" *Oxford English Dictionary.* Third edition, December 2009; online version December 2011. http://o-www.oed.com.fintel.roanoke.edu/view/Entry/269350. Accessed 13 February 2012.

"Adulthood, *N.*" *Oxford English Dictionary.* Third edition, October 2011; online version December 2011. http://o-www.oed.com.fintel.roanoke.edu/view/Entry/2846. Accessed 04 March 2012. An entry for this word was first included in *New English Dictionary*, 1884. Accessed 3 March 2012.

"Adulting, *N.*" *Oxford Dictionaries.* 2019. https://www.lexico.com/en/definition/adulting. Accessed 24 September 2019.

"Adulting: The Verb 'Adulting' Is All Grown Up." Words We're Watching. 2016. *Merriam-Webster Dictionary.* https://www.merriam-webster.com/words-at-play/adulting. Accessed 24 September 2019.

"Adultness, *N.*" *Oxford English Dictionary.* Third edition, October 2011; online version December 2011. http://o-www.oed.com.fintel.roanoke.edu/view/Entry/2848. Accessed 04 March 2012. An entry for this word was first included in *New English Dictionary*, 1884. Accessed 3 March 2012.

Armstrong, Louise. *A Child's Guide to Freud.* Illus. Whitney Darrow, Jr. New York: Simon & Schuster, 1963.

Barclay, Susan. "I'm Glad I Haven't 'Grown Up.'" *The Vancouver Province* (British Columbia). 15 January 2004: A21.

Barkham, Patrick. "Coming Soon to a Pavement Near You . . ." *The Times* (London). 6 September 2003: 8.

Basford, Johanna. *Secret Garden: An Inky Treasure Hunt and Colouring Book.* London: Laurence King, 2013.

Beckett, Sandra L. *Crossover Fiction: Global and Historical Perspectives.* London: Routledge, 2008.

——. *Crossover Picturebooks: A Genre for All Ages.* London: Routledge, 2013.

——, ed. *Transcending Boundaries: Writing for a Dual Audience of Children and Adults.* London: Routledge, 1999.

Behren, Christopher. *Penis Pokey.* New York: Quirk Books, 2006.

Bender, Kelli. "Remembering Tom Tierney." 22 July 2014. *People.* http://people.com/celebrity /tom-tierney-paper-doll-creator-dies-at-85/. Accessed 27 November 2017.

Bonjack, Stephanie. "Twisted and Wrong: 6 Children's Books Intended for Adults." *LitReactor.* 14 October 2013. https://litreactor.com/columns/twisted-and-wrong-6-childrens-books -intended-for-adults. Accessed 23 September 2019.

Brennan, William. "Coloring Books for Existential Angst." *The Atlantic.* April 2015.

Brunson, Martha L. "Children's Literature for Adults." *ADE Bulletin.* 68. (Summer 1981): 39–41.

Burton, Richard, and F. F. Arbuthnot. *The Pop-Up Kama Sutra*. New York: Stewart, Tabori, and Chang, 2003.

Cahalan, Susannah. "Hottest Trend in Publishing Is Adult Coloring Books." *New York Post*. 13 December 2015.

Calcutt, Andrew. *Arrested Development: Pop Culture and the Erosion of Adulthood*. London: Cassell, 1998.

Campbell-Dollaghan, Kelsey. "Why Millions of Grownups are Buying These Coloring Books for Adults." *Gizmodo*. 27 March 2015.

Cannon, Ann. "Coloring Books for Adults Are Red Hot for the Holidays." *The Salt Lake Tribune*. 1 December 2015.

Carter, Angela. *The Bloody Chamber*. 1979. New York: Penguin, 1990.

Carter, David. *One Red Dot*. New York: Little Simon, 2005.

———. *600 Black Spots: A Pop-Up Book for Children of All Ages*. New York: Little Simon, 2007.

———. *Yellow Square: A Pop-Up Book for Children of All Ages*. New York: Little Simon, 2008.

Cassidy, Julie Sinn. "Transporting Nostalgia: The Little Golden Books as Souvenirs of Childhood." *Children's Literature*. 36. (2008): 145–61.

Clark, Beverly Lyon. *Kiddie Lit: The Cultural Construction of Children's Literature in America*. Baltimore: Johns Hopkins UP, 2003.

Clerisse, Alexandre. *Now Playing: A Seek-and-Find Book for Film Buffs*. New York: Chronicle, 2017.

Collins, Suzanne. *Catching Fire*. New York: Scholastic, 2009.

———. *The Hunger Games*. New York: Scholastic, 2008.

———. *Mockingjay*. New York: Scholastic, 2010.

Conway, Alex. "Nostalgia and the Boom of Children's Literature for Adults." Children's Literature at the University of Cambridge blog. 31 October 2017. https://cambridge childrenslit.wordpress.com/2017/10/31/nostalgia-and-the-boom-of-childrens-literature -for-adults/. Accessed 23 September 2019.

Cope, Edward Drinker. *The Origin of the Fittest: Essays on Evolution*. New York: D. Appleton and Company, 1887. Google Books.

Côté, James. *Arrested Adulthood: The Changing Nature of Maturity and Identity*. New York: NYU Press, 2000.

Cross, Gary. *Men to Boys: The Making of Modern Immaturity*. New York: Columbia UP, 2008.

Dierksheide, Christa. "Thomas Jefferson and Slavery." Plantation and Slavery. Monticello. 2008. https://www.monticello.org/site/plantation-and-slavery/thomas-jefferson-and -slavery#footnote15_eqx540x. Accessed 24 November 2017.

Donahoo, Daniel. *Idolising Children*. Sydney, Australia: New South, 2007.

Dorr, Gregory P. *Santa's Lil' Gimp: A Book NOT For Children*. Illus. Michael E. Russell. Mahomet, IL: Mahven Publishing, 2003.

English, Leona M. "Children's Literature for Adults: A Meaningful Paradox." *PAACE: Journal of Lifelong Learning*. 9 (2000): 13–23.

Failure to Launch. Dir. Tom Dey. Perf. Matthew McConaughey, Sarah Jessica Parker, Kathy Bates. Paramount, 2006.

"Fast Facts." National Center for Education Statistics. Institute of Education Sciences. https://nces.ed.gov/fastfacts/display.asp?id=569.

Felsenthal, Julia. "Are Adult Coloring Books Really a Thing?" *Vogue*. 8 December 2015.

Field, Corinne T. "'Are Women . . . All Minors?': Woman's Rights and the Politics of Aging in the Antebellum United States." *Journal of Women's History*. 12.4 (Winter 2001): 113–37.

Fox, Margalit. "Tom Tierney, 85; Elevated Paper Dolls to an Art Form." *The New York Times*. 19 July 2014: B8.

Franklin, Benjamin. *Poor Richard's Almanack*. 1749. Waterloo, IO: U.S.C. Publishing, 1914.

Garin, Kristoffer. "Oh, To Play Like a Child Again." *The New York Sun*. 22 June 2006: 15.

Gould, Stephen Jay. *The Mismeasure of Man*. Rev. ed. New York: W. W. Norton, 1996.

Graham, Ruth. "Against YA." *Slate*. 5 June 2014. Accessed 18 March 2015.

Green, John. *The Fault in Our Stars*. New York: Penguin, 2012.

Greenberg, Gary, and Matthew Reinhart. *The Pop-Up Book of Nightmares*. New York: Rob Weisbach Books/William Morrow, 2001.

———. *The Pop-Up Book of Phobias*. New York: Rob Weisbach Books/William Morrow, 1999.

Griswold, Jerry. "The Disappearance of Children's Literature (or Children's Literature as Nostalgia) in the United States in the Late Twentieth Century." *Reflections of Change: Children's Literature Since 1945*. Ed. Sandra Beckett, Connecticut: Greenwood, 1997: 35–41.

Hall, Anthony L. *The Fear Equation: A Children's Book for Adults*. Bloomington, IN: Author House, 2006.

Hall, G. Stanley. *Adolescence: Its Psychology and Its Relation to Physiology, Anthropology, Sociology, Sex, Crime, Religion, and Education*. Vol 2. New York: D. Appleton and Company, 1904.

Hayden, P. A. *My Little Book of Bugbears: Nursery Rhymes for Grumpy Grown-ups*. Lexington, KY: CreateSpace, 2012.

Herzog, Brad. *D is for Dump Trump: An Anti-Hate Alphabet*. Illus. Amy Herzog. Why Not Books, 2016.

Hintz, Carrie, and Eric Tribunella. *Children's Literature: A Critical Introduction*. Boston, MA: Bedford, 2013.

Howlett, Georgina. "Why Are So Many Adults Reading YA and Teen Fiction?" *The Guardian*. 24 February 2015.

Hughes, Felicity A. "Children's Literature: Theory and Practice." *ELH*. 45.3 (Autumn 1978): 542–61.

Ishizuka, Katie, and Ramón Stephens. "The Cat is Out of the Bag: Orientalism, Anti-Blackness, and White Supremacy in Dr. Seuss's Children's Books." *Research on Diversity in Youth Literature*. 1.2 (2019).

Kane, Colleen. "Sleep Away Camps for Adults." *Fortune*. 14 July 2015.

Kelly, Kathy. *Menopop: A Menopause Pop-Up and Activity Book*. New York: Fill'er Up Productions, 2000.

"Kidult, *N*. and *Adj*." *Oxford English Dictionary*. Additions series, 1997; online version December 2011. http://0-www.oed.com.fintel.roanoke.edu/view/Entry/241026. Accessed 13 February 2012.

Kiley, Dan. *The Peter Pan Syndrome: Men Who Have Never Grown Up*. New York: Avon, 1983.

Knocked Up. Dir. Judd Apatow. Perf. Seth Rogin, Katherine Heigl, Paul Rudd. Universal Pictures, 2007.

Koslow, Sally. *Slouching Towards Adulthood: Observations from the Not-So-Empty Nest*. New York: Penguin, 2012.

Larrick, Nancy. "The All-White World of Children's Literature." *The Saturday Review*. 11 September 1965. 63–65.

Linn, Susan. *Consuming Kids: Protecting our Children from the Onslaught of Marketing & Advertising*. New York: Anchor, 2004.

Long, Amanda. "Book List: 23 of the Naughtiest Kids Parody Books for Adults." *Mum's Grapevine*. 6 January 2016. https://mumsgrapevine.com.au/2016/01/adult-parody-books/. Accessed 23 September 2019.

MacDonald, Robert. *Little Donnie Drumpf & the Magic Paintbrush*. Mouthy Primate, Inc., 2016.

Maley, Matt. *Little Donny Trump Needs a Nap*. Visualstuff Studios, 2016.

Maney, Mabel. *The Case of the Good-for-Nothing Girlfriend: A Nancy Clue Mystery*. San Francisco: Cleis, 1995.

———. *The Case of the Not-So-Nice Nurse: A Nancy Clue Mystery*. Pittsburgh, PA: Cleis, 1993.

———. *A Ghost in the Closet: A Hardly Boys Mystery*. Pittsburgh, PA: Cleis, 1995.

Mansbach, Adam. *Go the F**k to Sleep*. Brooklyn, NY: Akashic, 2011.

Mar, Jonathan, and Grace Norwich. *The Body Book for Boys: Everything You Need to Know About Growing Up*. New York: Scholastic, 2010.

Marston, Stephanie. *The Divorced Parent: Successful Strategies for Raising Your Children after Separation*. New York: Pocket Books, 1994.

Martinez, Joel. "Coloring Books for Adults are the New Craze." 2015. https://www.wwlp.com/news/coloring-books-for-adults-are-the-new-craze/amp/. Accessed 15 June 2020.

"Menstruation and the Menstrual Cycle Fact Sheet." Womenshealth.gov. US Department of Health and Human Services Office on Women's Health, 21 October 2009. http://www.womenshealth.gov/publications/our-publications/fact-sheet/menstruation.cfm#f. Accessed 21 February 2012.

Meyer, Stephanie. *Twilight*. New York: Little, Brown, 2005.

Milliot, Jim. "The Coloring Craze: Adult Coloring Books, 2015." *Publishers Weekly*. 13 November 2015.

Mintz, Steven. *The Prime of Life: A History of Modern Adulthood*. Cambridge, MA: Belknap Press/Harvard UP, 2015.

Mucha Jr., Alphonse Marie, and Ed Sibbett Jr. *Art Nouveau Design*. New York: Dover, 2015.

Nel, Philip. *Was the Cat in the Hat Black? The Hidden Racism of Children's Literature and the Need for Diverse Books*. Oxford, UK: Oxford UP, 2017.

Nelson, Claudia. *Precocious Children and Childish Adults: Age Inversion in Victorian Literature*. Baltimore, MD: Johns Hopkins UP, 2012.

Nixon, Sally. *Houseplants and Hot Sauce: An Adult Seek-and-Find Book*. New York: Chronicle, 2017.

Nodelman, Perry. *The Hidden Adult: Defining Children's Literature*. Baltimore, MD: Johns Hopkins UP, 2008.

Noxon, Christopher. *Rejuvenile: Kickball, Cartoons, Cupcakes, and the Reinvention of the American Grown-Up*. New York: Three Rivers, 2006.

Olson, Marilynn S. "John Ruskin and the Mutual Influences of Children's Literature and the Avant-Garde." *Children's Literature and the Avant-Garde*. Eds. Elina Druker, Bettina Kümmerling-Meibauer. Amsterdam: John Benjamins Publishing Company, 2015. 19–44.

Ommundsen, Åse Marie. "Picturebooks for Adults." *Picturebooks: Representation and Narration*. Ed. Bettina Kümmerling Meibauer. Routledge, 2014.

Orenstein, Peggy. "Kindergarten Cram." *The New York Times*. Magazine section. 3 May 2009: MM13.

Origen, Erich, and Gan Golan. *Don't Let the Republican Drive the Bus!* Berkeley, CA: Ten Speed Press, 2012.

———. *Goodnight Bush*. New York: Little, Brown, 2008.

Ouellette, Chris. *Dr. Paul*. YouTube video: https://www.youtube.com/watch?v=-vLiD6bK63Y. Uploaded 14 December 2011.

Park, Barbara. *MA! There's Nothing to Do Here!: A Word from Your Baby-in-Waiting*. Illus. Viviana Garofoli. New York: Random House, 2008.

Patterson, Thom. "For Adults Only: Sexy, Boozy, Summer Sleep-Away Camp." *CNN*. 9 June 2015.

Petras, Kathryn, and Ross Petras. *B is for Botox: An Alphabet Book for the Middle-Aged*. Kansas City: Andrews McMeel, 2009.

———. *1, 2, Can't Reach My Shoe: A Counting Book for the Middle-Aged*. Kansas City: Andrews McMeel, 2010.

Pierleoni, Allen. "Color Them Calm: Coloring Books for Adults." *The Sacramento Bee*. 6 December 2015.

Porter, Evan. "3 Reasons Why All the Adults You Know Have Started Coloring Again."
   Upworthy. 17 July 2015.

Postman, Neil. *The Disappearance of Childhood*. 1982. New York: Vintage, 1994.

Quinn, David, and Michael Davis. *The Littlest Bitch: A Not-for-Children Children's Book*. Illus.
   Devon Devereaux. South Portland, ME: Sellers Publishing, 2010.

Raphel, Adrienne. "Why Adults Are Buying Coloring Books (For Themselves)." *The New
   Yorker*. 12 July 2015.

Rogers, Dorothy. *The Adult Years: An Introduction to Aging*. 3rd ed. Edgewood Cliffs, NJ:
   Simon & Schuster, 1986.

Rose, Jacqueline. *The Case of Peter Pan; or, The Impossibility of Children's Literature*. New
   York: Macmillan, 1984.

Rosenthal, Lynne. "*Misunderstood*: A Victorian Children's Book for Adults." *Children's
   Literature*. 3. (1974): 94–102.

Rowling, J. K. *Harry Potter and the Chamber of Secrets*. New York: Scholastic, 1998.

——. *Harry Potter and the Deathly Hallows*. New York: Scholastic, 2007.

——. *Harry Potter and the Goblet of Fire*. New York: Scholastic, 2000.

——. *Harry Potter and the Half-Blood Prince*. New York: Scholastic, 2005.

——. *Harry Potter and the Order of the Phoenix*. New York: Scholastic, 2003.

——. *Harry Potter and the Prisoner of Azkaban*. New York: Scholastic, 1999.

——. *Harry Potter and the Sorcerer's Stone*. New York: Scholastic, 1998.

Rubess, Balvis and Kees Moerbeek. *The Pop-Up Book of Sex*. New York: HarperCollins, 2006.

Scott, A. O. "The Death of Adulthood in American Culture." *The New York Times Magazine*.
   11 September 2014.

Seuss, Dr. *You're Only Old Once!: A Book for Obsolete Children*. New York: Random House, 1986.

Silverstein, Shel. *Uncle Shelby's ABZ Book*. 1961. New York: Touchstone, 1985.

Smith, A. G. *Victorian House Coloring Book*. New York: Dover, 2016.

Spiegelman, Art. *In the Shadow of No Towers*. New York: Pantheon Graphics, 2004.

Stanger-Ross, Jordan, Christina Collins, and Mark J. Stern. "Falling Far from the Tree:
   Transitions to Adulthood and the Social History of the Twentieth Century." *Social Science
   History*. 29.4 (Winter 2005): 625–48.

Stein, Joel. "Adults Should Read Adult Books." *The New York Times*. 23 May 2012.

Steinhorn, Leonard. *The Greater Generation: In Defense of Baby Boomers*. New York:
   St. Martin's, 2006.

Sternbergh, Adam. "Up with the Grups." *New York*. 26 March 2006. http://nymag.com/news
   /features/16529/.

Stetterson, Richard A., Jr., and Barbara Ray. "What's Going on With Young People Today? The
   Long and Twisting Path to Adulthood." *Future Child*. 20.1 (Spring 2010): 19–41.

Sun, Ming-Ju. *Art Deco Fashions*. New York: Dover, 2014.

Tanaka, Ken. With David Ury. *Everybody Dies: A Children's Book for Grown-Ups*. New York:
   Harper Design, 2014.

Tatar, Maria. *The Hard Facts of the Grimms' Fairy Tales*. 2nd ed. Princeton, NJ: Princeton UP,
   2003.

Taylor, Stephanie K. "Delaying Adulthood: Society Shows a Reluctance to Grow Up." *The
   Washington Times*. 15 August 2003: A2.

Thomas, Robert McGill, Jr. "Dan Kiley, 54, Dies; Wrote 'Peter Pan Syndrome.'" *The New York
   Times*. 27 February 1996: 7.

Tierney, Tom. *Fashions of the Roaring Twenties Coloring Book*. Mineola, NY: Dover, 2013.

——. *New Attitude: An Adult Paper Doll Book*. Atglen, PA: Schiffer Publihsing Ltd, 2008.

Truth, Dr. *The Cat and the Mitt: A Parody for Conservatives*. 2012. Amherst, MA: Free Market
   Warrior Publications, 2011.

Tullo, Danielle. "Kindly Shut the Hell Up about Adulting." *Cosmopolitan.* 20 June 2016. https://www.cosmopolitan.com/lifestyle/news/a58946/stop-adulting/. Accessed 24 September 2019.

Twisted. Norman. *The Elf On Our Shelf Must Die: A Picture Book for Adult Children.* CreateSpace, 2015.

Unher, Susan C. "Children's Literature for Adults—Teaching English as a Foreign Language." *Morioka University English-American Literary Society Bulletin.* 11 (2000-03): 55–57.

Vachss, Andrew. *Another Chance to Get it Right: A Children's Book for Adults.* Milwaukie, OR: Dark Horse, 1995.

Walsh, Patricia Buchanan. *Growing Through Time: An Introduction to Adult Development.* Monterey, CA: Brooks/Cole Publishing, 1983.

Wolfe, Tom. "The 'Me' Decade and the Third Great Awakening." *New York.* 23 August 1976. Available full-text at http://nymag.com/news/features/45938/. Posted 3 March 2012.

Worden, Bruce, and Clare Cross. *Goodnight Keith Moon.* New York: Baker and Taylor, 2011.

Yablonovich, Mark, and Juliet Kaska. *The ABC's of Happiness: NOT for Children.* Santa Monica, CA: West Village Press, 2008.

Zusak, Markus. *The Book Thief.* New York: Knopf, 2005.

Chapter 1 · *"A Book for Obsolete Children"*

Abate, Michelle Ann. "'The Tricky Reverse Narration That Impels Our Entwined Stories': Alison Bechdel's *Fun Home* and Queer Temporalities." *The ALAN Review.* 44.1. (Fall 2016): 30–44.

Anderson, Virginia. "How Broadway Has Cared: The AIDS Epidemic and the Great White Way." *The 1980s: A Critical and Transitional Decade.* Eds. Kimberly R. Moffit and Duncan A. Campbell. Lanham, MD: Lexington Books, 2011.

"Antrum, N." *OED Online.* Oxford University Press, March 2015. Accessed 24 May 2015.

Bader, Barbara. *American Picturebooks from Noah's Ark to The Beast Within.* New York: Macmillan, 1976.

Barnes, Edward, and Anne Hollister. "The New Victims: AIDS Epidemic That May Change the Way America Lives." *Life* magazine. July 1985.

Barnes, Fred. "The Politics of AIDS." *The New Republic.* 4 November 1985: 11–14.

Barouh, Gail. *Support Groups: The Human Face of the HIV/AIDS Epidemic.* Huntington Station, NY: Long Island Association for AIDS Care, Inc., 1992.

Bayer, Ronald, and Gerald M. Oppenheimer. *AIDS Doctors: Voices from the Epidemic.* Oxford, UK: Oxford UP, 2000.

Brady, Danielle, Andrew Clifton, Viv Burr, and Stephen Curran. "The Infantilization of Older People: Is It a Problem?" *Mental Health Nursing.* 34.5 (2014): 22–24.

Couser, G. Thomas. *Recovering Bodies: Illness, Disability, and Life Writing.* Madison, WI: U of Wisconsin P, 1997.

Dolinsky, Elaine H., and Herbert B. Dolinsky. "Infantilization of Elderly Patients by Health Care Providers." *Special Care in Dentistry.* 4.4 (July/August 1984): 150–53.

Edelman, Lee. *No Future: Queer Theory and the Death Drive.* Durham, NC: Duke UP, 2004.

"Endoscope." United States National Library of Medicine. US Department of Health and Human Services. National Institutes of Health. 14 April 2014. http://www.nlm.nih.gov/medlineplus/ency/article/002360.htm. Accessed 15 Feburary 2015.

Freeman, Elizabeth. *Time Binds: Queer Temporalities, Queer Histories.* Durham, NC: Duke UP, 2010.

Halberstam, J. Jack. *In a Queer Time and Space: Transgender Bodies, Subcultural Lives.* New York: NYU Press, 2005.

Halkitis, Perry N. *The AIDS Generation: Stories of Survival and Resilience.* Oxford, UK: Oxford UP, 2014.

Horton, Randall. "Stop Infantilizing Old People, Please." *The Huffington Post.* 13 January 2016.

MacDonald, Ruth. *Dr. Seuss.* Boston: Twayne, 1988.

Marson, Stephen M., and Rasby M. Powell. "Goffman and the Infantilization of Elderly Persons: A Theory in Development." *Journal of Sociology and Social Welfare.* XLI.4 (December 2014): 143–58.

Miller, Frank. "Rock Hudson Profile." Turner Classic Movies. http://www.tcm.com/this -month/article/1001841%7C138977/Rock-Hudson-Profile.html. Accessed 15 February 2015.

Morgan, Judith, and Neil Morgan. *Dr. Seuss and Mr. Geisel: A Biography.* New York: Da Capo, 1995.

Mulvaney, Maria. "Spectral Histories: The Queer Temporalities of Emma Donoghue's *Slammerkin.*" *Irish University Review* (2013), 43(1): 157–168.

Murphy, J. E., and K. M. Bridgman. "A Comparative Clinical Trial of Mianserin (Norval) and Amitriptyline in the Treatment of Depression in General Practice." *Journal of International Medical Research.* 6.3 (1978): 199–206.

Quam, Michael D. "The Sick Role, Stigma, and Pollution: The Case of AIDS." *Culture and AIDS.* Ed. Douglas A. Feldman. New York: Praeger, 1990. 29–44.

Rudolph, Christopher. "Rock Hudson Announced He Had AIDS on July 25, 1985." *The Huffington Post.* 25 July 2013.

Salari, Sonia Miner, and Melinda Rich. "Social and Environmental Infantilization of Aged persons: Observations in Two Adult Day Care Centers." *International Journal of Aging and Human Development.* 52.2 (2001): 115–34.

Schmidt, Gary D. "Playing to an Audience: A Critical Look at Dr. Seuss." *Children's Literature Association Quarterly.* 16.1 (Spring 1991): 41–42.

Seuss, Dr. *You're Only Old Once!: A Book for Obsolete Children.* New York: Random House, 1986.

Shilts, Randy. *And the Band Played On: Politics, People, and the AIDS Epidemic.* 1987. New York: St. Martin's Griffin, 2007.

Smith, Jack. "Book Review: *You're Only Old Once! By Dr. Seuss.*" *The Los Angeles Times.* 9 March 1986.

Chapter 2 · *Off to Camp*

Abate, Michelle Ann, and Kenneth B. Kidd. Introduction. *Over the Rainbow: Queer Children's and Young Adult Literature.* Eds. Michelle Ann Abate and Kenneth B. Kidd. Ann Arbor, MI: University of Michigan, 2011.

Ballantyne, R. M. *The Coral Island.* 1857. Rockville, MD: Wildside Press, 2003.

Blume, Judy. *Forever.* 1975. New York: Atheneum, 2014.

Brown, Judith C. *Immodest Acts: The Life of the Lesbian Nun in Renaissance Italy.* New York: Oxford UP, 1986.

Brownworth, Victoria A. "Books: The Secret Life of Nancy Drew." *The Advocate.* 29 November 1994. 59–60.

Bruhm, Steven, and Natasha Hurley. Introduction. *Curiouser: On the Queerness of Children.* Eds. Steven Bruhm and Natasha Hurley. Minneapolis, MN: University of Minnesota Press, 2004. ix–xxxviii.

Carter, Angela. *The Bloody Chamber.* 1979. New York: Penguin, 1990.

Chamberlain, Kathleen. "The Secrets of Nancy Drew: Having Their Cake and Eating it Too." *The Lion and the Unicorn.* 18.1 (June 1994): 1–12.

Christie, Agatha. *Murder on the Orient Express.* 1934. New York: William Morrow, 2017.

Cifaldi Brothers. *Do You Want to Play with My Balls?* 2012. Illus. Santiago Ehzalde. Ann Arbor, MI: Bum Bum Books, 2015.

Cusack, Carole M. "Scarlet and Black: Non-Mainstream Religion as the 'Other' in Detective Fiction." The Buddha of Suburbia: Proceedings of the Eighth Australian and International

Religion, Literature and the Arts Conference, 2004. RLA Press, 2005: 159–74. Available online at https://ses.library.usyd.edu.au/handle/2123/1252.

Doty, Alexander. *Making Things Perfectly Queer: Interpreting Mass Culture*. Minneapolis, MN: U of Minnesota, 1997.

Dyer, Carolyn Stewart, and Nancy Tillman Romalov. "Part II: Reading Nancy Drew, Reading Stereotypes." *Rediscovering Nancy Drew*. Eds. Carolyn Stewart Dyer and Nancy Tillman Romalov. Iowa City: U of Iowa, 1995. 89–94.

Faderman, Lillian. *Odd Girls and Twilight Lovers: A History of Lesbian Life in Twentieth Century America*. New York: Columbia UP, 1991.

Foote, Stephanie. "Bookish Women: Reading Girls' Fiction: A Response to Julia Mickenberg." *American Literary History*. 19.2 (Summer 2007): 521–26.

Frank, Lawrence. *Victorian Detective Fiction and the Nature of Evidence: The Scientific Investigations of Poe, Dickens, and Doyle*. London: Palgrave, 2009.

Galvin, Gary. *Would You Like to Play with My Ass?* CreateSpace, 2017.

———. *Would You Like to Play with My Pussy?* CreateSpace, 2017.

Greenberg, Jerrold S., Clinton E. Bruess, and Sarah C. Conklin. *Exploring the Dimensions of Human Sexuality*. 4th ed. Sudbury, MA: Jones and Bartlett, 2011.

Hammett, Dashiell. *The Thin Man*. 1934. New York: Vintage, 1989.

Heilbrun, Carolyn G. "Nancy Drew: A Moment in Feminist History." *Rediscovering Nancy Drew*. Eds. Carolyn Stewart Dyer and Nancy Tillman Romalov. Iowa City: U of Iowa, 1995. 11–21.

Hills, Matt. *Fan Cultures*. New York: Routledge, 2002.

Hoeveler, Diane Long. *The Gothic Ideology: Hysteria and Anti-Catholicism in British Popular Fiction, 1780–1880*. University of Wales, 2014.

Hoff, Benjamin. *The Tao of Pooh*. New York: Dutton, 1982.

———. *The Te of Piglet*. New York: Dutton, 1992.

Hughes, Thomas. *Tom Brown's Schooldays*. 1857. CreateSpace, 2012.

Jamison, Anne. *Fic: Why Fanfiction is Taking Over the World*. Dallas, TX: Smart Pop Books, 2013.

Jenkins, Henry. *Textual Poachers: Television Fans and Participatory Culture*. New York: Routledge, 1992.

Kashay, Jennifer Fish. "From Kapus to Christianity: The Disestablishment of the Hawaiian Religion and Chiefly Appropriation of Calvinist Christianity." *The Western Historical Society*. 39.1 (Spring 2008): 17–39.

Kauka, Kanani. "Bookmarks: The Case of the Not-So-Nice Nurse." *Lambda Book Report*. 4.2 (January 1994): 36.

Keene, Carolyn. *The Haunted Showboat*. New York: Grosset and Dunlap, 1957.

———. *The Hidden Staircase*. 1930. Bedford, MA: Applewood, 1991.

———. *The Mystery of the Ivory Charm*. 1936. Bedford, MA: Applewood, 1999.

———. *The Secret of the Golden Pavilion*. New York: Grosset and Dunlap, 1959.

———. *The Secret of Red Gate Farm*. 1931. Bedford, MA: Applewood, 1994.

———. *The Witch Tree Symbol*. New York: Grosset and Dunlap, 1955.

Kent, Chris. *Coral Island Boys*. San Francisco, CA: GLB Publishers, 1998.

———. *The Real Tom Brown's Schooldays*. San Francisco, CA: GLB Publishers, 2002.

Kincaid, James R. *Child-Loving: The Erotic Child in Victorian Culture*. 1992. New York: Routledge, 1994.

———. *Erotic Innocence: The Culture of Child-Molesting*. Durham, NC: Duke UP, 1998.

Kuda, Marie. "Review: *The Case of the Not-So-Nice Nurse*." *Booklist*. 90.3 (1 October 1993): 257.

Levin, Stephanie Seto. "The Overthrow of the Kapu System in Hawaii." *The Journal of Polynesian Society*. 77.4 (December 1968): 402–30.

Lewis, C. S. *The Lion, the Witch and the Wardrobe*. 1950. New York: Harper Collins, 2008.

Maney, Mabel. *The Case of Good-for-Nothing Girlfriend.* San Francisco: Cleis,1994.

———. *The Case of the No-So-Nice Nurse.* San Francisco: Cleis, 1993.

———. *A Ghost in the Closet.* San Francisco: Cleis, 1995.

Moore, Alan, and Melinda Gebbie. *Lost Girls.* 1991. Top Shelf, 2009.

"Mystery, *N. 1.*" *Oxford English Dictionary.* 3rd edition, June 2003; online version June 2012. http://o-www.oed.com.fintel.roanoke.edu/view/Entry/124644. Accessed 26 August 2012.

Nash, Ilana. "Nancy Drew Mysteries." *Girlhood in America: An Encyclopedia.* Vol 1. Ed. Miriam Forman-Brunell. Santa Barbara, CA: ABC-CLIO, Inc., 2001. 465–72.

"The Official Website of Benjamin Hoff." https://www.benjaminhoffauthor.com/. Accessed 2 October 2019.

Pettis, Ruth. "Maney, Mabel." *Encyclopedia of Gay, Lesbian, Bisexual, Transexual and Queer Culture.* http://www.glbtqarchive.com/literature/maney_m_L.pdf. Accessed 30 November 2017.

Phillips, Bill. "Religious Belief in Detective Fiction." *Atlantis: Journal of the Spanish Association of Anglo-American Studies.* 36.1 (June 2014): 139–51.

Pugh, Tison. *Innocence, Heterosexuality, and the Queerness of Children's Literature.* New York: Routledge, 2011.

Reinders, Eric. "Taoism." Encyclopedia.com. 18 September 2019. https://www.encyclopedia.com/religion/legal-and-political-magazines/taoism. Accessed 20 October 2019.

"Religion in the Depression." The Covers in Historical Context: Religion, October 13th, 1934. *Urban and Urbane: The New Yorker Magazine in the 1930s.* American Studies Program at the University of Virginia. http://xroads.virginia.edu/~ug02/newyorker/religion.html. Accessed 20 August 2012.

Sendak, Maurice. *In the Night Kitchen.* 1970. New York: Harper Collins, 1996.

Severin, Werner Joseph, and James W. Tankard. *Communication Theories: Origins, Methods, Uses.* Longman, 1988.

Smith, Kevin Burton. "Nancy Drew, Cherry Aimless, and The Hardly Boys." *The Thrilling Detective.* 1998. http://www.thrillingdetective.com/more_eyes/nancy_clue.html. Accessed 30 August 2016.

Tayanita, Bimisi. *Brenda's Beaver Needs a Barber.* Illus. Sumguyen Bangladesh. Created by Matt Williams. St. George, UT: Reach Around Books, 2016.

———. *Come Swing with Us!* Illus. Sumguyen Bangladesh. Created by Matt Williams. St. George, UT: Reach Around Books, 2016.

———. *Put Tony's Nuts in Your Mouth!* Illus. Sumguyen Bangladesh. Created by Matt Williams. St. George, UT: Reach Around Books, 2016.

———. *Spank the Monkey Lends a Hand.* Illus. Sumguyen Bangladesh. Created by Matt Williams. St. George, UT: Reach Around Books, 2016.

———. *Suzy Likes to Look at Balls.* Illus. Sumguyen Bangladesh. Created by Matt Williams. St. George, UT: Reach Around Books, 2016.

"Transubstantiation, *N.*" *Oxford English Dictionary.* 2nd edition, 1989; online version June 2012. http://o-www.oed.com.fintel.roanoke.edu/view/Entry/205086. Accessed 26 August 2012.

Tribunella, Eric. "From Kiddie Lit to Kiddie Porn: The Sexualization of Children's Literature." *Children's Literature Association Quarterly.* 33.2 (Summer 2008): 135–55.

Velasco, Sherry Marie. *Lesbians in Early Modern Spain.* Nashville, TN: Vanderbilt, 2011.

Wilder, Laura Ingalls. *Little House in the Big Woods.* 1932. New York: Harper Collins, 2004.

Chapter 3 · *Material Matters*

Bader, Barbara. *American Picturebooks from Noah's Ark to The Beast Within.* New York: Macmillan, 1976.

Brown, Bill. *A Sense of Things: The Object Matter of American Literature*. Chicago: U of Chicago P, 2003.

Brown, Margaret Wise. *Goodnight Moon*. Illus. Clement Hurd. 1947. New York: Harper Collins, 2007.

Campbell, James. "Drawing Pains." *The Guardian*. 27 August 2004. Accessed 3 October 2015.

"Comments." *Papers*. 4.3 (December 1993): 2.

Duane, Anna Mae. Introduction. *The Children's Table: Childhood Studies and the Humanities*. Ed. Anna Mae Duane. Athens, GA: U of Georgia P, 2013. 1–14.

Genco, Barbara. "Great Reads for Grown-Ups." *School Library Journal*. 50.12 (December 2004): 54–57.

Gordon, Joan. "Surviving the Survivor: Art Spiegelman's *Maus*." *Journal of the Fantastic in the Arts* 5.2 (1993): 81–89.

Groensteen, Thierry. *The System of Comics*. Trans. Bart Beaty and Nick Nguyen. Jackson, MS: UP of Mississippi, 2009.

Gussow, Mel. "Dark Nights, Sharp Pens." *The New York Times*. 15 October 2003. 3 October 2015.

Harding, Louette. "Why I Left the Parenting Hothouse." *Mail on Sunday*, London. https://www.dailymail.co.uk/home/you/article-376836/Why-I-left-parenting-hothouse.html. 12 February 2009. Accessed 5 May 2012.

Joseph, Michael. "Seeing the Visible Book: How Graphic Novels Resist Reading." *Children's Literature Association Quarterly*. 37.4 (2012): 454–67.

Kaplan, Allison G. "From Board to Cloth and Back Again." *Children & Libraries: The Journal of the Association for Library Service to Children* 10.3 (2012): 41–44.

Kuhlman, Martha. "The Traumatic Temporality of Art Spiegelman's *In the Shadow of No Towers*." *Journal of Popular Culture* 40.5 (2007): 849–66.

Lewis, Michael J. "Op-Art." *Commentary* (December 2004): 73–75.

McGann, Jerome. *The Textual Condition*. Princeton, NJ: Princeton UP, 1991.

McKenzie, D. F. *Bibliography and the Sociology of Texts*. Cambridge: Cambridge UP, 1999.

Morris, William. "The Ideal Book." 1893. *The William Morris Internet Archive*. Marxists Internet Archive, n.d. http://www.marxists.org/archive/morris/works/1893/ideal.htm. Accessed 2 December 2015.

Orbán, Katalin. "Trauma and Visuality: Art Spiegelman's *Maus* and *In the Shadow of No Towers*." *Representations*. 97.1 (2007): 57–89.

Penaz, Mary Louise. "Drawing History: Interpretation in the Illustrated Version of the 9/11 Commission Report and Art Spiegelman's *In The Shadow of No Towers* as Historical Biography." *Auto/Biography Studies*. 24.1 (2009): 93–112.

Poulet, Georges. "Criticism and the Experience of Interiority." *The Structuralist Controversy: The Language of Criticism and the Sciences of Man*. Ed. Richard A. Macksey and Eugenio Donato. Baltimore, MD: Johns Hopkins UP, 1970. 56–72.

Sacco, Joe, and Art Spiegelman. "Only Pictures?" *The Nation*. 20 February 2006. 3 October 2015.

Santi, Avi. "Comics, Daily Newspapers." *Encyclopedia of Children, Adolescents, and the Media*. Ed. Jeffrey Jensen Arnett. Vol. 1. Thousand Oaks, CA: SAGE, 2005: 193–95. Google Books. 12 November 2014.

Schmidt, Brad, and Jeffrey Winters. "Anxiety After 9/11." *Psychology Today*. 1 January 2002. https://www.psychologytoday.com/us/articles/200201/anxiety-after-911. Accessed 28 August 2018.

Spiegelman, Art. *Breakdowns: Portrait of the Artist as a Young %@&*!* 1978. New York: Pantheon, 2008.

———. "Ephemera vs. the Apocalypse." *Indy Magazine*. http://64.23.98.142/indy/autumn_2004/spiegelman_ephemera/index.html. Autumn 2005. Accessed 3 October 2015.

————. *In the Shadow of No Towers*. New York: Pantheon, 2004.

————. *Maus I: A Survivor's Tale: My Father Bleeds History*. New York: Pantheon, 1986.

————. *Maus II: A Survivor's Tale: And Here My Troubles Began*. New York: Pantheon, 1991.

Terdiman, Richard. *Body and Story: The Ethics and Practice of Theoretical Conflict*. Baltimore: Johns Hopkins UP, 2005.

Thill, Scott. "In the Shadow of No Towers, by Art Spiegelman." *Salon*. 10 September 2004.

Thomas, Susan Gregory. *Buy, Buy Baby: How Consumer Culture Manipulates Parents and Harms Young Minds*. Boston: Houghton Mifflin, 2007.

Van Riper, Frank. "Ford to City: Drop Dead." *The New York Post*. 30 October 1975.

Versluys, Kristiaan. "Art Spiegelman's *In the Shadow of No Towers*: 9/11 and the Representation of Trauma." *Modern Fiction Studies* 52.4 (2006): 980–1003.

Whitlock, Gillian. "Autographics: The Seeing 'I' of the Comics." *Modern Fiction Studies* 52.4 (2006): 965–79.

Wright, Bradford W. *Comic Book Nation: The Transformation of Youth Culture in America*. Baltimore, MD: Johns Hopkins UP, 2001.

Young, James. "The Holocaust as Vicarious Past: Art Spiegelman's *Maus* and the Afterimages of History." *Critical Inquiry* 24 (1998): 666–99.

Chapter 4 · Baby Talk

1 US Code. Sec. 8. 2002. LexisNexis Academic. 2 July 2012.

"5 Steps to Enhance Your Unborn Baby's Brain Power." 2008. Health and Wellness. SevAfrica .com. http://www.sevafrica.com/modules/health/article.php?health_newsid=193. Accessed 14 May 2012.

"About the Series." Junie B. Jones. Random House. http://juniebjones.com/parents/. Accessed 23 December 2015.

Association for Psychological Science and World Science Staff. "Mom's Mood May Affect Developing Fetus." 17 November 2001. *World Science*. http://www.world-science.net /othernews/111117_depression.htm. Accessed 21 May 2012.

"BabyPlus—Your Unborn Baby Can *Learn!*" BabyPlus. http://www.babyplus.com/docs /EcoBaby11-08.pdf. 14 May 2012.

Becker, Daniel. *Personhood: A Pragmatic Guide to Prolife [sic] Victory in the 21st Century and the Return to First Principles in Politics*. Alpharetta, GA: TKS Publications, 2011.

Berlant, Lauren. *The Queen of American Goes to Washington: Essays on Sex and Citizenship*. Durham, NC: Duke UP, 1997.

Blakely, D. "super." Customer review *MA! There's Nothing to Do Here!* 2 March 2008. Amazon .com. Accessed 9 September 2016.

Blease, Kathleen. *I Can't Wait to Meet My Daddy*. Illus. Bruce Fackenthal. Easton, PA: Ncihe House, 1996.

Brazelton, T. Berry. *What Every Baby Knows*. Reading, MA: Addison-Wesley, 1987.

Calhoun, Ada. "The Criminalization of Bad Mothers." 25 April 2012. *The New York Times Magazine*. Accessed 21 November 2012. http://www.nytimes.com/2012/04/29/magazine /the-criminalization-of-bad-mothers.html?pagewanted=all.

Cohen-Scali, Sarah. *Max*. New York: Roaring Brook/Macmillan, 2017.

Doman, Regina. *Angel in the Waters*. Illus. Ben Hatke. Manchester, NH: Sophia Institute Press, 2004.

Douglas, Susan J., and Meredith Michaels. *The Mommy Myth: The Idealization of Motherhood and How It Has Undermined All Women*. New York: Free Press, 2004.

Dubow, Sara. *Ourselves Unborn: A History of the Fetus in Modern America*. Oxford, UK: Oxford UP, 2011.

Eckholm, Erik. "Push for 'Personhood' Amendment Represents New Track in Abortion Fight." 25 October 2011. *The New York Times.* http://www.nytimes.com/2011/10/26/us /politics/personhood-amendments-would-ban-nearly-all-abortions.html?pagewanted=all. Accessed 11 May 2012.

Eshleman, Adam. "Probing Question: Can Babies Learn in Utero?" 23 February 2009. Research Penn State. http://www.rps.psu.edu/probing/inutero.html. Accessed 19 May 2012.

Goodman, Eric. *Womb: A Novel in Utero.* Merge, 2017.

Grenby, M. O. "The Origins of Children's Literature." Discovering Literature: Romantics and Victorian. The British Library. 15 May 2014. https://www.bl.uk/romantics-and-victorians /articles/the-origins-of-childrens-literature. Accessed 11 November 2017.

Hays, Sharon. *The Cultural Contradictions of Motherhood.* New Haven: Yale UP, 1996.

"How to Maximize Unborn Baby Development." Baby Development News. http://www .babydevelopmentnews.com/unborn-baby-development.html. 21 May 2012.

Javerbaum, David. *What to Expect When You're Expected: A Fetus's Guide to the First Three Trimesters.* New York: Spiegel and Grau, 2009.

Kunhardt, Dorothy. *Pat the Bunny.* 1940. New York: Golden Books/Random House, 1968.

Langbauer, Laurie. *The Juvenile Tradition: Young Writers and Prolepsis, 1750–1835.* New York: Oxford UP, 2016.

Leach, Penelope. *Children First: What Our Society Must Do—and Is Not Doing—For Our Children Today.* New York: Random House, 1994.

Lilien-Harper, Amy. "Park, Barbara. Ma! There's Nothing to Do Here!: A Word from Your Baby-in-Waiting." *School Library Journal* Mar. 2008: 174. *Book Review Index Plus.* 9 September 2016.

Linn, Susan. *Consuming Kids: Protecting Our Children from the Onslaught of Marketing & Advertising.* New York: Anchor Books, 2004.

McClay, Jill Medersha. "World Enough and Tim: The Handmade Literacies of Young Adolescent Writers." *The Lion and the Unicorn.* 29.1. (January 2009): 87–101.

McEwan, Ian. *Nutshell: A Novel.* New York: Anchor/Knopf Doubleday, 2017.

McTasney, Marissa. *With Love: A Book to Be Read to You Child in Utero and Beyond.* Victoria, BC: Trafford Publishing, 2007.

Miller, John A. "Choosing to Make Children Your Life's Work." *Camping Magazine.* (July/ August 1994) http://findarticles.com/p/articles/mi_m1249/is_n6_v66/ai_15608018/. Accessed 17 May 2012.

Morales, Elena. "The Nag Factor: Measuring Children's Influence." *Admap* (March 2000): 35–37.

National Conference of State Legislatures. "Fetal Homicide Laws." (April 2012). Issues and Research: Health. http://www.ncsl.org/issues-research/health/fetal-homicide-state-laws .aspx. Accessed 1 July 2012.

Nelligan, Kate Merrow. *Pat the Bride.* Kennebunkport, ME: Cedar Mill, 2009.

Nessel, Jen, and Lizzy Ratner. *Goodnight Nanny-Cam: A Parody for Modern Parents.* Illus. Sara Pinto. New York: Plume, 2014.

Nicole M. "Great Pregnancy Gift for someone or Gift for yourself." Customer review *MA! There's Nothing to Do Here!* 28 July 2014. Amazon.com. Accessed 9 September 2016.

Nikolajeva, Maria, and Carol Scott. *How Picturebooks Work.* New York: Routledge, 2001.

Nodelman, Perry. *Words about Pictures: The Narrative Art of Children's Picture Books.* Athens, GA: U of Georgia, 1988.

Ommundsen, Åse Marie. "Who Are These Picturebooks For? Controversial Picturebooks and The Question of Audience." *Challenging and Controversial Picturebooks: Creative and Critical Responses.* Ed. Janet Evans. New York: Routledge, 2015. 71–94.

Origen, Erich, and Gan Golan. *Don't Let the Republican Drive the Bus!: A Parody for Voters.* Berkeley, CA: Ten Speed P, 2012.

———. *Goodnight Bush: An Unauthorized Parody.* New York: Little, Brown, 2008.
Ouellette, Chris. *Dr. Paul (A Parody of Dr. Seuss's Green Eggs And Ham featuring the Ron Paul Revolution).* 14 December 2011. http://www.youtube.com/watch?v=-vLiD6bK63Y. Accessed 3 February 2013.
Park, Barbara. Junie B. Jones series. New York: Random House, 1992–2013.
———. *MA! There's Nothing to Do Here!: A Word from Your Baby-in-Waiting.* Illus. Viviana Garofoli. New York: Random House, 2008.
Perk, Micah. *What Becomes Us.* New York: Outpost19/Ingram, 2016.
Pickert, Kate. "The Man Who Remade Motherhood." 21 May 2012. *Time Magazine.* http://www.time.com/time/magazine/article/0,9171,2114427,00.html. Accessed 21 May 2012.
"Prenatal Stimulation." *Make Way for Baby!* http://makewayforbaby.com/babies/prenatal-stimulation.html. Accessed 21 May 2012.
Rabe, Tish, adapted from Dr. Seuss. *Oh, Baby, the Places You'll Go!: A Book to Be Read in Utero.* New York: Random House, 1997.
Sadler, David. "Innocent Hearts: The Child Authors of the 1920s." *Children's Literature Association Quarterly.* 17.4. (Winter 1992): 24–30.
Schafer, Alyson. *Breaking the Good Mom Myth: Every Modern Mom's Guide to Getting Past Perfection, Regaining Sanity, and Raising Great Kids.* Mississauga, Ontario: John Wiley & Sons, 2007.
Sears, William, and Martha Sears. *The Baby Book: Everything You Need About Your Baby—From Birth to Age Two.* New York: Little, Brown, 1993.
Skurnick, Lizzie. "Chick Lit, the Sequel: Yummy Mummy." 17 December 2006. *The New York Times.* http://www.nytimes.com/2006/12/17/fashion/17MomLit.html?pagewanted=all. Accessed 4 May 2012.
Stearns, Peter N. *Anxious Parents: A History of Modern Childrearing in America.* New York: NYU Press, 2003.
Stonehouse, Cathy. "Feminism for a Strange Age." 12 May 1997. *The Globe and Mail.* D8.
Swaminathan, Nikhil. "Fact or Fiction? Babies Exposed to Classical Music End Up Smarter." *Scientific American.* 13 September 2007. http://www.scientificamerican.com/article.cfm?id=fact-or-fiction-babies-ex. Accessed 22 May 2012.
Truth, Dr. *The Cat and the Mitt: A Parody for Conservatives.* 2010. Amherst, MA: Free Market Warrior P, 2012.
Vandale, Susan A. Message to the author. 3 July 2012. E-mail.
Warner, Judith. *Perfect Madness: Motherhood in the Age of Anxiety.* New York: Riverhead Books, 2006.
Warren, Elisabeth M. "Clever Gift for Expectant Moms!" Customer review *MA! There's Nothing to Do Here!* 2 May 2008. Amazon.com. Accessed 9 September 2016.
Winterman, Denise. "Does Classical Music Make Babies Smarter?" 19 May 2005. *BBC News.* http://news.bbc.co.uk/go/pr/fr/-/2/hi/uk_news/magazine/4558507/stm. Accessed 17 May 2012.
Worden, Bruce, and Clare Cross. *Goodnight Keith Moon.* New York: Baker and Taylor, 2011.

Chapter 5 · Learning Left From Right

Abate, Michelle Ann. *Raising Your Kids Right: Children's Literature and American Political Conservatism.* Piscataway, NJ: Rutgers UP, 2010.
American Broadsides: Sixty Facsimiles Dated from 1680 to 1800 Reproduced from the Originals in the American Antiquarian Society. Selected and introduced by Georgia B. Bumgardner. Barre, MA: Imprint Society, 1971.
Bangs, John Kendrick. *Alice in Blunderland: An Iridescent Dream.* New York: Doubeday, 1907. Google Books.
Begbie, Harold. *The Political Struwwelpeter.* London: G. Richards, 1899.

Birkett, Terri. *Truax*. Chesterfield, MO: Wood Flooring Manufacturers Association, 1994.

Black, Michael Ian. *A Child's First Book of Trump*. Illus. Marc Rosenthal. New York: Simon and Schuster, 2016.

Blackburn, Katie. *Where the Wild Dads Went*. Illus. Sholto Walker. Faber and Faber, 2016.

———. *Where the Wild Moms Are*. Illus. Sholto Walker. Faber and Faber, 2015.

Blamires, David. *Telling Tales: The Impact of Germany on English Children's Books, 1750–1918*. Cambridge, UK: Open Book Publishers, 2009.

"Broadside." *Continuum Encyclopedia of Popular Music of the World: Media, Industry and Society*. London: Continuum, 2003. *Credo Reference*. Accessed 27 November 2012.

"Broadside, N." *OED Online*. December 2012. Oxford University Press. Accessed 3 February 2013.

Brown, Margaret Wise. *Goodnight Moon*. Illus. Clement Hurd. 1947. New York: HarperCollins, 2005.

Bryza, C. B. *Are You My Boyfriend? A Picture Book for Grown-Up Children*. Illus. Simon Greiner. New York: Gallery Books, 2014.

Bumgardner, Georgia B. Introduction. *American Broadsides: Sixty Facsimiles Dated from 1680 to 1800 Reproduced from the Originals in the American Antiquarian Society*. Barre, MA: Imprint Society, 1971. Unpaginated.

Cali, Davide, and Serge Bloch. *The Enemy*. New York: Schwartz and Wade, 2007.

"The Career of a Know-Nothing!" Library Company of Philadelphia. www.library-company .org/mcallisterexhibition/images/5-91.jpg. Accessed 23 January 2013.

Carle, Eric. *The Very Hungry Caterpillar*. 1969. New York: Philomel Books, 1994.

Carroll, Lewis. *Alice's Adventures in Wonderland*. 1865. New York: Penguin, 2013.

———. *Through the Looking-Glass*. 1871. New York: Dover, 1999.

Carter, Antonio. *Oh, the Sh*t You Don't Know!: College Graduate Edition*. Illus. Pyrink Hernandez. CreateSpace Publishing, 2016.

Charytan, Renee. *If You Give Mommy a Glass of Wine*. Illus. Rick Van Hattum. CreateSpace, 2016.

"Coffin Handbill." 1828. Winterthur Museum Collection. http://museumblog.winterthur. org/ files/2012/02/Summer-institute-research-009.jpg. Accessed 23 January 2013.

Cole, Matt. *Fuck You Sun*. Illus. Rigel Stumiller. Berkeley, CA: Tomorrow John Press, 2011.

Coombs, Kate. *Goodnight Mr. Darcy*. Illus. Alli Arnold. Layton, UT: Gibbs Smith, 2014.

Coover, Robert. "The End of Books." *The New York Times*. 21 June 1992.

Corsi, Jerome. *Goodnight Obama: A Parody*. Illus. M. G. Anthony. Post Hill Press, 2016.

Cunningham, Noble E., Jr. "Early Political Handbills in the United States." *The William and Mary Quarterly*. 14.1 (January 1957): 70–73.

de Valle, Elaine. "Street Vendors Get Economic Boost from the Republican National Convention." *VOXXI*. 29 August 2012. http://www.voxxi.com/street-vendors-eco-nomic -boost-rnc-convention/. Accessed 3 February 2013.

Droyd, Ann. *Goodnight iPad: A Parody for the Next Generation*. New York: Penguin, 2011.

Eastman, P. D. *Are You My Mother?* 1960. New York: Random House, 2002.

Gackley, Arthur C. *Bad Little Children's Books*. New York: Abrams, 2016.

"Hear a Sample of the Book." *The Cat and the Mitt*. http://obamaparody.com/sam-plereading .html. Accessed 4 February 2013.

Heller, Steven. "Once Upon a Time . . ." *Eye Magazine*. 69.18 (August 2008).

Hill, Simon Max, and Shannon Wheeler. *Grandpa Won't Wake Up*. Los Angeles, CA: BOOM! Studios, 2011.

Hodge, Hope. "Obama is the 'Cat' in Children's Book Spoof." *Human Events: Powerful Conservative Voices*. 28 August 2012. http://humanevents.com/2012/08/28/president -obama-is-the-cat-in-childrens-book-spoof/. Accessed 22 January 2016.

Hoffmann, Heinrich. *Struwwelpeter*. In English translation. 1845. New York: Dover, 1995.

Howell, William Huntting. "'Read, Pause, and Reflect!'" *Journal of the Early Republic*. 302. (Summer 2010): 293–300.

Hutcheon, Linda. *A Theory of Parody: The Teachings of Twentieth-Century Art Forms*. Chicago: U of Illinois P, 2000.

Johnson, Paul. *A Political Mother Goose*. New York: Non-Partisan Press, 1932.

Kanouse, Faye. *If You Give a Pig the White House*. Illus. Amy Zhing. New York: Castle Point Books, 2019.

Kunhardt, Dorothy. *Pat the Bunny*. 1940. New York: Golden Books/Random House, 1968.

Library of Congress. "Introduction to Printed Ephemera Collection." American Memory Project. http://memory/loc.loc.gov/ammem/rppehtml/pessay.A.html. Accessed 4 February 2013.

Ling, Reese. *Are You My Wine? A Children's Book Parody for Adults Exploring the World of Wine*. Berkeley, CA: Ulysses Press, 2017.

Lloyd, Josie, and Emlyn Rees. *The Very Hungover Caterpillar: A Parody*. Illus. Gillian Johnson. London: Constable, 2014.

——. *We're Going on a Bar Hunt!: A Parody*. Illus. Gillian Johnson. London: Constable, 2013.

MacDonald, Ross, and James Victore. *In and Out with Dick and Jane: A Loving Parody*. New York: Harry N. Abrams, 2011.

Marcus, Julie, and Susan Carp. *Pat the Politician: A Political Pull and Poke Parody*. San Francisco: Imagineering, 2004.

——. *Pat the Politician #2*. San Francisco: Imagineering, 2008.

Mason, Paul. *Why It's Kicking Off Everywhere: The New Global Revolutions*. New York: Verso, 2012.

McDowell, Paula. "'The Manufacture and Lingua-facture of *Ballad-Making*': Broadside Ballads in Long Eighteenth-Century Ballad Discourse." *The Eighteenth Century*. 47.2/3 (2006): 151–78.

McShane, Angela. "Ballads and Broadsides." *The Oxford History of Popular Print Culture*. Vol. 1: Cheap Print in Britain and Ireland to 1660. Ed. Joad Raymond. Oxford, UK: Oxford UP, 2011. 339–62.

Mickenberg, Julia L. *Learning from the Left: Children's Literature, the Cold War, and Radical Politics*. New York: Oxford UP, 2005.

Mickenberg, Julia L., and Philip Nel. "Radical Children's Literature Now!" *Children's Literature Association Quarterly*. 36.4 (2011): 445–73.

——, eds. *Tales for Little Rebels: A Collection of Radical Children's Literature*. New York: New York UP, 2008.

Nebeker, Eric. "The Broadside Ballad and Textual Publics." *Studies in English Literature, 1500–1900*. 51.1 (2011): 1–19.

Nelligan, Kate Merrow. *Pat the Bride*. Kennebunkport, ME: Cedar Mill, 2009.

——. *Pat the Daddy*. Kennebunkport, ME: Cedar Mill, 2010.

——. *Pat the Husband*. Kennebunkport, ME: Cedar Mill, 2008.

Newton, Phil and J. Edward. *If You Give a Guy a Beer*. Illus. William Adams. If You Give a Guy Publications, 2013.

Oceanak, Karla. *Good Morning Brew: A Parody for Coffee People*. Illus. Allie Ogg. Ft. Collins, CO: Bailiwick Press, 2015.

——. *Goodnight Brew: A Parody for Beer People*. Illus. Allie Ogg. Ft. Collins, CO: Bailiwick Press, 2014.

Olson, Alison Gilbert. "Political Humor, Deference, and the American Revolution." *Early American Studies: An Interdisciplinary Journal*. 3.2 (2005): 36–82.

Origen, Erich, and Gan Golan. *Don't Let the Republican Drive the Bus!: A Parody for Voters*. Berkeley, CA: Ten Speed P, 2012.

———. *Goodnight Bush: An Unauthorized Parody*. New York: Little, Brown and Company, 2008.

Ouellette, Chris. *Dr. Paul (A Parody of Dr. Seuss's Green Eggs And Ham featuring the Ron Paul Revolution)*. 14 December 2011. http://www.youtube.com/watch?v=-vLiD6bK63Y. Accessed 3 February 2013.

Pat the Foodie: A Culinary Pull and Poke Parody. San Francisco, CA: The Imagineering Company, 2011.

Paul, Ron. *End the Fed*. New York: Grand Central P, 2009.

———. *Liberty Defined: 50 Essential Issues That Affect Our Freedom*. New York: Grand Central P, 2011.

———. *The Revolution: A Manifesto*. New York: Grand Central P, 2008.

Reynolds, Amy, and Gary R. Hicks. *Prophets of the Fourth Estate: Broadsides by Press Critics of the Progressive Era*. Los Angeles: Litwin Books, 2011.

Reynolds, Kimberley. "Understanding Alice." The British Library. 15 May 2014. https://www.bl.uk/romantics-and-victorians/articles/understanding-alice. Accessed 10 October 2019.

Schuessler, Jennifer. "Inside the List." Times Book Review. *The New York Times*. Accessed 15 January 2009.

Scieszka, Jon, and Lane Smith. *The Stinky Cheese Man and Other Fairly Stupid Tales*. New York: Viking, 1992.

Seuss, Dr. *The Butter Battle Book*. New York: Random House, 1984.

———. *The Cat in the Hat*. 1957. New York: Random House, 1985.

———. *Green Eggs and Ham*. 1960. New York: Random House, 1988.

———. *Horton Hears a Who!* New York: Random House, 1954.

———. *The Lorax*. New York: Random House, 1971.

———. *Oh, the Places You'll Go!* New York: Random House, 1990.

———. *Yertle the Turtle and Other Stories*. New York: Random House, 1958.

Shaw, John MacKay. *The Parodies of Lewis Carroll and Their Originals: A Catalogue of an Exhibition*. Florida State University Library, 1960.

Shires, Linda M. "Fantasy, Nonsense, Parody, and the Status of the Real: The Example of Carroll." *Victorian Poetry*. 26.3. (Autumn 1988): 267–83.

"Show Your Faith in the Women of Massachusetts, Vote Yes on the Amendment Enabling Women to Vote." 1916. www.tc.pbs.org/wnet/need-to-know/files/2012/11/mtholyoakesuffrage.jpg. Accessed 23 January 2013.

Silverstein, Shel. *The Giving Tree*. New York: Harper and Row, 1964.

Simonian, Andrew. *Bi-Curious George: An Unauthorized Parody*. Kennebunkport, ME: Cider Mill Press, 2012.

Slauter, Eric. "Revolutions in the Meaning and Study of Politics." *American Literary History*. 22.2 (2010): 325–40.

Spence, Robert, and Philip Spence. *Struwwelhitler: A Nazi Story*. Haycock Press, 1941.

Stangel, Eric, and Justin Stangel. *Goodnight Husband, Goodnight Wife*. San Rafael, CA: Insight Editions, 2012.

Suits, Dr. *Oh, The Meetings You'll Go To!: A Parody*. New York: Portfolio / Penguin, 2017.

Teitelbaum, Michael. *The Very Hungry Zombie: A Parody*. Illus. John Apple. New York: Skyhorse Publishing, 2012.

Toffler, Alvin. *Future Shock*. New York: Random House, 1970.

Travesty, Shrill. *The Taking Tree: A Selfish Parody*. Illus. Lucy Ruth Cummins. New York: Simon and Schuster, 2010.

Truth, Dr. *The Cat and the Mitt: A Parody for Conservatives*. 2010. Amherst, MA: Free Market Warrior P, 2012.

Villa, Luis. "Political Information Overload and the New Filtering." 3 October 2008. Freedom to Tinker: Research and Expert Commentary on Digital Technologies in Public Lie.

https://freedom-to-tinker.com/blog/luis/political-information-overload-and-new-filtering/. Accessed 3 February 2013.

Warner, Michael. *The Letters of the Republic: Publication and the Public Sphere in Eighteenth-Century America.* Cambridge, MA: Harvard UP, 1990.

Weiner, Ellis, and Barbara Davilman. *Yiddish with George and Laura.* New York: Little, Brown and Company, 2006.

Willems, Mo. *Don't Let the Pigeon Drive the Bus!* New York: Hyperion, 2003.

Williams, Vera. *Amber Was Brave, Essie Was Smart.* 2001. New York: Greenwillow/Harper-Collins, 2004.

Wong, Janet S., and David Roberts. *The Dumpster Diver.* Somerville, MA: Candlewick, 2007.

Worden, Bruce, and Clare Cross. *Goodnight Keith Moon.* New York: Baker and Taylor, 2011.

Wortis, Joseph. *Tricky Dick and His Pals: Comical Stories, All in the Manner of Dr. Henrich Hoffmann's Der Struwwelpeter.* Illus. David Arkin. New York: Quadrangle Books, 1974.

Ximm, Aaron. *Pat the Zombie: A Cruel (Adult) Spoof.* Illus. Kaveh Soofi. Berkeley, CA: Ten Speed Press, 2012.

Zevin, Dan. *Mr. Selfie: A Parody.* New York: Three Rivers Press, 2015.

Chapter 6 · Not Kidding Around

Abate, Michelle Ann. *Bloody Murder: The Homicide Tradition in Children's Literature.* Baltimore, MD: Johns Hopkins UP, 2013.

Anonymous. "Raw Honesty." Customer review of *Go the F**k to Sleep.* 15 May 2011. www.amazon.com. Accessed 11 August 2011.

"Baby, Mix Me a Drink." *Baby, Mix Me a Drink.* By Lisa Brown. Amazon.com. Accessed 29 December 2015.

Basford, Johanna. *Secret Garden: An Inky Treasure Hunt and Colouring Book.* London: Laurence King, 2013.

Beaman, Rhonda. *You're Only Young Twice: 10 Do-Overs to Reawaken Your Spirit.* St. Louis, MO: VanderWyk & Burhham, 2006.

Brown, Lisa. *Baby, Make Me Breakfast.* San Francisco, CA: McSweeney's, 2005.

——. *Baby, Mix Me a Drink.* San Francisco, CA: McSweeney's, 2005.

——. *Baby Do My Banking.* San Francisco, CA: McSweeney's, 2006.

——. *Baby Fix My Car.* San Francisco, CA: McSweeney's, 2006.

——. *Baby Get Me Some Lovin'.* San Francisco, CA: McSweeney's, 2009.

——. *Baby Plan My Wedding.* San Francisco, CA: McSweeney's, 2009.

Cedar, White. *Baby Don't Sh!t Your Pants.* Illus. Vivian Mineker. Bambino, 2017.

Childress, Alice. *A Hero Ain't Nothin' But a Sandwich.* 1973. New York: Puffin, 2000.

"Customer Discussions" about *Go the F**k to Sleep.* Amazon.com. 10 August 2011. http://www.amazon.com/Go-F-Sleep-Adam-Mansbach/dp/1617750255/ref=sr_1_1?s=books&ie=UTF8&qid=1313088624&sr=1-1

Goldman, Abigail. "A Grown-Up Barbie for Older Girls." *The Los Angeles Times.* 22 July 2002. http://articles.latimes.com/2002/jul/22/business/fi-mattel22. Accessed 15 September 2018.

Greenberg, Gary, and Matthew Reinhart. *The Pop-Up Book of Nightmares.* New York: Rob Weisbach Books/William Morrow, 2001.

——. *The Pop-Up Book of Phobias.* New York: Rob Weisbach Books/William Morrow, 1999.

Grimm, Wilhelm, and Jacob Grimm. *Hansel and Gretel.* Trans. Elizabeth D. Crawford. Illus. Lisbeth Zwerger. New York: Penguin, 2008.

——. "The Juniper Tree." *The Juniper Tree and Other Tales from Grimm.* vol 2. Selected by Lore Segal and Maurice Sendak. Trans. Lore Segal and Randall Jarrell. New York: Farrar, Straus and Giroux, 1973. 314–32.

———. "Snow White." *The Classic Fairy Tales*. Ed. Maria Tatar. New York: W. W. Norton, 1999. 83–89.

Harmanci, Reyhan. "'Go the F--- to Sleep': The Case of the Viral PDF." *The Bay Citizen*. 12 May 2011.

———. "A Whim, a Book, and, Wow!" *The New York Times*. 28 April 2011.

Higonnet, Anne. *Pictures of Innocence: The History and Crisis of Ideal Childhood*. New York: Thames and Hudson, 1998.

Hoffman, Jan. "Nancy Drew's Granddaughters." *The New York Times*. 17 July 2009. https:// www.nytimes.com/2009/07/19/fashion/19drew.html. Accessed 11 September 2018.

Kann, Victoria, and Elizabeth Kann. *Pinkalicious*. New York: Harper Collins, 2006.

Linn, Susan. *Consuming Kids: Protecting Our Children from the Onslaught of Marketing & Advertising*. New York: Anchor Books, 2004.

Lyubomirsky, Sonja. *The Myths of Happiness: What Should Make You Happy, But Doesn't, What Shouldn't Make You Happy, But Does*. New York: Penguin, 2013.

Mandel, G. Thomas. *T is for Trump: A Candidate's ABC Book*. Ridge Street, 2016.

Maney, Mabel. *The Case of the Not-So-Nice Nurse: A Nancy Clue Mystery*. Pittsburgh, PA: Cleis, 1993.

Mansbach, Adam. *Go the F**k to Sleep*. Illus. Ricardo Cortés. Brooklyn, NY: Akashic, 2011.

———. *You Have to F**king Eat*. Illus. Owen Brozman. Brookyln, NY: Akashic Books, 2014.

Mucklow, Lacy. *Color Me Calm: 100 Coloring Templates for Meditation and Relaxation*. Illus. Angela Porter. London: Race Point, 2014.

National Children's Book and Literacy Alliance. "Why Do Kids Need Books?" Supporting Arguments: Literacy, Literature and Library Statistics. http://www.thencbla.org/BPOSpages /supportarguments.html. 12 August 2011.

Numeroff, Laura. *If You Give a Mouse a Cookie*. Illus. Felicia Bond. 1985. New York: Harper Collins, 2015.

Orenstein, Peggy. "Kindergarten Cram." *The New York Times*. Magazine section. 3 May 2009: MM13.

Origen, Erich, and Gan Golan. *Don't Let the Republican Drive the Bus!* New York: Little, Brown and Company, 2012.

———. *Goodnight Bush*. New York: Little, Brown and Company, 2008.

Paper Moon. Dir. Peter Bogdanovich. Perfs. Tatum O'Neal, Ryan O'Neal, Madeline Kahn. Paramount, 1973.

Park, Barbara. *MA! There's Nothing to Do Here!: A Word from Your Baby-in-Waiting*. Illus. Viviana Garofoli. New York: Random House, 2008.

Petras, Kathryn, and Ross Petras. *B is for Botox: An Alphabet Book for the Middle-Aged*. Kansas City: Andrews McMeel, 2009.

———. *1, 2, Can't Reach My Shoe: A Counting Book for the Middle-Aged*. Kansas City: Andrews McMeel, 2010.

Postman, Neil. *The Disappearance of Childhood*. 1982. New York: Vintage, 1994.

Quinn, David, and Michael Davis. *The Littlest Bitch: A Not-for-Children Children's Book*. Illus. Devon Devereaux. South Portland, ME: Sellers Publishing, 2010.

Rich, Adrienne. *Of Woman Born: Motherhood as Experience and Institution*. 1976. New York: W. W. Norton, 1995.

Rickett, Joel. *H is for Hummus: A Modern Parent's ABC*. Illus. Spencer Wilson. New York: Viking, 2013.

Roznick, Marcy. *If You Give a Kid a Cookie, Will He Shut the F**k Up?* Illus. Miranda Lemming. New York: St. Martin's Griffin, 2012.

Sarnat, Marjorie. *Cats Coloring Book*. Mineola, NY: Dover, 2015.

Seinfeld, Jerry. *I'm Telling You for the Last Time.* Originally aired on HBO on August 8, 1998. Netflix.

Sopp, Kelly, and David Sopp. *The New Parents' Fun Book: Laugh Yourself Silly Through Baby's First Year!* Philadelphia: Running Press, 2008.

———. *Safe Baby Handling Tips.* Philadelphia: Running Press, 2005.

Telnaes, Ann. *Trump's ABC.* Fantagraphics, 2018.

Tillman, Nancy. *It's Time To Sleep, My Love.* Illus. Eric Metaxas. Feiwel and Friends, 2008.

Zacharias, Karen Spears. "'Go the F**k to Sleep' Not Funny." CNN.com. 27 June 2011.

Zelizer, Viviana A. *Pricing the Priceless Child: The Changing Social Value of Children.* New York: Basic Books, 1987.

Conclusion · Both Radical and Reinforcing

Butler, Judith. *Gender Trouble.* 1991. New York: Routledge, 2006.

Carpenter, Susan. "Adam Mansbach Writes 'Seriously, Just Go to Sleep' for the Kids." *The Los Angeles Times.* 10 April 2012. http://articles.latimes.com/2012/apr/10/entertainment/la-et -0411-adam-mansbach-20120411. Accessed 24 September 2016.

Donahoo, Daniel. *Idolising Children.* Sydney, Australia: New South, 2007.

Maney, Mabel. *The Case of the Not-So-Nice Nurse: A Nancy Clue Mystery.* Pittsburgh, PA: Cleis, 1993.

Mansbach, Adam. *Go the F**k to Sleep.* Illus. Ricardo Cortés. Brooklyn, NY: Akashic, 2011.

———. *Seriously, Just Go to Sleep.* Illus. Ricardo Cortés. Brooklyn, NY: Akashic, 2012.

Nestle, Joan, Clare Howell, and Riki Wilchins, eds. *GenderQueer: Voices from Beyond the Sexual Binary.* New York: Alyson Books, 2002.

Origen, Erich, and Gan Golan. *Goodnight Bush.* New York: Little, Brown and Company, 2008.

Park, Barbara. *MA! There's Nothing to Do Here!: A Word from Your Baby-in-Waiting.* Illus. Viviana Garofoli. New York: Random House, 2008.

Seuss, Dr. *You're Only Old Once!: A Book for Obsolete Children.* New York: Random House, 1986.

Spiegelman, Art. *In the Shadow of No Towers.* New York: Pantheon Graphics, 2004.

Stryker, Susan. *Transgender History.* Berkeley, CA: Seal Press, 2008.

Truth, Dr. *The Cat and the Mitt: A Parody for Conservatives* 2012.: Amherst, MA Free Market Warrior Publications, 2011.

Page numbers in *italics* refer to figures.

Bryne, Kathyne, 61
Bumgardner, Georgia B., 146, 151
Burr, Viv, 40
Burton, Richard, 34
Bush, George W., parodies of, 143. See also *Goodnight Bush*
Butler, Judith, 190

Cahalan, Susannah, 1, 2, 3
Calcutt, Andrew, 18
Cali, Davide, 150
Camel, Thomas, 153
Campbell, James, 94
Cannon, Ann, 1
Carle, Eric, 140
Carpenter, Susan, 192
Carroll, Lewis, 138
Carter, Antonio, 140
Case of the Good-for-Nothing Girlfriend, The (Maney), 60–61
Case of the Not-So-Nice Nurse, The (Maney): concept of mystery in, 66–69; as fanfiction, 64; *The Haunted Showboat* compared to, 75–76; LGBTQ+ community and, 4; overview of, 29–30, 57–58, 59, 189; as parody, 65–66; queer content in, 59–60; religion in, 69–70; *The Secret of the Golden Pavilion* compared to, 78, 80; as slash fiction, 64–65
Cassidy, Julie Sinn, 21
Cat and the Mitt, The (Truth): broadside tradition and, 145–46, 149, 151–53; call for engagement in, 164–65; disclaimer for, 163; illustration from, 158; language of, 161; overview of, 31, 136–37, 144; as political parody, 150–51, 157–58, 167, 192; pseudonym for author of, 164; sales of, 168
categories of children's literature for adults, 6, 7
Cat in the Hat, The (Seuss), 144, 161, 165
Cedar, White, *Baby Don't Sh!t Your Pants*, 177–78
Chamberlain, Kathleen, 59
Charytan, Renee, 140
Cheney, Dick, 167
Cherry Ames series, retellings of, 29–30, 59. See also *Case of the Not-So-Nice Nurse, The*
Chesterton, G. K., 73
childhood: adulthood as antithesis of, 12–13; duration of, 6–7; idolization of, 191; perception of, 172; politicization of, 97–99, 101–6; as stage of

development, 186–87; as subsumed into adulthood, 173, 183–86, 187–88
childhood studies, 105–6
children: boredom of, 125–26; in classic comics reproduced in *In the Shadow of No Towers*, 95; feelings of helplessness of, 93; ill, infirm, and elderly treated as, 38, 39–41; likening of adults to, 13–16, 18; "Nag Factor" and, 126; politicization of, 97–99, 101–6, 105; prenatally advantaged, 130–34. See also parenting
children's literature: authorship of, 112, 135–36; as endpoint, 192; materiality and, 106; nature of, 134–35; parodies of, 27, 138–42; parody in, 138; political parodies of, 142–46; race and ethnicity in, 50–51; retellings of, 61–62, 81–85; sociopolitical issues in, 149–50, 167. See also board books; picture books
children's literature for adults: board books, 24, 95–96; as challenging boundaries, 4, 21–26, 189–93; commercial success of, 3–4; as genre, 3, 5, 36–37, 38, 41; literary implications for, 28–29; as phenomenon, 27–28, 171–72; pop-up books, 33–34, 171; scholarly study of, 4–5; topics of, 6. See also fanfiction; parodies; political parodies
Child's Guide to Freud, A (Armstrong), 26, 27
Christie, Agatha, 74
Churchyard, Thomas, 153
citizenship: definition of, 116–17; fetal, 112, 114–15, 117–19
Clark, Beverly Lyon, 13
Clerisse, Alexandre, 34
Clifton, Andrew, 40
"Coffin Handbill," 155, 156
Collins, Christina, 8, 13
coloring books for adults, 1–3, 23–24, 171; as stress-relief tools, 20
comic strips, 95, 98–99
Conan Doyle, Arthur, 73, 74
consumerism, 21, 98, 125–29, 184, 190
Continuum Encyclopedia of Popular Music of the World, 147, 149, 163
Conway, Alex, 4, 27
Coover, Robert, 169
Cope, Edward Drinker, 14
copyright, fair use, and parodies, 162–64
Coral Island Boys (Kent), 82, 84
Cortés, Ricardo, 180
Côté, James, 7, 12